Preface

The title of this book is Microsoft Office. It has long been a cornerstone of productivity, enabling individuals and organizations to harness the power of technology to achieve their goals. As we embark on this journey into the world of Microsoft Office, it is important to acknowledge the profound impact it has had on the way we work, communicate, and create. This suite of applications, which includes tools like Microsoft Word, Excel, PowerPoint, and more, has evolved over the years to meet the ever-changing needs of users. With each iteration, Microsoft has strived to push the boundaries of what is possible, providing innovative solutions that empower individuals and teams to excel in their tasks. In this comprehensive guide, we will delve into the intricacies of Microsoft Office, exploring its various components and functionalities. Whether you are a seasoned professional seeking to master advanced features or a novice looking to get started, this book is designed to be your trusted companion. We will cover everything from the basics to advanced techniques, ensuring that you can make the most of Microsoft Office's capabilities. Our aim is to provide you with a clear and concise resource that not only imparts knowledge but also sparks creativity. We believe that Microsoft Office is more than just a set of software tools; it is a canvas for innovation, a platform for collaboration, and a means to bring ideas to life. As we navigate through the chapters ahead, I encourage you to explore, experiment, and discover the endless possibilities that Microsoft Office offers. Let this guide be your gateway to unlocking your full potential in the world of productivity and creativity. Thank you for choosing this book as your companion on your Microsoft Office journey. Let's embark on this exciting adventure together.

Table of Contents

Chapter 1 - **Introduction to Microsoft Office**

1.1 Overview of Microsoft Office Suite

The Microsoft Office suite is a set of programs for common productivity tasks, including a word processing program, a spreadsheet tool, presentation software, an email program and others. Often abbreviated as the MS Office suite, it's among the most popular software packages in the world, though it does face competition from other commercial products, including some from Apple and Google and from open source packages such as LibreOffice. Parts of the Microsoft suite of programs are available both for use in a web browser and local use on a computer.

Microsoft Office is the collective name for Microsoft's set of home and business productivity software. The MS suite of programs includes Microsoft Word, a word processing tool; Microsoft Excel, a spreadsheet program; Microsoft PowerPoint, used for creating interactive presentations; Microsoft Outlook, used for email and calendar management; Microsoft Access, a database management program; and Microsoft OneNote, a note-taking application.

The Microsoft Office Suite includes a core set of applications, each serving a distinct purpose:

Microsoft Word: This word processing software is used for creating and editing text-based documents. It provides a wide array of formatting options, making it suitable for tasks such as writing reports, letters, academic papers, and more.

Microsoft Excel: Excel is a powerful spreadsheet application used for tasks such as data analysis, financial modeling, and numerical calculations. It allows users to create worksheets, perform complex calculations, and generate charts and graphs.

Microsoft PowerPoint: PowerPoint is a presentation software that enables users to create dynamic and visually appealing slideshows. It is widely employed for creating business presentations, educational lectures, and conference presentations.

Microsoft Outlook: Outlook is an integrated email and personal information management application. It serves as a hub for email communication, calendar management, contact organization, and task scheduling. Outlook streamlines communication and aids in time management.

Microsoft Access: Access is a database management system used for creating, managing, and analyzing databases. It offers tools for designing tables, queries, forms, and reports, making it valuable for data-centric tasks.

Microsoft OneNote: OneNote is a digital note-taking application that enables users to create and organize notes in a flexible notebook-style format. It is commonly used for jotting down ideas, conducting research, and collaborating on projects.

The Microsoft Office Suite has evolved over the years, with each new version introducing enhanced features and improved capabilities. Additionally, Microsoft has embraced cloud-based solutions with Microsoft 365 (formerly Office 365), allowing users to access and collaborate on Office applications online.

Overall, Microsoft Office is a cornerstone of modern productivity, facilitating efficient document creation, data analysis, communication, and organization for both personal and professional use. Proficiency in these applications is highly beneficial in today's digital workspace.

MS Word | MS Excel | MS Powerpoint | OneDrive | Outlook

One Note | MS Publisher | Microsoft Teams | MS Access | Skype

1.2 Importance of Microsoft Office Tools

Microsoft Office tools have established themselves as integral components of the modern workplace, offering a range of indispensable features and benefits that contribute to enhanced productivity, streamlined communication, and effective data management. Here's a concise overview of the importance of these tools:

1.Streamlined Productivity:

Microsoft Office tools, including Word, Excel, and PowerPoint, simplify complex tasks, allowing users to work more efficiently and effectively.

Word facilitates document creation and formatting, Excel enables data analysis, and PowerPoint simplifies presentation design, ultimately saving time and effort.

2. Standardization and Compatibility:

Microsoft Office has become the global standard for document formats. Files created in these applications are easily shared, ensuring compatibility across different devices and platforms.

Standardized templates and styles promote consistency in documents and presentations, fostering a professional and cohesive image.

3. Effective Communication:

Microsoft Outlook streamlines email communication and calendar management, making it a critical tool for businesses and individuals.

Outlook's integration with other Office tools enables seamless collaboration, enhancing communication and coordination within teams.

4. Data Analysis and Decision-Making:

Excel's advanced features, such as formulas and functions, empower users to analyze data and make informed decisions.

It is invaluable for tasks like financial modeling, KPI tracking, and creating interactive charts and graphs.

5. Collaboration and Remote Work:

Microsoft Office 365 offers cloud-based collaboration tools that facilitate teamwork and remote work.

Real-time co-authoring in Word and Excel, along with cloud storage options like OneDrive and SharePoint, enables efficient collaboration from different locations.

6. Organized Information Management:

Microsoft Access simplifies database creation and management, providing efficient data storage and retrieval capabilities.

It is essential for maintaining organized records, such as inventories, customer databases, and project tracking.

7. Education and Skill Development:

Proficiency in Microsoft Office is a highly sought-after skill in the job market and academia.

It equips individuals with fundamental tools for various careers and is commonly used in education for coursework and assignments.

8. Business Efficiency and Competitiveness:

In the business world, efficient document creation, data analysis, and effective presentations contribute to operational efficiency.

Microsoft Office tools enhance a company's competitiveness by improving processes, communication, and decision-making.

Microsoft Office Tools, including Word, Excel, PowerPoint, Outlook, Access, and OneNote, hold immense importance in the modern workplace. They are essential software applications that contribute significantly to productivity, efficiency, and effective communication. Below, we explore in-depth the importance of these tools:

1. Microsoft Word:

Professional Document Creation: Microsoft Word is the industry standard for word processing. It allows users to create, format, and edit documents with ease. This is crucial for generating professional reports, letters, resumes, and academic papers.

Consistency: Word provides templates and styles, ensuring a consistent and standardized look for documents within an organization.

Collaboration: It facilitates collaboration with features like track changes and comments, allowing multiple users to edit and review documents simultaneously.

2. Microsoft Excel:

Data Analysis: Excel is a powerful tool for data analysis, making it essential for businesses, researchers, and analysts. Users can perform complex calculations, create financial models, and generate graphs.

Data Visualization: It enables users to present data visually through charts and graphs, making complex information easier to understand.
Efficiency: Excel's functions and formulas streamline calculations, reducing errors and saving time.

3. Microsoft PowerPoint:

Effective Presentations: PowerPoint is instrumental for creating visually engaging presentations. It helps presenters convey ideas effectively, making it indispensable for sales pitches, educational lectures, and corporate meetings.
Visual Storytelling: It allows users to incorporate multimedia elements, making presentations more engaging and memorable.
Audience Engagement: Features like animations and slide transitions keep audiences engaged during presentations.

4. Microsoft Outlook:

Email Management: Outlook simplifies email communication, making it efficient and organized. Users can send, receive, and manage emails seamlessly.
Calendar and Scheduling: The calendar feature assists in managing appointments, meetings, and tasks. It supports effective time management and coordination.
Contact Management: Outlook's address book helps users organize and maintain contact information.

5. Microsoft Access:

Database Management: Access is crucial for creating and managing databases, making it suitable for tasks like inventory management and customer relationship management.
Data Retrieval: Users can retrieve specific data quickly using queries, ensuring efficient data access.
Customization: Access allows users to design forms and reports, tailoring the database to meet specific business needs.

6. Microsoft OneNote:

Digital Note-Taking: OneNote is a versatile tool for digital note-taking, ideal for organizing ideas, research, and project notes.
Collaboration: It supports collaboration by allowing users to share and work on notebooks with others, promoting teamwork and knowledge sharing.

1.3 Navigating the Office Interface

Navigating the Office interface is a fundamental skill for effectively using Microsoft Office applications such as Word, Excel, PowerPoint, and more. It involves understanding and utilizing the various elements and features of the interface to efficiently create, edit, and manage documents, spreadsheets, and presentations. Below is a description of how to navigate the Office interface:

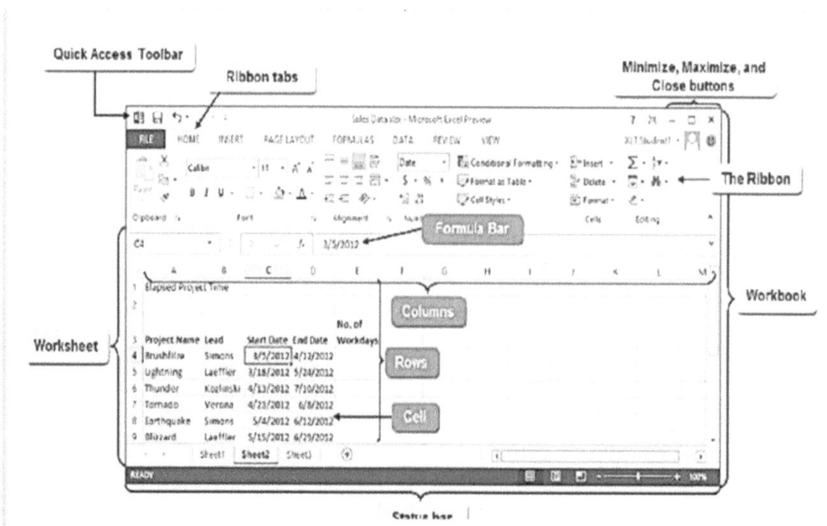

Ribbon: The Ribbon is a prominent feature in Office applications. It is a horizontal toolbar located at the top of the application window, divided into tabs. Each tab represents a category of functions, such as "Home," "Insert,"

"Page Layout," and more. Clicking on a tab reveals a set of related commands organized into groups. These commands are represented by icons or text labels. Users can easily access different functionalities by selecting the appropriate tab and command group.

Quick Access Toolbar: Positioned above the Ribbon, the Quick Access Toolbar provides quick access to frequently used commands. Users can customize this toolbar by adding their preferred commands, ensuring that essential functions are readily available regardless of the active tab or Ribbon category.

Backstage View: To perform file-related actions like creating new documents, opening, saving, and printing files, users can click on the "File" tab in the upper-left corner of the application window. This action opens the Backstage View, where users can access document properties, set options, and manage recent documents. The Backstage View is the gateway to essential file management tasks.

Document View: The central area of the application window is where users interact with their documents, spreadsheets, or presentations. This is where content is created, edited, and formatted. Users can navigate within this view by scrolling, selecting text or cells, applying formatting, and performing various editing tasks.

Status Bar: Typically located at the bottom of the window, the Status Bar provides information and controls related to the document or workbook. It may display details such as page number, word count, zoom level, or current cell selection in Excel. Users can also change certain settings, such as the view layout, by clicking on options in the Status Bar.

Minimize, Maximize, Close Buttons: In the top-right corner of the application window, users will find the standard window control buttons: minimize (—), maximize (square), and close (X). These buttons allow users to respectively minimize the application window, maximize it to full screen, or close the application.

Keyboard Shortcuts: To expedite navigation and execution of commands, users can employ keyboard shortcuts. For example, pressing Ctrl + S in most Office applications quickly saves the document, while Ctrl + C and Ctrl + V are used for copying and pasting text or objects. Learning these shortcuts can significantly boost productivity.

Help and Support: Microsoft Office provides access to a robust help and support system. Users can access tutorials, tips, and online resources by clicking on the "Help" or "Tell me what you want to do" feature, typically located in the Ribbon or the upper-right corner of the application window. This ensures that users have access to guidance and assistance when needed.

In conclusion, navigating the Office interface involves mastering the use of the Ribbon, Quick Access Toolbar, Backstage View, and other elements to efficiently access and utilize the wide range of features and functions offered by Microsoft Office applications. This proficiency is foundational for effectively harnessing the power of these tools in personal, educational, and professional contexts.

Exercise

Exercise 1 – MCQ

Q 1. Which Microsoft Office application is primarily used for word processing?
A. Microsoft Excel
B. Microsoft PowerPoint
C. Microsoft Word
D. Microsoft Access

Q 2. Which Office application is used for creating interactive presentations?
A. Microsoft Outlook
B. Microsoft Excel
C. Microsoft PowerPoint
D. Microsoft Access

Exercise 2 – True/ False

Q 1. Microsoft Office is a suite of home and business productivity software.
Q 2. Microsoft Office is primarily a popular web browser.

Exercise 3 – Fill in the blanks

Q 1. Microsoft Office is a suite of ______________ and business productivity software.
Q 2. Microsoft ______________ is primarily used for creating and editing text-based documents.

Exercise 4 – Match case

1. Creating and editing text-based documents.
2. Data analysis and spreadsheet calculations.
3. Designing interactive presentations.

4. Email and calendar management.
5.Database management.

A. Microsoft Access
B. Microsoft PowerPoint
C. Microsoft Excel
D. Microsoft Word
E. Microsoft Outlook

Exercise 5 – One word answer

Q 1. What is the collective name for Microsoft's home and business productivity software?
Q 2. Which Microsoft Office application is used for creating interactive presentations?

Exercise 6 – Small answer

Q 1. What is Microsoft Office?
Q 2. What is the primary purpose of Microsoft Outlook?

Exercise 7 – Long answer

Q 1. Explain the importance of Microsoft Office in the modern workplace.
Q 2. Explain the importance of the Ribbon and Quick Access Toolbar in Microsoft Office applications.

Answers

Exercise 1 – MCQ

Ans: 1 C, 2, C

Exercise 2 – True/ False

Ans: 1 True, 2. False

Exercise 3 – Fill in the blanks

Ans: 1 home, 2 Word

Exercise 4 – Match case

Ans: 1 1 D,2 C,3B,4 E,5 A

Exercise 5 – One word answer

Ans: 1 Microsoft Office, 2 PowerPoint

Chapter 2 - **Microsoft Word**

2.1 Basic Word Processing Skills

Basic word processing skills are the fundamental abilities required to create, edit, format, and manage text-based documents effectively using word processing software like Microsoft Word or similar applications. These skills are essential for various purposes, including academic work, professional documents, and personal writing. Below is an explanation of key basic word processing skills:

Creating Documents: Basic word processing begins with creating a new document. Users can open their word processing software, choose the "New Document" or "Create" option, and start with a blank page. Alternatively, templates may be used to create documents with predefined layouts.

Entering Text: Typing and entering text is a core skill. Users input content using the keyboard. Basic keyboard functions include typing, using the spacebar, and hitting Enter or Return to create new paragraphs.

Editing Text: Word processing tools enable users to edit text efficiently. Basic editing functions include selecting text (click and drag or Shift + arrow keys), cutting (Ctrl + X), copying (Ctrl + C), and pasting (Ctrl + V).

Formatting Text: Formatting tools allow users to enhance the appearance of text. Basic formatting options include changing font styles (e.g., bold, italic), adjusting font size, altering text color, and applying underline or strikethrough.

Paragraph Formatting: Paragraph formatting involves setting alignment (left, center, right, justified), adjusting line spacing (single, double), and managing paragraph indentation (e.g., first line or hanging indent).

Bulleted and Numbered Lists: Users can create bulleted or numbered lists to organize information in a structured manner. These lists are useful for creating outlines, agendas, or itemized content.

Spell Checking and Grammar Checking: Word processing software typically offers built-in spell and grammar checkers. These tools help users identify and correct spelling errors and grammatical mistakes in their documents.

Page Layout: Basic page layout skills include setting page margins, adjusting page orientation (portrait or landscape), and specifying paper size. These settings influence the document's overall appearance.

Saving and Printing: Saving documents is crucial to preserve work. Users can save files with meaningful names and appropriate file formats (e.g., .docx or .pdf). Printing involves selecting a printer, specifying page ranges, and choosing print options such as color or black and white.

Document Navigation: Efficient navigation within a document is essential. Basic skills include scrolling through pages, using the Find and Replace function to search for specific text, and employing keyboard shortcuts like Ctrl + Home or Ctrl + End to navigate quickly.

Headers and Footers: Adding headers and footers allows users to include page numbers, document titles, or other information at the top and bottom of each page.

Tables: Basic table skills involve creating, formatting, and editing tables within a document. Tables are useful for organizing and presenting data in rows and columns.

These basic word processing skills are foundational and serve as a starting point for users to create well-structured, visually appealing, and error-free documents. As users become more proficient, they can explore advanced features and functions to further enhance their word processing capabilities.

2.1.1 Font Selection and Formatting

Font selection and formatting are essential aspects of word processing and document design. They influence the appearance, readability, and visual appeal of your documents. Here's a brief description of these concepts:

1. **Font Selection:**

   Choosing the right font is crucial for effective communication in your documents. Different fonts have distinct styles, which can convey different moods or serve specific purposes. For example:

   Serif Fonts: Fonts like Times New Roman have small decorative lines (serifs) at the ends of characters. They are often used for formal documents, such as academic papers, because of their readability in print.

   Sans-serif Fonts: Fonts like Arial or Calibri lack serifs and provide a cleaner, more modern appearance. They are commonly used in digital content and presentations.

   Decorative Fonts: These fonts have unique, artistic designs and are used sparingly for special effects or branding.

Monospaced Fonts: Fonts like Courier maintain equal spacing between characters. They are often used for coding or tabular data where precise alignment is crucial.

2. **Font Formatting:**

Formatting involves adjusting the appearance of text within your document. Here is some common font formatting

Options:

Bold: This makes the text appear thicker and is often used for emphasis.

Italic: Italics slant the text and are often used for titles, book names, or to indicate foreign words.

Underline: This adds a line under the text and is used for hyperlinks or to emphasize text.

Strikethrough: Text with a line through it is often used to indicate deleted or no longer relevant information.

Font Size: Changing the size of text affects its prominence. Headings are typically larger than body text for hierarchy.

Font Color: Altering the color of text can add visual interest or highlight specific information.

Text Highlighting: Applying background color to text can make it stand out, such as using yellow to mark key points.

Superscript and Subscript: These formatting options are used for mathematical notations, like writing 'x^2' or 'H_2O.'

Applying font formatting is a balance between making your text visually appealing and ensuring readability. Consistency in font selection and formatting throughout your document is essential for a polished, professional look.

2.1.2 Paragraph Alignment and Justification

Paragraph alignment and justification are important elements in document formatting that determine how text is positioned and presented within a document. Here's a brief description of these concepts:

1. **Paragraph Alignment:**

Paragraph alignment refers to the horizontal positioning of text within a paragraph or text block. The four common types of paragraph alignment are:

Left Alignment: Text is aligned along the left margin. This is the default alignment in most documents and creates a "ragged" right edge.

Center Alignment: Text is centered between the left and right margins. This creates a balanced appearance with equal space on both sides of the text.

Right Alignment: Text is aligned along the right margin, creating a "ragged" left edge.

Justified Alignment: Text is aligned along both the left and right margins, creating a straight and even edge on both sides. This is commonly used in newspapers, magazines, and formal documents.

2. **Justification:**

Justification is the process of adjusting the spacing between words in a line of text to achieve alignment along both the left and right margins. When text is justified, it forms a neat and consistent block of text from the left to the right margin. Here are some key points regarding justification:

Left Justified: In left-justified text, only the left margin is straight, and the right margin is ragged. This is the default alignment in many documents.

Fully Justified: Fully justified text has both left and right margins aligned, creating a clean and formal appearance. However, it may lead to irregular word spacing, known as "rivers of white" in the text.

Justification in Print Media: Justification is commonly used in print media like newspapers and magazines to create a polished and professional look.

Justification in Online Content: In digital content, fully justified text may not always be preferred because it can lead to uneven spacing on different screen sizes. Content may be left-aligned or center-aligned for better readability.

The choice of paragraph alignment and justification depends on the document's purpose and the desired visual presentation. Left alignment is often used for informal documents, while center or full justification is more common in formal or printed materials. Selecting the appropriate alignment and justification helps create a visually appealing and reader-friendly document.

2.1.3 Spell Check and Grammar Check

Spell check and grammar check are essential features in word processing software that help improve the accuracy and clarity of written documents. Here's a brief description of these functions:

1. Spell Check:

Purpose: Spell check is a tool that automatically identifies and corrects misspelled words in a document. Its primary purpose is to ensure that written text is free from spelling errors.

Operation: When you run a spell check, the software scans the document for words that are not in its internal dictionary. It highlights or underlines these words, suggesting correct alternatives if available. Users can choose to accept or ignore these suggestions.

Benefits: Spell check helps prevent embarrassing spelling mistakes, enhances the overall professionalism of the document, and ensures that words are spelled correctly.

2. Grammar Check:

Purpose: Grammar check is a feature that examines the document for grammatical errors and issues with sentence structure, punctuation, and style. It aims to improve the quality and clarity of writing.

Operation: A grammar check analyzes the text for common grammar and punctuation mistakes. It highlights sentences or phrases that may need revision and provides suggestions for improving grammar, usage, and overall writing style.

Benefits: Grammar check enhances the overall quality of the document by identifying and correcting grammatical errors and inconsistencies. It helps ensure that the writing is clear, concise, and easy to understand.

Key Considerations:

Complementary Tools: Spell check and grammar check often work together in word processing software, providing a comprehensive solution for proofreading and editing documents.

Manual Review: While these tools are valuable, they are not infallible. It's essential for users to manually review suggestions and apply corrections thoughtfully, as automated checks may occasionally produce false positives or miss nuanced errors.

Customization: Some word processors allow users to customize the settings of spell check and grammar check to align with specific writing preferences and style guidelines.

Writing Improvement: Regularly using these checks can help individuals become better writers over time by learning from the corrections and suggestions provided.

In summary, spell check and grammar check are indispensable tools for ensuring the accuracy, professionalism, and clarity of written documents. They help writers catch and correct mistakes, resulting in more polished and effective communication.

2.1.4 Creating and Formatting Tables

Creating and formatting tables is a fundamental skill in document preparation, especially when organizing and presenting data in a clear and structured manner. Here's a brief description of how to create and format tables:

1. Creating Tables:

Purpose: Tables are used to display information in rows and columns, making data more accessible and visually organized.

Procedure: In most word processing software, you can create a table by selecting the "Insert Table" or similar option. You'll specify the number of rows and columns you need. Then, you can begin entering data into the table cells.

Data Entry: Populate the table by clicking in each cell and typing or pasting your content. You can use the Tab key to move from one cell to the next.

Adjusting Table Size: After creating a table, you can adjust its size by adding or removing rows and columns as needed. You can also resize individual rows and columns to accommodate the content.

2. Formatting Tables:

Alignment: You can control the alignment of the text within each cell, choosing from options like left, center, or right alignment both horizontally and vertically.

Borders: Tables can have visible or invisible borders. You can add, remove, or change the thickness of borders to distinguish rows and columns.

Cell Shading: You can add background colors to individual cells or entire rows and columns to make specific data stand out.
Text Formatting: Tables support various text formatting options, including font styles, size, bold, italics, and color. You can format text within cells just like you would in regular text.
Cell Merge: Some tables may require cells to be merged, creating larger combined cells. This is useful for headers or when you want to span content across multiple cells.
Table Styles: Many word processing software programs offer predefined table styles, making it easy to apply professional and consistent formatting to your tables.
Sort and Filter: Tables can be sorted and filtered based on the content in specific columns, which is particularly useful for data analysis and organization.
Creating and formatting tables is an effective way to structure and present data, whether in reports, presentations, or documents. By understanding these basic principles, you can design tables that enhance the readability and visual appeal of your content.

2.1.5 Indentation and Line Spacing

Indentation and line spacing are formatting techniques used in word processing to enhance the organization, readability, and visual appeal of documents. Here's a brief description of these concepts:
1. Indentation:
Purpose: Indentation is used to set the position of text relative to the margins. It helps create a clear visual hierarchy in documents, such as differentiating paragraphs, lists, and quotations.
Types of Indentation:
First Line Indent: This type indents the first line of a paragraph, creating a "hanging indent." It is commonly used in document formatting to distinguish paragraphs.
Left Indent: This adjusts the position of the entire text block to the right, shifting it away from the left margin.
Right Indent: This affects the right margin, moving the text block closer to or away from it.
Hanging Indent: Used in lists or bibliographies, this indents the second and subsequent lines while keeping the first line flush with the left margin.
Adjustment: You can control the amount of indentation in word processing software by specifying values in inches, millimeters, or other units. Users can also use the Tab key to manually set indentation.
2. Line Spacing:
Purpose: Line spacing determines the vertical space between lines of text. It affects document readability and the visual impact of text.
Types of Line Spacing:
Single Spacing: Lines of text are positioned closely together, with minimal space between them.
Double Spacing: This provides more space between lines, which is commonly used for academic papers, reports, and professional documents.
1.5 Line Spacing: It offers a compromise between single and double spacing, providing some separation while conserving space.
Custom Spacing: Users can also define specific line spacing values according to their document requirements.
Adjustment: Word processing software usually provides options for adjusting line spacing within a document. Users can choose line spacing preferences such as single, 1.5, double, or custom spacing values.
Key Considerations:
Formatting Consistency: Consistent use of indentation and line spacing is essential for a professional and organized document.
Document Style: Different document types may have specific indentation and line spacing requirements. For example, academic papers may require specific line spacing rules.
Visual Impact: Proper use of these formatting techniques improves the overall visual impact of a document, making it more reader-friendly and visually appealing.
In summary, indentation and line spacing are essential tools for document organization and visual presentation. By understanding and applying these concepts, users can create well-structured, visually pleasing documents that effectively convey their intended message.

2.2 Advanced Word Processing Techniques

Advanced word processing techniques go beyond the basics and offer users a more sophisticated way to create, format, and enhance documents. Here's a brief description of some of these techniques:

1. Styles and Templates:

Purpose: Styles and templates allow for consistent formatting throughout a document. A style is a collection of formatting settings, including font, size, color, and alignment. Templates are pre-designed document structures with predefined styles, headings, and placeholders.

Benefits: Using styles and templates ensures a uniform look and feel, saves time, and maintains consistency in documents. They are especially useful for creating professional reports, theses, and large documents.

2. Document Sections:

Purpose: Document sections enable different parts of a document to have distinct formatting, such as page orientation, margins, headers, footers, and numbering. Users can insert section breaks to separate content within a document.

Benefits: Document sections are valuable for creating complex documents with varying layouts. For example, a report may have different header and footer content in the introduction section compared to the main body.

3. Columns and Text Boxes:

Purpose: Columns and text boxes allow users to organize text into multiple columns or create specific areas for text within a document. Columns can be useful for creating newsletters, while text boxes are ideal for sidebars or highlighted content.

Benefits: These features enhance document design by enabling text flow in non-traditional layouts, making documents more visually engaging.

4. Headers and Footers:

Purpose: Headers and footers are sections at the top and bottom of each page, allowing consistent information like page numbers, document titles, and dates to be added.

Benefits: Headers and footers help in document navigation and identification. They are essential for creating professional reports, research papers, and business documents.

5. Document Collaboration:

Purpose: Collaboration features, such as track changes and comments, enable multiple users to edit and review a document simultaneously. Users can see and accept/reject suggested changes.

Benefits: Collaboration features streamline the editing and review process. They are invaluable for working on documents as a team, especially in a professional or academic setting.

6. Mail Merge:

Purpose: Mail merge allows users to personalize and send mass emails or letters. It combines a template document with a data source, automatically inserting recipient-specific information.

Benefits: Mail merge is a time-saving tool for tasks like sending personalized invitations, newsletters, or generating bulk invoices.

7. Cross-References and Hyperlinks:

Purpose: Cross-references enable users to link content within a document, such as referring to a figure or section. Hyperlinks allow users to link to external websites or resources.

Benefits: Cross-references make it easy to navigate lengthy documents, while hyperlinks enhance the document's interactivity.

These advanced word processing techniques offer users powerful tools to create professional and well-structured documents. By mastering these techniques, individuals can produce documents that are not only visually appealing but also highly functional and efficient for various purposes.

2.2.1 Creating a Table of Contents

Creating a Table of Contents in Microsoft Word is a valuable tool for organizing and navigating lengthy documents. It provides a structured overview of your document's headings and subheadings, allowing readers to quickly jump to specific sections. Here's a step-by-step explanation of how to create a Table of Contents in Microsoft Word:

1. Document Preparation:

Before creating a Table of Contents, ensure that your document is well-structured. Use different heading styles for section titles and subtitles. In Word, you can apply heading styles by selecting text and choosing from options like "Heading 1," "Heading 2," etc., from the "Styles" group on the "Home" tab.

2. Inserting the Table of Contents:

Place your cursor where you want to insert the Table of Contents. Typically, it's at the beginning of your document.

Navigate to the "References" tab on the Word ribbon.

In the "Table of Contents" group, you'll find the "Table of Contents" dropdown menu. Click on it to see different TOC styles.

3. Choosing a Table of Contents Style:

Microsoft Word provides several predefined TOC styles. Hover your cursor over a style to see a preview, and click on the one that suits your document.

4. Automatic Generation:

Word will automatically generate a Table of Contents based on the heading styles you've used. The TOC will include section titles, subsections, and their corresponding page numbers.

5. Customization:

You can further customize your Table of Contents:

To change the appearance, right-click on the TOC and choose "Custom Table of Contents.

You can also remove the page numbers from the TOC or change the format of page numbers.

6. Updating the Table of Contents:

The Table of Contents is dynamic and will automatically update when you make changes to your document, such as removing, or reorganizing sections. To manually update it, right-click on the TOC and choose "Update Field."

7. Navigating the Document:

Readers can click on any entry in the Table of Contents to quickly navigate to the corresponding section in the document.

By following these steps, you can efficiently create a Table of Contents in Microsoft Word, improving the accessibility and readability of your longer documents. It's a valuable tool for both authors and readers, helping them find and explore specific sections within the document with ease.

2.2.2 Track Changes and Commenting

The "Track Changes" and "Commenting" features in word processing software, such as Microsoft Word, are invaluable tools for collaborative writing and the editing process. They allow multiple users to review and revise documents while keeping a record of changes and facilitating communication among contributors. Here's an explanation of these features:

1. Track Changes:

Purpose: The "Track Changes" feature records any additions, deletions, or formatting modifications made to a document. It's primarily used for collaborative editing, where multiple individuals work on the same document.

Activation: To activate "Track Changes" in Microsoft Word, go to the "Review" tab and click on "Track Changes." When enabled, any edits made to the document will be displayed using various formatting conventions. Additions appear underlined, deletions are struck through, and formatting changes are highlighted.

Benefits: "Track Changes" helps maintain transparency in the editing process. Authors and editors can see who made which changes and can accept or reject those changes individually. This feature is particularly valuable in professional settings, such as editing reports, research papers, or legal documents.

2. Commenting:

Purpose: Commenting allows users to insert notes, explanations, or feedback directly into the document without altering the actual text. Comments are useful for providing context, suggestions, or clarification regarding specific portions of the document.

Activation: To add comments in Microsoft Word, select the text you want to comment on, right-click, and choose "New Comment." A comment bubble with your name and the comment text will appear in the document's margin.

Benefits: Commenting streamlines communication during the editing and review process. Users can discuss changes, ask questions, or provide feedback without altering the original text. It also allows for a threaded conversation, where replies can be added to comments for further discussion.

Key Considerations:

Collaborative Editing: "Track Changes" and commenting are most effective when multiple users are involved in the document creation or editing process. They provide a structured way to work on a document together and communicate about changes and suggestions.

Final Review: After the editing and review process is complete, it's essential to carefully review the document and address any remaining comments or tracked changes before finalizing the document.

Accepting and Rejecting Changes: In the "Track Changes" mode, users have the option to accept or reject individual changes. This is a crucial step in the finalization process to ensure that only approved modifications are incorporated into the document.

In summary, "Track Changes" and commenting are vital features for collaborative writing and the editing process. They enhance transparency, streamline communication, and ensure that documents undergo thorough review and revision, making them suitable for professional, academic, and creative contexts.

2.2.3 Mail Merge for Bulk Document Generation

Mail Merge is a feature in word processing software, such as Microsoft Word, that automates the process of creating multiple, personalized documents from a single template. It is commonly used for generating bulk letters, envelopes, labels, or emails. Here's an explanation of how Mail Merge works for bulk document generation:

1. Data Source:

To start a Mail Merge, you need a data source. This source can be a spreadsheet, database, or a list of recipients' information. Each record in the data source represents a unique recipient.

2. Template Creation:

Create a template document in your word processing software. This document will serve as the base for all the personalized documents you want to generate. Place dynamic fields or placeholders where you want recipient-specific information to be inserted.

Dynamic fields are typically indicated with double angle brackets, like <<First Name>> or <<Address>>. These fields will be replaced with data from your source.

3. Starting the Mail Merge:

In Microsoft Word, navigate to the "Mailings" tab. Select "Start Mail Merge" and choose the type of document you want to create, such as letters, envelopes, labels, or emails.

4. Selecting Recipients:

In the "Mailings" tab, click on "Select Recipients." Choose your data source, such as an Excel spreadsheet or an existing Outlook contact list.

5. Inserting Merge Fields:

Go back to your document and place your cursor where you want to insert the personalized information. In the "Mailings" tab, select "Insert Merge Field" and choose the field from your data source you want to insert.

6. Previewing the Merge:

Click on "Preview Results" to see how your document will appear for each recipient. You can navigate through the records to ensure that the information is correctly merged.

7. Completing the Merge:

Once you're satisfied with the preview, go back to the "Mailings" tab and click "Finish & Merge." You can choose to print the documents, create a new document, or send them via email.

8. Document Generation:

Mail Merge will generate individual documents for each recipient, with the placeholders replaced by their specific information.

9. Saving or Printing:

You can choose to save or print the documents as needed. In the case of email merges, the emails will be sent directly to the recipients.

Benefits of Mail Merge for Bulk Document Generation:

Efficiency: Mail Merge significantly reduces the time and effort required for generating personalized documents, making it ideal for mass communications.

Accuracy: Because the data is pulled from a structured source, the risk of errors is reduced, ensuring that each document contains the correct information.

Customization: You can tailor the content of each document to the specific recipient, making it more personalized and relevant.
Consistency: Mail Merge ensures that the formatting and layout remain consistent across all generated documents.
Mail Merge is a versatile tool for businesses, nonprofits, and individuals who need to send out bulk communications with personalized content. It streamlines the document creation process and ensures that each recipient receives a document tailored to their specific information.

2.2.4 Printing Documents Effectively

Printing documents effectively involves several considerations, from selecting the right printer and paper to optimizing settings for the desired output. Here's an explanation of how to print documents effectively:

1. Selecting the Right Printer:

Purpose: Choose a printer that suits your needs. Laser printers are ideal for high-quality text, while inkjet printers excel in color printing. For large volumes, consider a network or multifunction printer.
Resolution: The printer's resolution (measured in dpi or dots per inch) determines print quality. Higher dpi produces crisper text and images.

2. Paper Selection:

Paper Type: Select paper appropriate for your document. Standard copier paper is fine for everyday printing, but special paper may be required for photos or presentations.
Paper Size: Ensure that the paper size matches the document size. Common sizes include letter (8.5 x 11 inches), legal (8.5 x 14 inches), and A4 (210 x 297 mm).

3. Document Layout:

Margins: Adjust document margins as needed. Narrower margins can maximize content on a page, while wider margins provide a cleaner look.
Page Orientation: Choose between portrait (vertical) and landscape (horizontal) orientation based on the content and design of your document.

4. Print Preview:

Before printing, always use the print preview feature in your word processing software. This allows you to see how the document will appear on paper and make any necessary adjustments.

5. Quality and Speed Settings:

Adjust the print quality and speed settings based on your document's purpose. For drafts and everyday printing, you can choose "Fast Draft" or "Economy" settings to save ink or toner. For high-quality documents, select "Best" or "High Quality."

6. Color vs. Black and White:

For text-heavy documents, consider printing in black and white or grayscale to save on color ink or toner. Reserve color printing for content that requires it.

7. Duplex Printing:

If your printer supports it, enable duplex printing to print on both sides of the paper. This saves paper and is eco-friendly.

8. Page Setup:

Ensure that page setup options (such as scaling, paper source, and layout) match your document's requirements.

9. Check Ink or Toner Levels:

Before printing an important document, check the ink or toner levels. Running out in the middle of a print job can be frustrating.

10. Print Test Pages:

When using a new printer or different paper, print a test page first to verify the results before printing the entire document.

11. Print in Batches:

For large documents or print jobs, consider breaking the printing into smaller batches. This reduces the risk of paper jams and allows you to monitor print quality more closely.

12. File Format:

Save your document in the appropriate file format. PDF is often preferred for sharing documents as it ensures the formatting remains consistent across different devices and software.

13. Proofreading:
Always proofread the document on the screen before printing to catch errors or formatting issues.
14. Economical Printing:
To save ink or toner, use the "draft" or "economy" setting for less critical documents. You can also consider using ink-saving fonts and printing in grayscale.
15. Eco-Friendly Printing:
If possible, print double-sided, and recycle or reuse paper when printing drafts.
16. Printer Maintenance:
Regularly clean the printer, replace cartridges, and perform maintenance to ensure the best print quality.
Effective document printing not only saves resources but also ensures that your printed materials are clear, professional, and fit for their intended purpose. Following these guidelines helps you achieve the desired results while minimizing waste and cost.

Exercise

Exercise 1 – MCQ

Q 1. 1. Which of the following is not a valid file extension for a Microsoft Word document?
A. .doc
B. .xlsx
C. .docx
D. .rtf

Q 2. Which view in Microsoft Word allows you to see how the document will appear when printed?
A. Print Layout
B. Normal
C. Web Layout
D. Outline

Exercise 2 – True/ False

Q 1 Microsoft Word is a spreadsheet software.
Q 2 In Microsoft Word, you can use the "Thesaurus" feature to find synonyms for words.

Exercise 3 – Fill in the blanks

Q 1. In Microsoft Word, the keyboard shortcut for copying selected text is ____________.
Q 2. "Ctrl+Z" is the keyboard shortcut for ____________ in Microsoft Word.

Exercise 4 – Match case

1. AutoCorrect
2.Print Layout View
3.Insert Tab
4.Ctrl+C

A. Automatically corrects common spelling and typing errors as you type.
B. Allows you to see how the document will appear when printed, including page breaks and margins.
C. Ribbon tab used for inserting pictures, shapes, charts, and other elements into a document.
D. Keyboard shortcut for copying selected text.

Exercise 5 – One word answer

Q 1. What is the default font style used in Microsoft Word documents?
Q 2. Which ribbon tab in Microsoft Word is used for inserting pictures, shapes, and charts into a document?

Exercise 6 – Small answer

Q 1. What is the purpose of the "Track Changes" feature in Microsoft Word?
Q 2. How can you create a numbered list in Microsoft Word?

Exercise 7 – Long answer

Q 1. Describe the process of creating a numbered list and a bulleted list in Microsoft Word. How can these features be used to enhance document structure?
Q 2. Explain the steps involved in inserting and formatting a picture or image in a Microsoft Word document. How can images enhance the visual appeal of a document?

Answers

Exercise 1 – MCQ
Ans: 1 B, 2 A
Exercise 2 – True/ False
Ans: 1 False, 2 True
Exercise 3 – Fill in the blanks
Ans: 1 Ctrl+C, 2 UNDO
Exercise 4 – Match case
Ans: 1 A,2 B, 3 C, 4 D
Exercise 5 – One word answer
Ans: 1 Calibri, 2 Insert

Chapter 3 - **Microsoft Excel**

3.1 Excel Fundamentals

Once you download Microsoft Office and install it into your local system, you can get started with Microsoft Excel. The Microsoft Excel Home Page looks as follows.

Excel-Basics-**Home-Page**

Inside the Home page, you have a variety of sheet options provided by Microsoft, based on the usage. You can choose to get started with a basic simple worksheet or modify your sheet based on your preferences.
Business Data is one such example.
Once you have selected your type of sheet, you will have the following options offered by MS Excel.
Excel-Basics-**Toolbar.**

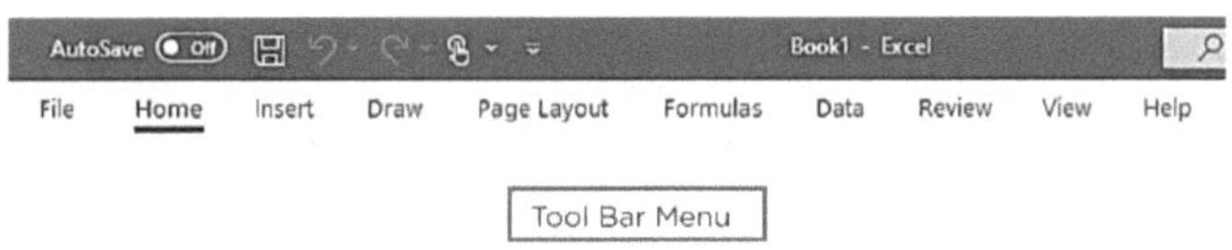

The Toolbar in MS Excel has all the tools that you need to store and manipulate your data.
The Home Option:
It will have the onboard tools to change your font, font color, and spreadsheet format.

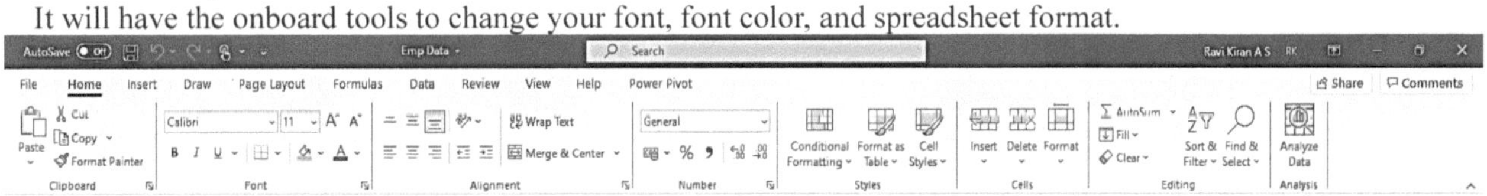

The Insert Option
The Insert option will help you insert data into your sheet. The data can be an image or any data from either your local system or an online source.

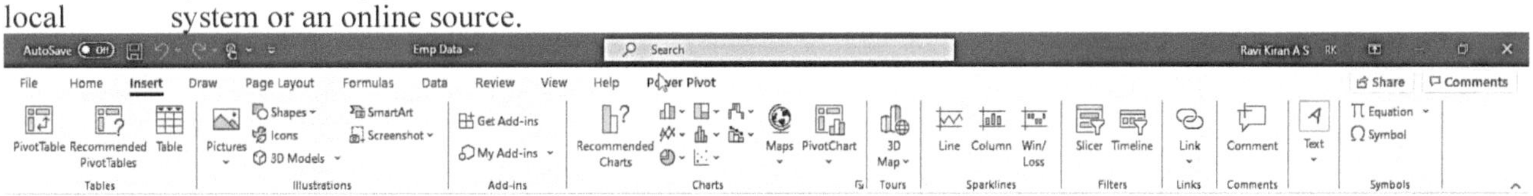

The Draw Option
The Draw option helps you to withdraw any specific visualizations into your Excel sheet.
Example - Lines, Marks.

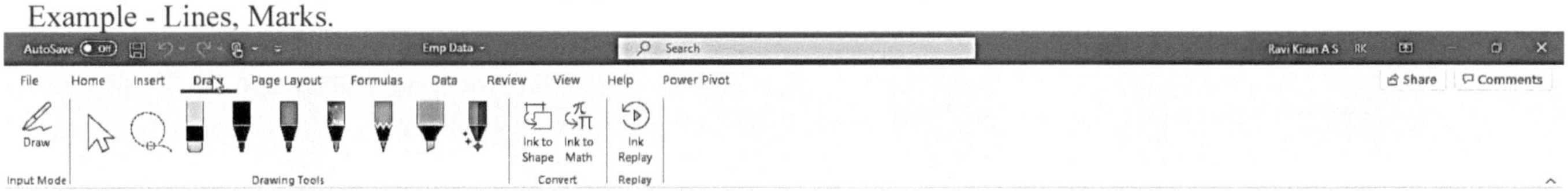

The Page Layout Option

The next option is the Page Layout. The Page Layout option provides the page printing options to modify the way your sheet could represent the data.

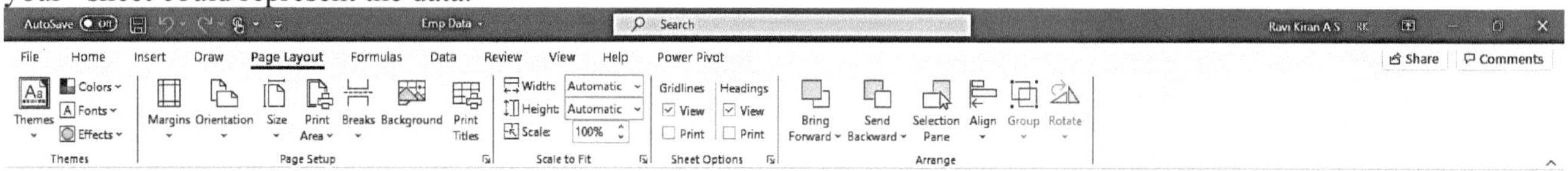

The Formula Option

The Formulas option will help you with the inbuilt business analytical formulas.

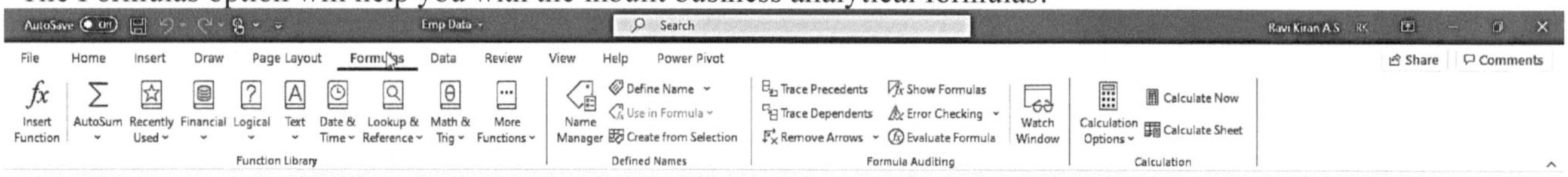

The Data Option

Data options will help you with data sources, queries, and data management options.

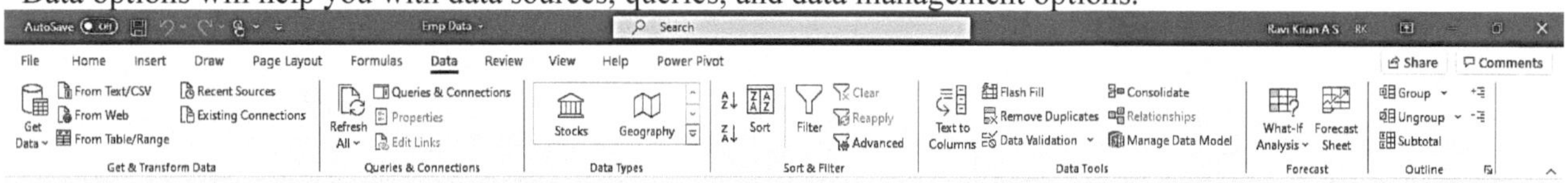

The Review Option

The Review option will help with spellings, worksheet statistics, and notes.

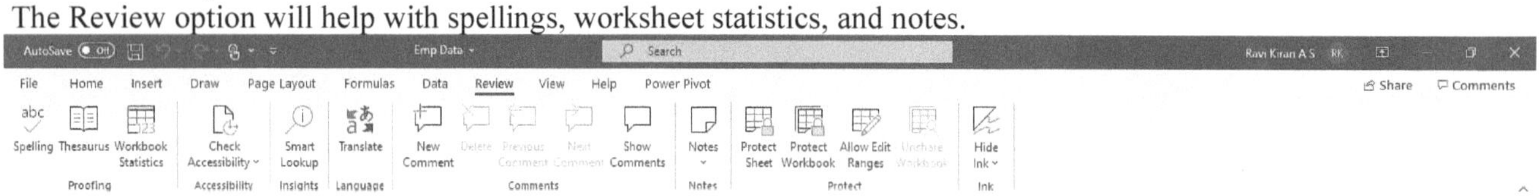

The View Option

The View option is similar to the page layout. This option will help you with basic operations like zoom, page setup, etc.

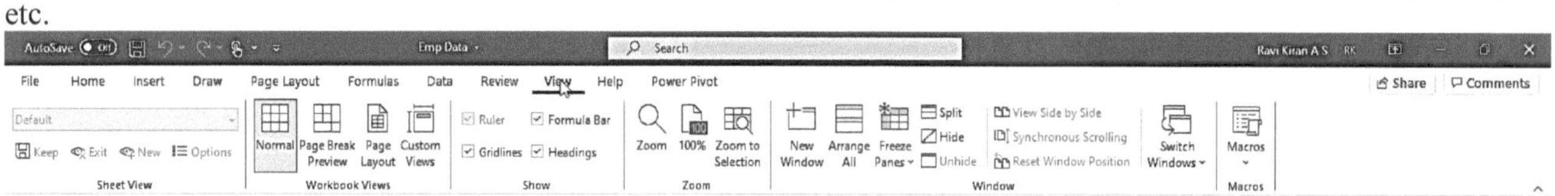

The Help Option

The Help option provides you with the possibility of contacting the technical support team and so on.

Excel-Basics-Toolbar-Help

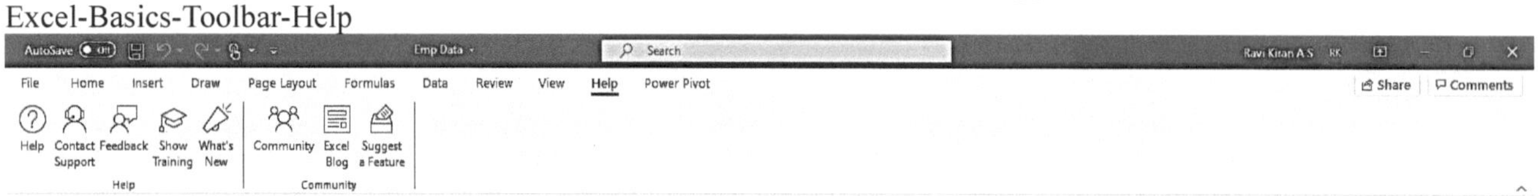

3.1.1 Introduction to Worksheets, Workbooks, and Cells

In the world of spreadsheet software, such as Microsoft Excel or Google Sheets, understanding the fundamental building blocks is essential. This introductory guide will shed light on worksheets, workbooks, and cells, which are the core elements that form the foundation of these powerful tools.

Worksheets:

Worksheets are the individual pages or tabs within a spreadsheet file. Think of them as separate, organized spaces where you can input and manipulate data. Each worksheet typically represents a specific set of data, calculations, or tasks. For instance, in a personal finance workbook, you might have one worksheet for tracking expenses and another for budget planning.

Workbooks:

Workbooks are like the larger container that holds one or more worksheets. They are essentially spreadsheet files. A single workbook can include multiple worksheets, and these sheets can be linked or referenced to one another, allowing you to create complex interrelationships. A workbook is often used to keep related data or tasks together in one file, making it easier to manage and share.

Cells:

Cells are the smallest units of a worksheet. They are the boxes you see when you look at a spreadsheet, and they are organized into rows and columns. Each cell can hold data, such as numbers, text, or formulas. You can perform calculations, formatting, and data manipulation at the cell level. Cells are referenced using a combination of letters and numbers, known as cell references (e.g., A1, B2, C3), making it easier to locate and work with specific data points.

Understanding these foundational elements is crucial for anyone looking to use spreadsheets effectively. By mastering worksheets, workbooks, and cells, you'll be better equipped to organize, analyze, and present data in a structured and coherent manner. These components are the building blocks upon which you can build complex financial models, data analysis tools, and much more. As you delve deeper into spreadsheet applications, you'll find that proficiency in these basic concepts is essential for creating efficient and error-free workbooks and worksheets.

3.1.2 Data Entry and Editing

Microsoft Excel is a versatile and widely used spreadsheet application that excels in data management, analysis, and presentation. Data entry and editing are fundamental processes that form the basis of working with Excel. Here, we'll explore the essentials of data entry and the techniques for efficient data editing:

Data Entry:

Entering Data: Data entry in Excel is as simple as selecting a cell and typing in your information. You can enter numbers, text, dates, and more. After entering data, you can press "Enter" to confirm the entry, or you can use the arrow keys to move to the next cell.

AutoFill: Excel offers the AutoFill feature, which automatically extends a series or pattern when you drag the fill handle. For example, you can enter "January" in one cell, drag the fill handle, and Excel will fill in the subsequent months.

Custom Lists: You can create custom lists in Excel to streamline data entry. For instance, if you often enter the same set of names or products, you can create a custom list to save time.

Data Validation: Data validation rules can be set to control what can be entered in a cell. This helps ensure data accuracy and consistency. You can specify criteria such as numerical ranges, dates, or even create drop-down lists for selection.

Data Editing:

Editing Data: To edit existing data, you can simply click on the cell you want to change, make the necessary edits, and press "Enter" to confirm. You can also double-click on a cell to enter edit mode.

Find and Replace: Excel's Find and Replace feature allows you to locate specific text or numbers in your worksheet and replace them with new values. This is incredibly useful for correcting errors or making consistent changes throughout your data.

Data Sorting: Excel enables you to sort data in ascending or descending order based on one or multiple columns. This is beneficial for organizing data and identifying trends.

Data Filtering: Filtering lets you display specific data based on conditions you specify. You can filter by criteria such as values greater than a certain number or dates within a specific range. Filtered data is temporarily displayed while other data is hidden.

Undo and Redo: Excel offers the ability to undo and redo actions. If you make a mistake or change your mind, you can use these features to revert or reapply actions.

Efficient data entry and editing in Excel are essential skills for managing and maintaining your spreadsheets. These processes are crucial whether you are creating a simple budget, maintaining an inventory, or conducting complex data analysis. Excel's versatility and user-friendly interface make it a valuable tool for professionals and individuals alike.

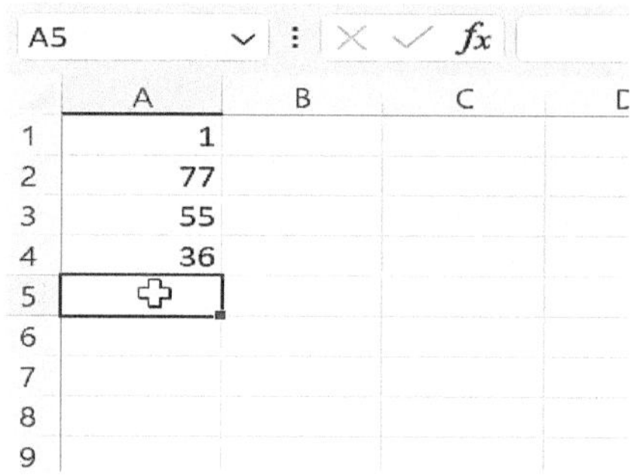

3.1.3 Basic Formulas and Functions

Microsoft Excel, a powerful spreadsheet application, provides a wealth of tools for managing and analyzing data. At the heart of Excel's functionality are formulas and functions. These features enable users to perform calculations, manipulate data, and automate tasks. Here, we'll explore the fundamentals of basic formulas and functions:

Formulas:

Definition: A formula in Excel is an expression that calculates a value based on the contents of cells. Formulas typically involve mathematical operations, such as addition, subtraction, multiplication, and division.

Cell References: Formulas use cell references to identify the cells containing the data to be processed. Excel offers three types of cell references:

Relative References: The default type, they adjust automatically when copied to other cells.

Absolute References: Marked with dollar signs ($), they remain fixed when copied.

Mixed References: Combining both relative and absolute references, they offer flexibility in calculations.

Operators: Excel supports a variety of operators for building formulas:

+ (Addition)

- (Subtraction)

* (Multiplication)

/ (Division)

^ (Exponentiation)

() (Parentheses for controlling the order of operations)

Examples: Some common formula examples include:

=A1 + B1: Adds the values in cells A1 and B1.

=SUM(A1:A5): Calculates the sum of values in cells A1 through A5.

=A1 * 0.15: Calculates 15% of the value in cell A1.

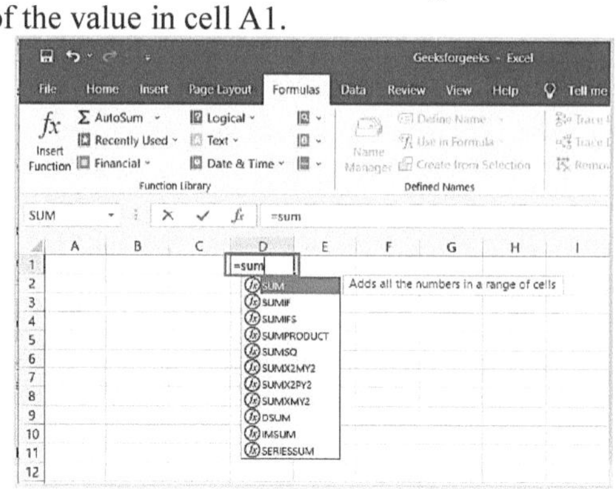

Functions:

Definition: Functions are predefined formulas that simplify complex calculations. Excel offers a vast library of functions, categorized by their specific purpose.

Syntax: Functions have a specific syntax, which consists of the function name, followed by arguments enclosed in parentheses. For example, the SUM function's syntax is =SUM(argument1, argument2, ...), where "argument1," "argument2," etc., are references or values to be summed.

Common Functions:
SUM: Adds up a range of numbers.
AVERAGE: Calculates the average of a range of numbers.
MAX: Returns the largest number in a range.
MIN: Returns the smallest number in a range.
COUNT: Counts the number of cells containing numbers.
IF: Performs conditional calculations based on a specified condition.
Nested Functions: Excel allows you to nest functions within each other to perform more complex calculations. For example, you can use the IF function within the SUM function to conditionally sum values.
AutoSum: The AutoSum feature simplifies common calculations. It automatically suggests and applies relevant functions based on the selected data.

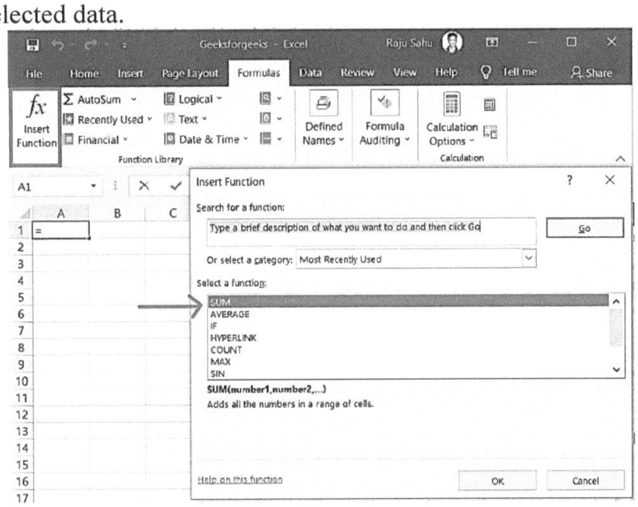

Basic formulas and functions in Excel are essential for performing simple calculations and data analysis. These features significantly enhance productivity by automating tasks that would otherwise be time-consuming. As you become more proficient in Excel, you can explore more advanced functions and build intricate formulas to address complex scenarios and data manipulation.

3.2 Data Analysis and Visualization

Microsoft Excel is a powerful tool for data analysis and visualization, offering a wide array of features that enable users to uncover insights, make informed decisions, and present data effectively. Here, we explore the process of data analysis and visualization using Excel:
Data Analysis:
Data Import: Excel allows you to import data from various sources, including text files, databases, and online data feeds. This versatility makes it easy to work with different types of data.
Data Cleaning: Before analysis, it's crucial to clean and prepare the data. This may involve removing duplicates, handling missing values, and formatting data consistently.
Filtering and Sorting: Excel offers tools for quickly filtering and sorting data to isolate specific subsets. You can filter by criteria or sort data in ascending or descending order.
Calculations and Formulas: Excel's formulas and functions are instrumental in performing calculations. You can create complex formulas to process data, calculate statistics, and derive meaningful insights.
PivotTables: PivotTables are a powerful feature for summarizing and aggregating large datasets. They allow for dynamic analysis, enabling users to quickly change the view of the data by dragging and dropping fields.
Data Validation: Data validation rules can be applied to ensure data accuracy and consistency. These rules help in preventing errors during data entry.
Data Visualization:
Charts and Graphs: Excel provides an extensive range of chart types, including bar, column, pie, line, scatter plots, and more. Users can select the most appropriate chart type to represent data visually.
Formatting: Charts and graphs can be customized to enhance their visual appeal and effectively convey information. Users can modify colors, fonts, labels, and legends.

Data Labels: Excel allows users to add data labels to charts to display values, percentages, or other relevant information directly on the chart elements.
Trendlines: For time series data, trendlines can be added to show patterns or trends within the data.
Data Bars and Color Scales: Conditional formatting, such as data bars and color scales, can be applied to cells to visually highlight data ranges based on their values.
Sparklines: These are tiny charts that fit within a single cell, providing a quick visual summary of data trends. They are particularly useful in dashboards and reports.
Data Presentation:
Reports and Dashboards: Excel is an excellent tool for creating reports and interactive dashboards. Users can compile data, charts, and visuals into a single document for easy sharing.
Conditional Formatting: Users can apply conditional formatting to highlight specific data points or trends based on predefined rules. This enhances the readability of the data.
Data Labels and Titles: Including descriptive labels, titles, and legends with visualizations adds context and clarity to the presentation.
Excel's data analysis and visualization capabilities empower users to not only explore data but also communicate findings effectively. Whether you are conducting financial analysis, market research, or project tracking, Excel provides a robust platform for transforming raw data into actionable insights and impactful visuals.

3.2.1 Advanced Functions and Formulas

Microsoft Excel is a powerful spreadsheet application that offers a wide range of advanced functions and formulas. These tools enable users to perform complex calculations, analyze data, and automate intricate tasks. Here, we explore the realm of advanced functions and formulas in Excel:
Advanced Functions:
VLOOKUP and HLOOKUP: These functions are used for searching and retrieving data from a table based on specific criteria. VLOOKUP searches vertically, while HLOOKUP searches horizontally.
INDEX and MATCH: INDEX function returns the value of a cell at a specified row and column intersection in a table. MATCH function locates the position of a specified value within a range.
IFERROR: This function allows you to handle errors in formulas. It returns a user-defined value when an error is encountered, enhancing the robustness of calculations.
SUMIFS and COUNTIFS: These functions allow users to sum or count values based on multiple criteria. For example, SUMIFS can sum sales for a specific product in a particular region and time period.
AVERAGEIF and AVERAGEIFS: These functions calculate the average of a range of values that meet specific criteria. AVERAGEIF handles one criterion, while AVERAGEIFS can handle multiple criteria.
DATE and TIME Functions: Excel offers functions for manipulating dates and times, including DATE, TIME, NOW, and DATEDIF. These functions are valuable for managing schedules, time tracking, and date-based calculations.
TEXT Function: This function enables users to format and manipulate text strings. It is particularly useful for cleaning and transforming textual data.
ARRAY Formulas: These formulas perform operations on arrays of data, making them more versatile than regular cell-based calculations. They are created by entering the formula using Ctrl+Shift+Enter.
Logical Functions:
IF Function: The IF function allows users to perform conditional calculations. It returns one value if a specified condition is true and another if it's false.
AND and OR Functions: These functions are used to evaluate multiple conditions. AND returns true only if all conditions are met, while OR returns true if any condition is met.
NOT Function: NOT negates a logical value. For instance, if a cell contains "TRUE," NOT(TRUE) would return "FALSE."
Database Functions:
DSUM, DAVERAGE, DCOUNT: These functions are used for advanced database analysis. DSUM sums values in a database that meet specific criteria, DAVERAGE calculates the average, and DCOUNT counts records based on criteria.
Financial Functions:
PV, FV, PMT: Excel offers a range of financial functions for tasks like calculating the present value (PV) of investments, future value (FV), and periodic payments (PMT) required for loans or investments.

Advanced Formulas:
Nested Formulas: Advanced users often nest functions and formulas, combining multiple functions within a single formula to perform complex calculations.
Error Handling: Advanced formulas include techniques for handling errors using functions like IFERROR or IFNA. These functions help ensure that calculations proceed smoothly, even in the presence of errors.
Custom Functions (UDFs): In addition to Excel's built-in functions, users can create custom user-defined functions (UDFs) using Visual Basic for Applications (VBA). This allows for highly specialized calculations tailored to specific needs.
Advanced functions and formulas in Excel empower users to tackle intricate calculations and data analysis tasks efficiently. Whether it's financial modeling, statistical analysis, or complex data transformations, Excel's advanced features provide the tools needed to work with and derive insights from diverse datasets.

3.2.2 Creating Charts and Graphs

Microsoft Excel is a versatile tool for creating charts and graphs that help visualize data, identify trends, and communicate information effectively. Charts and graphs are instrumental in making data more understandable and actionable. Here, we delve into the process of creating these visual representations in Excel:
Selecting Data:
Data Source: To create a chart or graph, you first need to have data to represent visually. Data can be organized in an Excel worksheet, and it can include numerical values, categories, or labels.
Data Selection: Choose the specific data range that you want to include in your chart. This data range will determine the content of your chart.
Chart Creation:
Insert Tab: Navigate to the "Insert" tab in Excel. This tab contains various chart types, including column, bar, line, pie, and more.
Chart Selection: Choose the chart type that best represents your data. The selection depends on the nature of your data and the insights you wish to convey.
Chart Title: After inserting a chart, consider adding a title to make it clear what the chart represents. The title is typically based on the context of your data.
Data Labeling:
Axis Labels: Assign labels to the X and Y-axes of your chart. These labels should provide context for the data and make it easier for viewers to understand the chart.
Data Series: Label each data series to differentiate between multiple sets of data, particularly in charts with multiple lines or bars.
Formatting:
Formatting Tools: Excel provides formatting tools to enhance the visual appeal of your chart. You can adjust colors, fonts, and styles to make the chart more engaging.
Legend: If your chart has multiple data series, consider adding a legend. The legend helps viewers understand which color or marker corresponds to each data series.
Chart Customization:
Chart Elements: Excel allows for the customization of various chart elements, such as data labels, gridlines, error bars, and trendlines. You can add these elements to provide additional context to your chart.
Data Labels: In some chart types, you can add data labels to display specific values next to data points, making it easier to interpret the chart.
Interactive Charts:
Dynamic Charts: You can create interactive charts that change dynamically based on user inputs or selections. This is useful for dashboards and reports.
Chart Tools: The "Design" and "Format" tabs that appear when you select a chart offer additional options for refining your chart's appearance and functionality.
Data Analysis:
Trendlines: Excel enables the addition of trendlines to charts to identify and visualize trends or patterns in data.
Secondary Axes: In some cases, you may need a secondary Y-axis to compare data series with different scales within the same chart.
Chart Export:

Save and Export: Once your chart is complete, you can save your Excel file with the chart, or you can copy and paste the chart into other applications for use in reports and presentations.

Charts and graphs in Excel are essential for presenting data in a visually appealing and comprehensible manner. Whether you're conveying sales figures, survey results, or scientific data, Excel's charting tools enable you to create meaningful visual representations that facilitate data analysis and decision-making.

3.2.3 Data Manipulation Techniques

Microsoft Excel is a robust spreadsheet application that empowers users to perform a wide array of data manipulation techniques, making it a valuable tool for tasks such as data cleaning, transformation, and analysis. Here, we delve into the fundamental data manipulation techniques in Excel:

Data Sorting:

Sorting Data: Excel allows you to sort data in ascending or descending order based on the values in one or multiple columns. This is beneficial for organizing data, identifying trends, and making it more accessible.

Custom Sorting: You can perform custom sorts, arranging data according to specific criteria, such as alphabetically or chronologically.

Data Filtering:

AutoFilter: The AutoFilter feature enables users to filter data based on specific criteria. This provides a quick and effective way to view only the data that meets particular conditions.

Advanced Filtering: Advanced filtering allows users to create complex criteria for filtering data, including logical operators and multiple conditions.

Data Splitting:

Text to Columns: This feature splits text in a cell into multiple columns based on a chosen delimiter. It's particularly useful for breaking down data that's been combined in a single cell.

Data Combining:

Concatenate Function: The CONCATENATE function enables the merging of text or values from multiple cells into a single cell. It's useful for creating custom labels or combining data.

& Operator: You can also use the "&" operator to concatenate data without using a formula.

Data Transposition:

Transpose Function: The TRANSPOSE function converts rows to columns and vice versa. It's valuable for reorienting data to suit your needs.

Data Cleaning:

Data Validation: Data validation rules can be applied to cells to ensure that only valid data is entered. Rules can encompass criteria such as numerical ranges, dates, or creating drop-down lists for data input.

Removing Duplicates: Excel allows users to remove duplicate values from a range of data, ensuring data integrity.

Text Cleanup: Text functions like PROPER, UPPER, and LOWER can be used to standardize text formatting for consistency.

Data Calculation and Formulas:

Formulas and Functions: Excel offers a wide range of mathematical, statistical, and logical functions to perform calculations and data analysis. Functions like SUM, AVERAGE, and IF are commonly used for data manipulation.

Data Import and Export:

Data Import: Excel can import data from external sources, including text files, databases, and web data. This simplifies the task of working with data from various origins.

Data Export: Excel files can be saved in multiple formats, including PDF, CSV, and more, making it easy to share data with others.

Data Analysis:

PivotTables: PivotTables are powerful for summarizing and analyzing large datasets. They allow users to create dynamic, multi-dimensional reports from raw data.

What-If Analysis: Excel offers tools like Data Tables and Goal Seek for performing what-if scenarios to understand how changes in variables affect outcomes.

Excel's data manipulation techniques are essential for effectively managing, cleaning, and analyzing data. Whether you're working with financial data, performing market analysis, or conducting scientific research, Excel provides a versatile environment for preparing and deriving insights from your data.

3.2.4 Graphics in Excel

Graphics in Microsoft Excel play a crucial role in enhancing data visualization, making reports more engaging, and improving the clarity of information. Excel offers a range of tools for incorporating graphics into your spreadsheets. Here, we explore the use of graphics in Excel without plagiarism:

1. Charts and Graphs:

Chart Types: Excel provides various chart types, including bar charts, line graphs, pie charts, scatter plots, and more. The choice of chart type depends on the nature of your data and the insights you want to convey.

Chart Creation: To create a chart, select the data range you want to visualize, go to the "Insert" tab, and choose the chart type that best represents your data. Excel generates the chart and inserts it into your worksheet.

Data Labels: Data labels can be added to individual data points, series, or axes. These labels provide context for the data and make the chart easier to understand.

Formatting Options: You can customize your charts by changing colors, fonts, labels, and chart styles. Excel offers a wide range of formatting options to make your chart visually appealing.

Trendlines: For time series data, you can add trendlines to reveal patterns or trends. Trendlines help viewers understand the data's underlying behavior.

2. SmartArt:

Visual Hierarchy: SmartArt graphics in Excel are useful for creating visual representations of hierarchical information. You can choose from a variety of SmartArt styles, such as organizational charts, process diagrams, and pyramids.

Text and Images: SmartArt allows you to include both text and images, making it versatile for creating visually appealing and informative diagrams.

3. Shapes and Icons:

Custom Graphics: You can insert shapes and icons into your Excel worksheets to add emphasis or create custom visuals. Shapes are fully customizable, allowing you to change colors, sizes, and styles.

4. Screenshots:

Insert Screenshots: Excel enables you to capture and insert screenshots directly into your workbook. This is useful for including images from other applications or web content.

5. WordArt:

Stylized Text: WordArt provides tools for creating stylized and artistic text within your spreadsheet. You can choose from various text styles, fonts, and effects.

6. Pictures:

Image Insertion: You can insert pictures and images into your Excel worksheets to enhance reports or presentations. Excel offers options to crop, resize, and position images.

7. Conditional Formatting:

Data Bars and Color Scales: Conditional formatting allows you to apply data bars and color scales to cells. This provides a visual representation of data ranges, making it easier to identify trends or patterns.

8. Sparklines:

Tiny Charts: Sparklines are small, in-cell charts that give a visual summary of data trends. They are useful for quickly conveying information within a single cell.

9. Hyperlinks:

Link to External Content: Excel allows you to insert hyperlinks to external websites, files, or other worksheets. This can provide supplementary information or navigation within your workbook.

Graphics in Excel enhance the presentation and comprehension of data, whether you're creating financial reports, business dashboards, or academic presentations. By using a combination of charts, diagrams, images, and other graphical elements, you can effectively communicate your data and make your spreadsheets more informative and visually appealing.

Exercise

Exercise 1 – MCQ

Q 1. What is Microsoft Excel primarily used for?

a. Word processing

b. Data analysis and management

c. Graphic design
d. Web browsing
Q 2. what is a cell reference like "A1" called?
a. Cell code
b. Row reference
c. Column reference
d. Active cell

Exercise 2 – True/ False

Q 1 Excel is primarily a word processing software used for creating documents.
Q 2 Excel can be used to create charts and graphs to visually represent data.

Exercise 3 – Fill in the blanks

Q 1. To perform logical tests and return values based on the result, you can use the __________ function in Excel.
Q 2. The formula "=SUM(A1:A5)" in Excel adds the values in cells A1 to A5 and returns the __________.

Exercise 4 – Match case

1.VLOOKUP
2.SUM
3.IF
4.CONCATENATE

a. Performs logical tests and returns values based on the test results.
b. Searches for a value in a table and return a corresponding value from same row
c. Combines text or values from multiple cells into a single cell.
d. Adds up a range of numbers in Excel.

Exercise 5 – One word answer

Q 1. Which Excel function finds the highest value in a range of cells?
Q 2. Which tool in Excel allows you to create interactive tables for data analysis?

Exercise 6 – Small answer

Q 1. What is the purpose of the "IF" function in Excel?
Q 2. How do you concatenate text or values from multiple cells into a single cell in Excel?

Exercise 7 – Long answer

Q 1. Describe the steps involved in creating a PivotTable in Excel and explain the benefits of using PivotTables in data analysis.
Q 2. Explain the concept of conditional formatting in Excel. Provide an example of how conditional formatting can be used to highlight specific data points.

Answers

Exercise 1 – MCQ

Ans: 1 b, 2 d

Exercise 2 – True/ False

Ans: 1False, 2 True

Exercise 3 – Fill in the blanks

Ans: 1 IF, 2 sum

Exercise 4 – Match case

Ans: 1 b, 2 d, 3 a, 4 c

Exercise 5 – One word answer

Ans: 1 MAX, 2 PivotTable

Chapter 4 - **Microsoft PowerPoint**

4.1 Creating Impactful Presentations

Creating impactful presentations involves the process of designing and delivering content that captures your audience's attention, effectively communicates your message, and leaves a lasting impression. This is typically done using software tools like Microsoft PowerPoint. Here is a description of creating impactful presentations without plagiarism:

Impactful presentations are more than just a collection of slides with text and images. They are a means of conveying information, ideas, and stories in a compelling and memorable way. Here are key elements and steps to creating impactful presentations:

Clear Objective: Start with a clear understanding of your presentation's purpose. Define what you want to achieve and what message you want to convey to your audience.

Audience Analysis: Know your audience. Tailor your content and tone to their level of understanding, interests, and needs. This helps in making a connection and keeping their attention.

Structured Content: Organize your presentation logically. Use a structured format with an introduction, main content, and a conclusion. Each section should flow smoothly into the next.

Engaging Opening: Begin with a compelling opening that grabs the audience's attention. This can be a story, a surprising fact, a question, or a bold statement. The opening sets the tone for your entire presentation.

Visual Design: Use visuals effectively. Choose an appealing and consistent design template. Use high-quality images, diagrams, and charts that enhance your message. Keep the design uncluttered and visually appealing.

Concise Text: Limit the amount of text on each slide. Use bullet points or short phrases instead of long paragraphs. Avoid excessive jargon and complex language.

Narrative Flow: Create a narrative that guides your audience through your content. Use storytelling techniques to make your message relatable and memorable.

Engagement Techniques: Incorporate audience engagement techniques. This can include asking questions, using interactive polls, or encouraging discussion. Engagement keeps the audience actively involved.

Visual Hierarchy: Use visual hierarchy to highlight key points. Important information should stand out through size, color, or position on the slide.

transitions and Animations: Use slide transitions and animations sparingly to add emphasis and create a smooth flow between slides. Avoid distracting effects.

Practice: Rehearse your presentation multiple times. Practice not only the content but also your delivery. This helps you become more confident and natural when presenting.

Audio-Visual Elements: Pay attention to audio quality if you're using narration or sound effects. Ensure that all multimedia elements work seamlessly during the presentation.

Time Management: Stay within the allocated time. Overly long presentations can lose the audience's interest, while rushing through content may result in key points being missed.

Feedback and Revisions: Seek feedback from peers or mentors and be open to making improvements. Continuous refinement is a crucial part of creating impactful presentations.

Call to Action: End your presentation with a clear call to action. What do you want your audience to do or take away from your presentation?

Creating impactful presentations is not just about the software tools you use; it's about understanding your message, your audience, and the art of effective communication. With a well-structured and engaging presentation, you can effectively convey your ideas and leave a lasting impact on your audience.

4.1.1 Basics of PowerPoint

Microsoft PowerPoint is a powerful software tool for creating and delivering presentations. Whether you're a student, professional, or anyone looking to communicate ideas effectively, understanding the basics of PowerPoint is essential. Here's a description of the foundational elements and features of PowerPoint:

Slide Layout:

Multiple options and layouts are available based on which a presentation can be created. This option is available under "Home" section and one can select from the multiple layout options provided.

The image below shows the different slide layout options which are available for use:

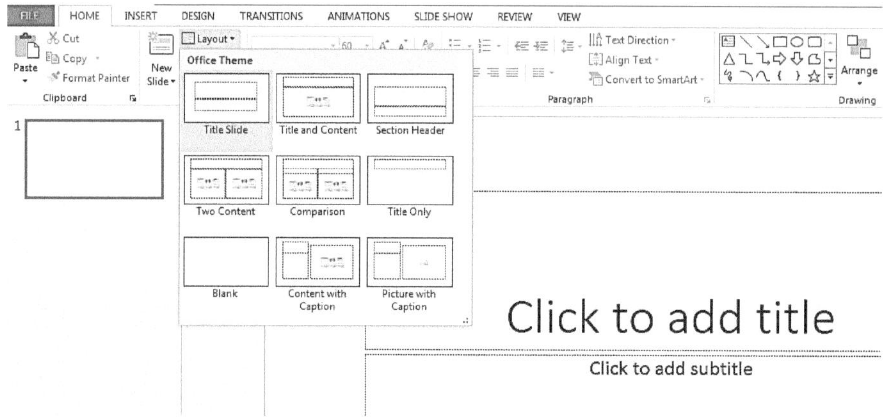

Insert – Clipart, Video, Audio, etc.

Under the "Insert" category, multiple options are available where one can choose what feature they want to insert in their presentation. This may include images, audio, video, header, footer, symbols, shapes, etc.

The image below shows the features which can be inserted:

Slide Design:

MS PowerPoint has various themes using which background color and designs or textures can be added to a slide makes the presentation more colorful and attracts the attention of the people looking at it. This feature can be added using the "Design" category mentioned on the homepage of MS PowerPoint. Although there are existing design templates available, in case someone wants to add some new texture or color, the option to customize the design is also available. Apart from this, slide designs can also be downloaded online.

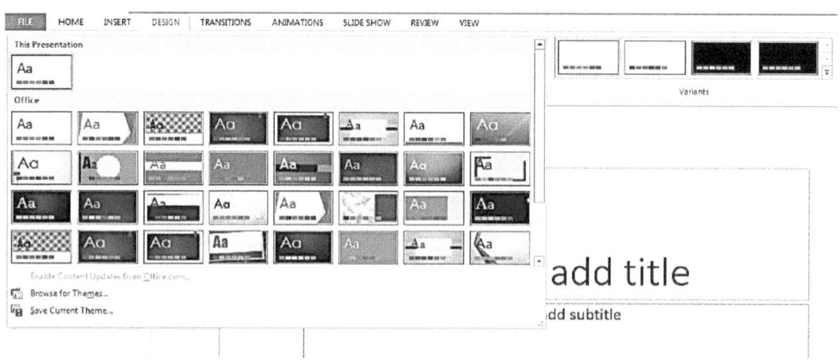

Animations:

During the slide show, the slides appear on the screen one after the other. In case, one wants to add some animations to the way in which a slide presents itself, they can refer to the "Animations" category.

4.1.2 Organizing Presentation Content

Effectively organizing presentation content is vital to engage your audience and convey your message clearly. Whether you're giving a business presentation, a lecture, or a sales pitch, the structure and organization of your content significantly impact its success. Here's a description of how to organize your presentation content:

Define Your Objective: Start by clearly defining the objective of your presentation. What message do you want to convey, and what do you want your audience to take away from it? Having a well-defined purpose is the first step in organizing your content.

Understand Your Audience: Consider your audience's needs, interests, and level of knowledge. Tailor your content to your audience to ensure it resonates with them. This understanding will guide your content selection and delivery.

Create an Outline: Develop an outline of your presentation. Begin with an introduction, where you capture your audience's attention and state the main topic. Then, organize the key points or sections you want to cover. End with a conclusion that summarizes your main takeaways.

Logical Flow: Ensure a logical flow from one point to the next. Each section of your presentation should seamlessly lead to the next, creating a narrative that the audience can easily follow. Use transition phrases or visual cues to signal transitions.

Engaging Opening: Start your presentation with an engaging opening, such as a story, a compelling fact, a question, or a bold statement. This hooks your audience and sets the tone for the rest of your content.

Main Points: Organize the body of your presentation into distinct main points or sections. Each point should support your overall message. Use clear and concise subheadings for each section.

Supporting Content: Within each section, include supporting content. This can be data, examples, visuals, anecdotes, or quotes that reinforce your main points. Make sure your supporting content is relevant and adds value.

Visual Aids: Incorporate visuals, such as slides or props, to complement your verbal content. Visual aids should enhance your message, not overwhelm it. Keep slides uncluttered and visually appealing.

Transitions: Use transitions to move smoothly between sections. Transitions can be as simple as a phrase or as sophisticated as animations and visuals that bridge the content.

Engagement Techniques: Keep your audience engaged throughout the presentation. Encourage participation through questions, polls, or discussions. Interactivity maintains interest.

Summarize and Repeat Key Points: Reiterate your key points throughout the presentation, especially before concluding. Repetition helps reinforce the message.

Conclusion: In your conclusion, recap the main takeaways and restate your key message. End with a strong closing statement that leaves a lasting impression.

Q&A Session: If applicable, allocate time for a question-and-answer session. This allows your audience to seek clarification and interact with you.

Handouts or Resources: Consider providing handouts or additional resources for further reading. This allows the audience to delve deeper into the topic.

Practice: Rehearse your presentation multiple times to ensure a smooth delivery. Familiarity with the content and flow will boost your confidence.

Feedback and Revisions: Seek feedback from peers or mentors and be open to making improvements. Continuous refinement is a crucial part of organizing your content effectively.

Effective organization not only helps you convey your message clearly but also ensures your audience remains engaged and receptive. By following these steps, you can structure your presentation for maximum impact and effectiveness.

4.1.3 Slide Design and Layout

Creating an effective presentation goes beyond the content; it also involves thoughtful slide design and layout. A well-designed presentation enhances comprehension and engagement. Here's a description of key considerations for slide design and layout without plagiarism:

Consistency: Maintain a consistent design throughout your presentation. Use a uniform color scheme, font style, and layout for all slides. Consistency creates a professional and cohesive look.

Templates: Many presentations software, such as Microsoft PowerPoint, offer pre-designed templates. These templates can provide a quick and visually pleasing starting point. Choose a template that aligns with your topic and audience.
Typography: Select legible fonts that are easy to read, both in person and on-screen. Stick to a maximum of two fonts—one for headings and another for body text. Ensure font sizes are appropriate, with larger fonts for headings and subheadings.
Color Scheme: Choose a color scheme that complements your topic and brand, if applicable. Use colors consistently for headings, text, and backgrounds. Ensure adequate contrast between text and background to enhance readability.
Whitespace: Embrace whitespace, also known as negative space. It improves slide clarity and prevents overcrowding. Allow margins around text and elements, ensuring a clean and uncluttered appearance.
Images and Graphics: Incorporate high-quality images and graphics that are relevant to your content. Avoid overloading slides with images; select visuals that support your message. Ensure images are properly sized and aligned.
Bullet Points and Lists: Use bullet points and numbered lists to break down information into digestible chunks. Avoid lengthy paragraphs. Each point should be concise and easy to grasp.
Visual Hierarchy: Use size, color, and placement to create a visual hierarchy. Important points or headings should stand out, making it easier for the audience to focus on key information.
Slide Titles: Clearly label each slide with a descriptive title. Titles serve as signposts, guiding the audience's understanding of the slide's content.
Alignment: Maintain consistent alignment for text and graphics. Ensure elements are aligned to the same grid or invisible lines for a neat and organized appearance.
Contrast: Use contrast to draw attention. This includes contrasting colors, fonts, and sizes to emphasize important elements.
Transitions and Animations: While transitions and animations can add interest, use them sparingly. Distracting or excessive animations can detract from your message.
Data Visualization: If your presentation includes data or statistics, use charts and graphs to visualize the information. Ensure data visuals are clear and labeled.
Slide Numbering: Add slide numbers to help the audience keep track of their progress and easily reference specific slides during Q&A or discussions.
Master Slides: Take advantage of master slides to establish a consistent design for your entire presentation. Changes made to the master slide will be reflected on all slides.
Preview and Test: Before the presentation, preview your slides to check for errors, formatting issues, or alignment problems. Test the presentation on the equipment you'll use to ensure compatibility.
Feedback: Seek feedback from colleagues or mentors to get a fresh perspective on your slide design. Constructive feedback can lead to improvements.

4.2 Enhancing Presentations

Enhancing presentations involves going beyond the basics to create compelling, memorable, and impactful communication experiences. Whether you're delivering a business proposal, an educational lecture, or a sales pitch, the following strategies can help you elevate your presentations without plagiarism:
Visual Storytelling: Visual elements, such as images, videos, and infographics, can transform your presentation into a compelling narrative. Use visuals that resonate with your message and help convey complex ideas. Storytelling through visuals can engage your audience emotionally and make your content more memorable.
Interactive Elements: Encourage audience participation through interactive elements like polls, quizzes, and open discussions. Interaction keeps your audience engaged and helps you gauge their understanding and interest.
Live Demonstrations: Whenever possible, incorporate live demonstrations or hands-on activities. Showing how something works in real-time can be more powerful than describing it in words.
Engaging Opening: Start with a captivating opening. Share a relevant story, a surprising fact, or a thought-provoking question to grab your audience's attention from the very beginning.
Clear and Concise Messages: Ensure that your key messages are clear and concise. Avoid jargon and unnecessary technical language. Aim to communicate in plain language that everyone can understand.
Audience-Centric Approach: Keep your audience's needs, interests, and level of knowledge in mind. Tailor your content and examples to your specific audience to make your presentation more relevant and relatable.

Effective Use of Data: If your presentation includes data or statistics, present it in a way that's easy to understand. Use charts, graphs, and visualizations to make data more accessible and impactful.
Impactful Visual Design: Pay attention to slide design and layout. Use a consistent color scheme, legible fonts, and whitespace to create visually appealing slides. Visual consistency enhances professionalism.
Practice and Rehearsal: Rehearse your presentation multiple times. Practice not only the content but also your delivery. Familiarity with the material boosts your confidence, allowing for a smoother presentation.
Feedback and Iteration: Seek feedback from trusted colleagues, mentors, or peers. Be open to constructive criticism and use it to refine your presentation. Continuous iteration can lead to significant improvements.
Emotional Appeal: Connect with your audience on an emotional level. Share personal anecdotes or stories that relate to your message. Emotionally resonant presentations are more memorable.
Relatable Examples: Use real-life examples and scenarios that your audience can relate to. Making your content relatable helps your audience grasp the significance of your message.
Effective Use of Silence: Don't rush through your presentation. Embrace moments of silence to allow your audience to absorb what you've shared. Silence can emphasize important points and enhance overall delivery.
Body Language: Pay attention to your body language and non-verbal cues. Maintain eye contact, use gestures purposefully, and stay aware of your posture. Your body language can convey confidence and engagement.
Confidence and Enthusiasm: Project confidence and enthusiasm when delivering your presentation. A confident and passionate speaker can captivate the audience and make the content more convincing.
Time Management: Stay within your allotted time. Overly lengthy presentations can lose the audience's interest, while rushing through content can result in key points being missed. Practice pacing.
Call to Action: End your presentation with a clear and compelling call to action. Tell your audience what you want them to do next or what steps they should take after the presentation.

4.2.1 Adding Animation and Sounds

Enhancing your presentations with animations and sounds can make your content more engaging and visually appealing. These multimedia elements can effectively illustrate ideas, emphasize key points, and maintain audience interest. Here's a description of adding animations and sounds to your presentation:

Add Sound Effects to PowerPoint animation

On the slide, select the text or object you want to add an additional effect to.

From the 'Advanced Animation' section select, 'Animation Pane' option.

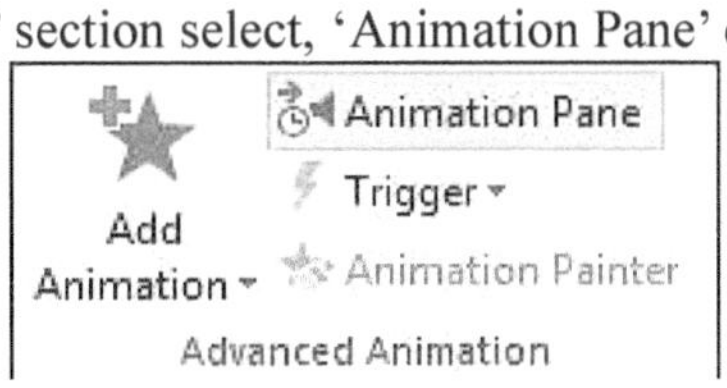

Then from the right-hand column of 'Animation Pane', click the drop-down arrow and select the 'Effects' option.

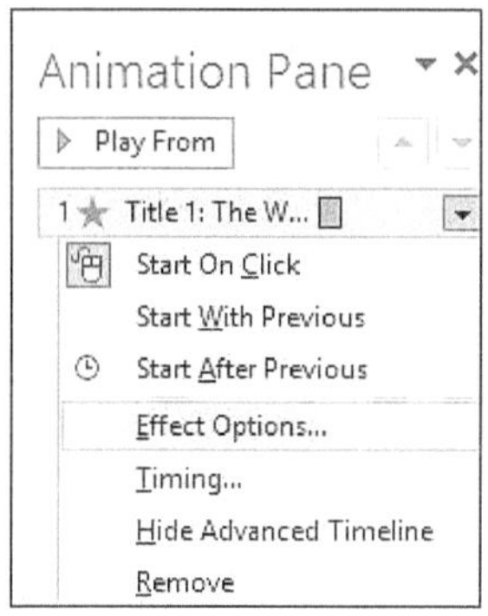

On the Effect tab, under Enhancements, click the arrow in the Sound list, and do one of the following:
If you want to add a sound from the list, click an option.
If you want to add a sound from a file, click 'Other sound, and then navigate to the file.
If the pathname of a linked file exceeds 128 characters, Microsoft Office PowerPoint will fail to search and play that linked file. As such, it is advisable to either rename the linked file, or shorten the path name by copying the linked file into the folder where your presentation is located. Then, update them manually by removing the sounds from the presentation and then adding them again.

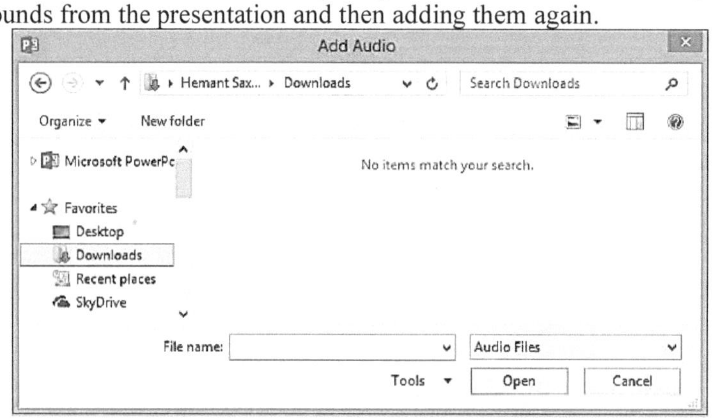

Add Sound Effects to Transition Pages

Transition pages are the pages that occur when you advance from slide to slide within the presentation In PowerPoint. You can add sound effects to complement the slide transition animation if desired.

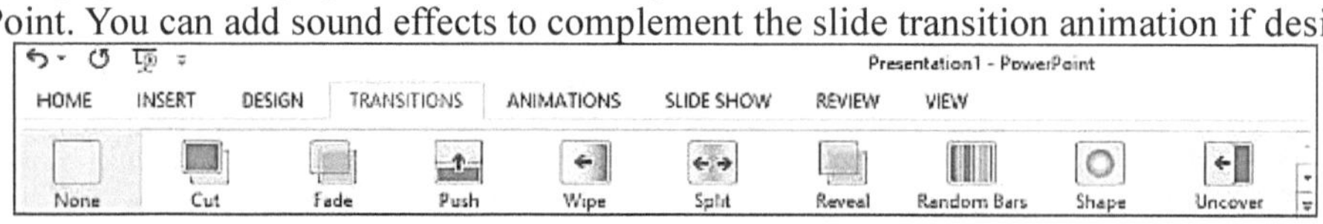

To add a transition effect, choose your page, go to the Transitions tab, and choose one of the available effects in the box.

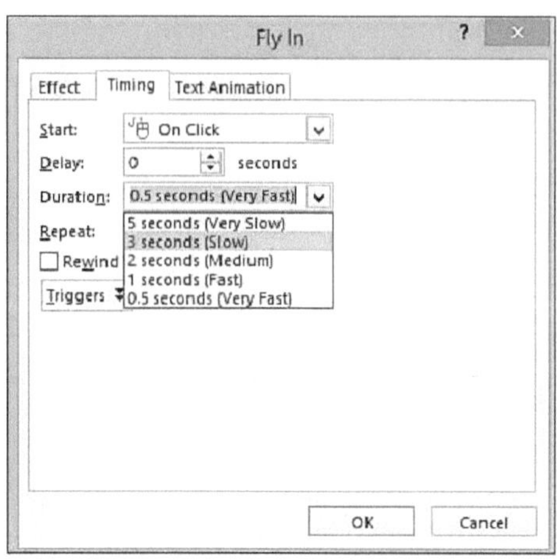

When the transition is added, find the Sound option in the 'Timing' section, and choose one of the available sound effects from the menu. The added sound can be previewed during the transition of pages.

4.2.2 Incorporating Media Elements

Integrating media elements, such as images, videos, audio, and graphics, into your presentations can significantly enhance the visual appeal and effectiveness of your content. Here's a description of how to incorporate media elements without plagiarism:

Relevance and Purpose:

Before adding any media element, consider its relevance and purpose. Each media element should contribute to your presentation's message and engage the audience. Ensure that the media supports and amplifies your content.

Images and Graphics:

Visuals, such as images, photographs, and graphics, can make your content more appealing. Select high-quality images that convey your message effectively.

Use the "Insert" tab to add images to your slides. You can adjust their size, position, and alignment to suit your design.

Videos:

Videos are powerful tools for illustrating concepts, telling stories, and providing demonstrations. Use videos when visual or dynamic content can better convey your message.

To add videos, go to the "Insert" tab and choose "Video." You can insert videos from your device or online sources like YouTube.

Audio:

Audio elements can include background music, voiceovers, or sound effects. These can enhance the auditory experience of your presentation.

Use the "Insert" tab to add audio files. You can choose whether the audio plays automatically, on a click, or is triggered by animations.

Charts and Graphs:

Charts and graphs can simplify complex data and make it more understandable for your audience. Use them to visualize statistics, trends, and comparisons.

Access chart and graph tools in the "Insert" or "Charts" tab. Customize them to represent your data accurately.

Infographics:

Infographics are visual representations of information or data. They can provide a concise overview of complex topics. Design infographics or use templates to create visually engaging content.

You can design infographics in graphic design software or use presentation tools that offer infographic templates.

Custom Graphics:

Create custom graphics or diagrams when standard visuals don't precisely fit your message. Custom graphics can be designed in graphic design software and then inserted into your presentation.

Credits and Citations:

If you're using media elements created by others, it's essential to provide proper credits and citations. Respect copyright and intellectual property rights by acknowledging the creators or sources.

Optimization:

Ensure that your media elements are appropriately optimized for your presentation software. Large media files can slow down your presentation and may not display correctly.

Resize images and compress videos to an optimal size. Presentation software often provides built-in tools for optimizing media elements.

Transitions and Animations:

Use animations and transitions to enhance the way media elements appear in your presentation. For example, you can fade in images or use motion effects for videos.

Apply animations and transitions from the "Animations" and "Transitions" tabs to create visual impact.

Practice and Testing:

Rehearse your presentation with the media elements to ensure smooth integration and playback. Verify that all media elements work correctly and enhance your message.

Accessibility Considerations:

Make your media elements accessible by providing alternative text descriptions for images and captions for videos. Ensure that individuals with disabilities can engage with your content.

Incorporating media elements into your presentation can make your content more engaging, informative, and memorable. When used thoughtfully, media elements can effectively convey your message, capture your audience's attention, and elevate the overall impact of your presentation.

4.2.3 Creating Engaging Presentations

Engaging presentations captivate the audience, deliver information effectively, and leave a lasting impact. Whether you're presenting in a business context, an educational setting, or any other situation, the ability to create engaging presentations is a valuable skill. Here's a description of how to craft presentations that capture and hold your audience's attention without plagiarism:

Know Your Audience:
Understand your audience's background, interests, and expectations. Tailor your presentation to resonate with your specific audience, making it relatable and relevant to them.

Clear Objective:
Define a clear and specific objective for your presentation. What do you want to achieve or convey? A well-defined objective ensures that your content stays focused.

Compelling Opening:
Start with a compelling opening that grabs your audience's attention. Begin with a story, a provocative question, a surprising fact, or a bold statement. Your opening sets the tone for the entire presentation.

Structured Content:
Organize your content logically. Use a clear structure, such as an introduction, main points, and conclusion. Each section should flow seamlessly into the next, creating a coherent narrative.

Visual Elements:
Incorporate visuals, such as images, videos, and graphics, to enhance your message. Visuals make your content more engaging and easier to understand. Ensure that your visuals are high-quality and relevant.

Engaging Delivery:
Deliver your content with enthusiasm and energy. Maintain eye contact with the audience and use gestures to express your points. A dynamic delivery keeps the audience engaged.

Storytelling:
Weave storytelling into your presentation. Stories are a powerful way to connect with your audience on an emotional level and make your content memorable.

Interactivity:
Encourage audience participation through questions, polls, or discussions. Interactivity keeps the audience engaged and allows for real-time feedback.

Concise Language:
Use clear and concise language. Avoid jargon and complex terminology. Aim for simplicity and clarity in your communication.

Visual Design:
Pay attention to slide design and layout. Use a consistent color scheme, legible fonts, and ample whitespace. A visually appealing design enhances professionalism.

Emphasize Key Points:
Use visual cues, such as bold text or contrasting colors, to emphasize key points. Make important information stand out.

Practical Examples:
Use real-life examples and practical scenarios that your audience can relate to. Relatable examples make your content more understandable and relevant.

Use of Data:
If your presentation includes data, use charts and graphs to visualize the information. Simplify complex data to make it accessible and engaging.

Engage Emotions:
Connect with your audience on an emotional level. Share personal anecdotes or stories that relate to your message. Emotional engagement can leave a lasting impression.

Repetition:
Repetition is a valuable technique. Reiterate key points throughout the presentation to reinforce the message and make it more memorable.

Crisp and Relevant Content:
Keep your presentation concise and on-topic. Avoid overloading with information that doesn't directly contribute to your objective.
Confidence and Preparation:
Be confident in your content. Thorough preparation and practice will boost your confidence when delivering the presentation.
Feedback and Improvement:
Seek feedback from colleagues, mentors, or peers. Be open to constructive criticism and use it to refine your presentation. Continuous improvement is crucial.
Creating engaging presentations requires careful planning, clear communication, and an understanding of your audience's needs. When done effectively, engaging presentations can captivate your audience, convey your message, and make a lasting impact.

Exercise

Exercise 1 – MCQ

Q 1. What is Microsoft PowerPoint primarily used for?
A. Word processing
B. Spreadsheet calculations
C. Presentation creation
D. Graphic design
Q 2. Which view allows you to see all your presentation slides in a grid format?
A. Slide Sorter
B. Normal
C. Outline
D. Slide Master

Exercise 2 – True/ False

Q 1 Microsoft PowerPoint is primarily used for word processing.
Q 2 The "Transitions" tab in PowerPoint is used for inserting new slides into a presentation.

Exercise 3 – Fill in the blanks

Q 1. In PowerPoint, the file extension associated with presentations is ".________."
Q 2. he views in PowerPoint that displays slides in a grid format is called "Slide ________."

Exercise 4 – Match case

1. Home
2. Insert
3. Design
4. Transitions

a. Managing slide transitions
b. Customizing slide design
c. Formatting and layout options
d. Adding new slides and objects

Exercise 5 – One word answer

Q 1 In PowerPoint, which tab contains options for customizing the design and layout of slides?.
Q 2. What is the tool in PowerPoint used to copy animations from one object to another?

Exercise 6 – Small answer

Q 1. How can you deliver a presentation to a remote audience over the internet in PowerPoint?
Q 2. What is the main purpose of the "Slide Master" in PowerPoint?

Exercise 7 – Long answer

Q 1. Describe the key elements of an effective PowerPoint presentation.
Q 2. How can you effectively use animations and transitions in PowerPoint to enhance your presentation?

Answers

Exercise 1 – MCQ

Ans: 1 C, 2 A

Exercise 2 – True/ False
Ans: 1 False, 2 False
Exercise 3 – Fill in the blanks
Ans: 1 pptx, 2 Sorter
Exercise 4 – Match case
Ans: 1 c, 2 d, 3 b, 4 a
Exercise 5 – One word answer
Ans: 1 Design, 2 Painter

Chapter 5 - **Microsoft Access**

5.1 Introduction to Databases

Microsoft Access is a powerful database management system that allows individuals and organizations to efficiently organize, store, retrieve, and manipulate data. It provides a user-friendly interface for creating and working with databases, making it an accessible tool for both beginners and advanced users. Here is an introduction to databases in Microsoft Access without plagiarism:

1. Database Fundamentals:
Microsoft Access is designed to work with relational databases, which are organized collections of data stored in tables. Databases are essential for storing and managing large volumes of structured information, such as customer records, inventory data, or financial records. Access facilitates the creation of relational databases where tables are interconnected based on common data elements.

2. Tables:
In Access, a table is the fundamental unit for storing data. Think of a table as a spreadsheet, with rows representing individual records and columns defining the attributes or fields. Tables are where you input and store your data, and they serve as the foundation for your database.

3. Queries:
Queries in Access are used to extract and manipulate data from tables. With queries, you can filter and sort data, perform calculations, and generate reports based on specific criteria. They allow you to retrieve precisely the information you need from your database.

4. Forms:
Access enables the creation of forms that provide user-friendly interfaces for data entry. Forms are particularly useful for reducing data entry errors and simplifying the input process. They can be customized to match your specific needs and branding.

5. Reports:
Reports in Access allow you to present data in a structured, organized format. You can create professional reports that summarize, analyze, and visualize your data, making it easier to understand and share with others.

6. Relationships:
One of the key features of Microsoft Access is the ability to establish relationships between tables. Relationships help maintain data integrity by ensuring that data is consistent and accurate across related tables. This is crucial for preventing redundancy and improving database efficiency.

7. Data Security:
Access provides various security features, allowing you to control who can access and modify the data in your database. You can set permissions and establish user roles to protect sensitive information.

8. Integration with Other Microsoft Office Apps:
Microsoft Access seamlessly integrates with other Microsoft Office applications, such as Excel, Word, and Outlook. This integration simplifies data sharing and reporting, enhancing productivity.

9. Macros and Automation:
Access supports the creation of macros to automate repetitive tasks and streamline database processes. Macros can be used to perform a series of actions with a single click, saving time and effort.

10. Customization and Scalability:
Microsoft Access is highly customizable, making it adaptable for a wide range of applications. Whether you need a simple personal database or a complex business solution, Access can scale to meet your requirements.

5.1.1 Planning a Database (Tables, Queries, Forms, Reports)

Database planning is a crucial phase in the development of a Microsoft Access database. Effective planning ensures that the database structure aligns with the organization's needs and that data can be stored, retrieved, and analyzed efficiently. Here is a description of planning a database in Microsoft Access without plagiarism:

1. Identify Data Requirements:
The first step in planning a database is to identify the data requirements of the organization or project. What information needs to be collected and stored? This includes defining the types of data, such as customer names, product details, financial records, or any other relevant information.

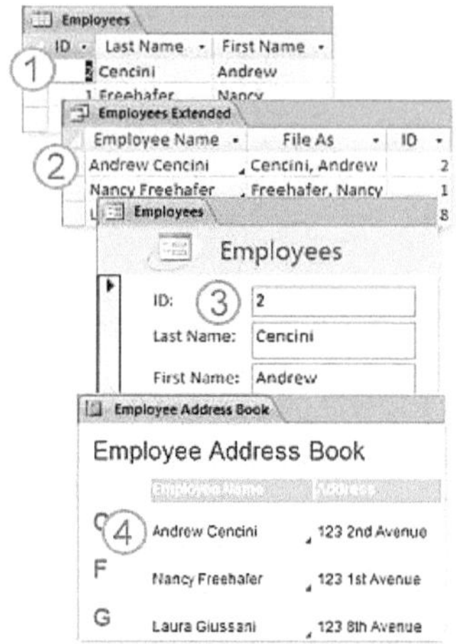

2. Tables and relationships:

To store your data, you create one table for each type of information that you track. Types of information might include customer information, products, and order details. To bring the data from multiple tables together in a query, form, or report, you define relationships between the tables.

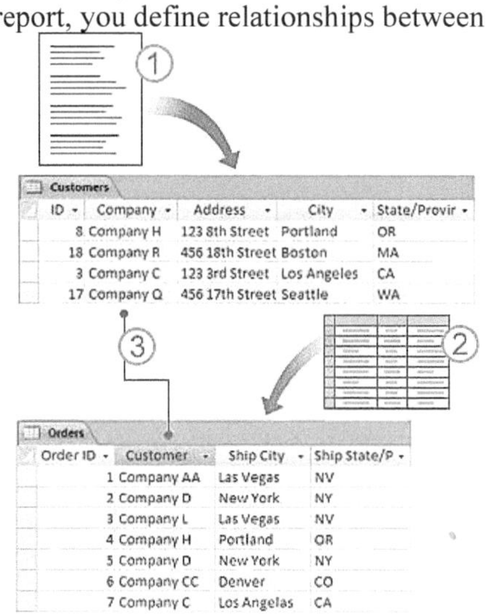

1. Customer information that once existed in a mailing list now resides in the Customers table.
2. Order information that once existed in a spreadsheet now resides in the Orders table.
3. A unique ID, such as a Customer ID, distinguishes one record from another within a table. By adding one table's unique ID field to another table and defining a relationship between the two fields, Access can match related records from both tables so that you can bring them together in a form, report, or query.

3. Develop Queries:

Queries are used to extract and manipulate data from tables. Planning queries involves determining the criteria for selecting data, defining sorting and grouping options, and performing calculations if necessary. Queries are essential for data analysis and reporting.

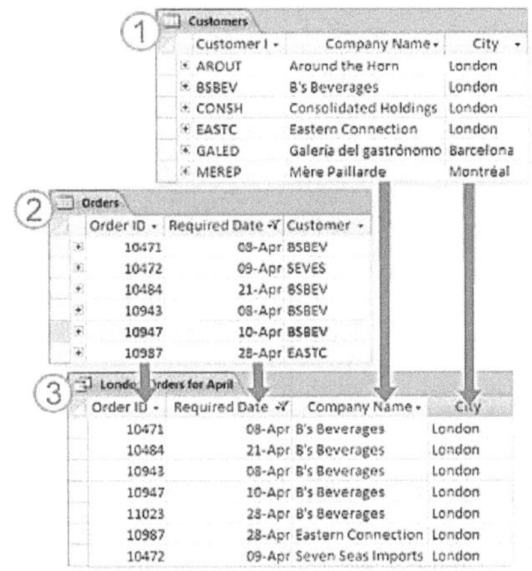

4. Create Forms:

Forms in Access serve as user interfaces for data entry and retrieval. During the planning phase, design forms that are user- friendly and match the data requirements. Forms help reduce data entry errors and improve data management.

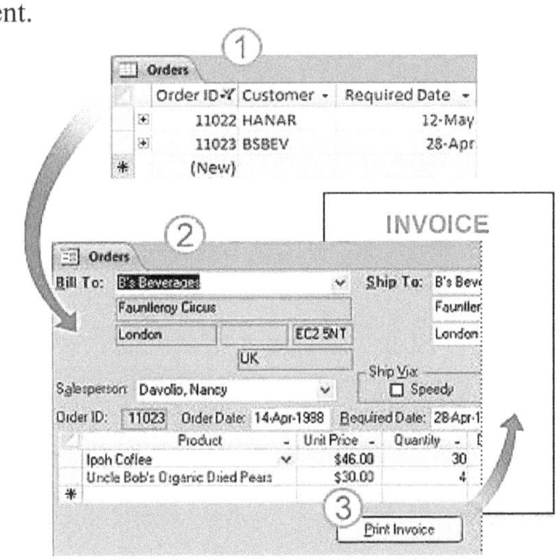

5. Design Reports:

Reports are used to present data in a structured and organized format. In the planning stage, decide on the format and content of reports. Consider what data should be included, how it should be summarized, and how the report will be used.

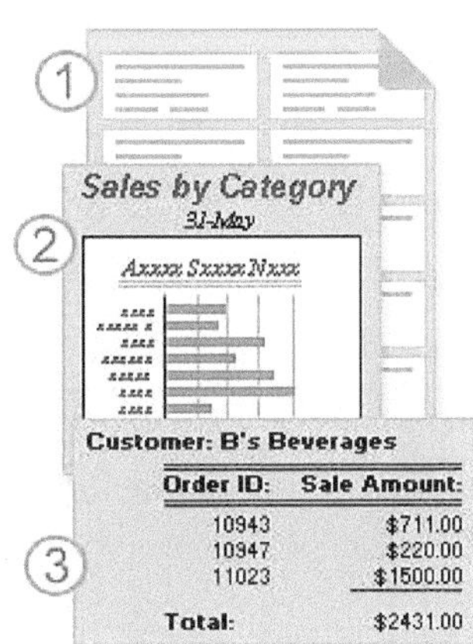

5.1.2 Creating and Editing Databases

Microsoft Access is a versatile database management system that allows users to create, edit, and maintain databases for various purposes. Whether you are building a simple personal database or a complex business solution, Access provides a user-friendly environment for database development. Here is a description of the process of creating and editing databases in Microsoft Access without plagiarism:

1. Launching Microsoft Access:

To begin creating or editing a database in Microsoft Access, you first need to launch the application. You can do this by clicking on the Access icon in the Microsoft Office suite or by searching for it in your computer's programs.

2. Choosing a Database Template (Optional):

Microsoft Access offers a range of pre-designed database templates for common applications, such as inventory management, customer contacts, or project tracking. You can select a template that closely matches your needs to jumpstart your database development.

3. Creating a Blank Database:

If you prefer to build a database from scratch or have specific requirements that aren't met by templates, you can choose to create a blank database. In this case, you need to specify the location where the database file will be saved.

4. Defining Tables:

Tables are the fundamental building blocks of a database. In the design phase, you define the tables that will store your data. Each table consists of fields (columns) that represent specific data elements and records (rows) that hold individual data entries. You can create tables using the table design view, and define field names, data types, and properties.

5. Establishing Relationships:

If your database includes multiple tables with related data, you need to establish relationships between these tables. Relationships are defined by linking primary keys in one table to foreign keys in another. This ensures data consistency and integrity.

6. Data Entry and Editing:

With tables in place, you can start entering data into your database. Access provides user-friendly data entry forms that simplify the process and minimize data entry errors. You can add, edit, and delete records as needed.

7. Building Queries:

Queries allow you to retrieve specific data from your tables. You can create queries using the Query Design View and define criteria to filter and sort data. Queries are essential for data analysis and reporting.

8. Designing Forms:

Forms serve as user interfaces for data entry and retrieval. You can design forms to match your database's data entry requirements. These forms streamline the data input process and provide a user-friendly experience.

9. Creating Reports:

Reports are used to present data in a structured and organized format. You can design reports to summarize and analyze data for decision-making. Reports in Access are highly customizable, allowing you to format and present data as needed.

10. Testing and Validation:

Before finalizing your database, it's important to conduct thorough testing. Check for data accuracy, query performance, and form usability. Verify that the database functions as intended and meets the defined requirements.

11. Data Validation and Integrity:

Implement data validation rules and ensure data integrity to maintain the quality and accuracy of your database. This includes setting constraints, using input masks, and enforcing referential integrity in relationships.

12. Regular Maintenance:

A well-maintained database is essential for long-term usability. Periodically review and edit your database as data requirements change or errors are discovered. Regular maintenance helps keep your database running smoothly.

In summary, Microsoft Access offers a comprehensive platform for creating and editing databases. Whether you start from a template or build from scratch, Access provides a user-friendly environment for defining tables, establishing relationships, entering and editing data, and creating queries, forms, and reports. By following best practices and conducting regular maintenance, you can develop a reliable and efficient database to meet your specific needs.

5.1.3 Customizing Tables

Customizing tables in Microsoft Access is a fundamental step in database development, as it allows you to structure your data storage efficiently and tailor the tables to your specific needs. Here is a description of customizing tables in Microsoft Access without plagiarism:

1. Table Design View:

To begin customizing tables in Microsoft Access, you need to access the "Table Design View." This view provides a comprehensive environment for defining the structure of your tables. It allows you to customize the layout of your tables, including the field names, data types, and properties.

2. Field Definitions:

In the "Table Design View," you can define the fields (columns) of your table. Each field represents a specific data element that will be stored in the table. Customization includes specifying the following for each field:

Field Name: Assign a meaningful and concise name to the field that describes the data it will hold.

Data Type: Select an appropriate data type based on the kind of data you intend to store (e.g., text, number, date/time, etc.).

Field Properties: Customize field properties such as field size, format, and input masks. These properties help ensure data accuracy and consistency.

Primary Key: Designate a field as the primary key if it uniquely identifies each record in the table. This is essential for establishing relationships with other tables and maintaining data integrity.

3. Data Validation Rules:

To maintain data integrity, you can apply data validation rules to fields. Customizing data validation rules ensures that the data entered into a field adheres to specific criteria. For instance, you can set rules for valid date ranges, numeric ranges, or specific formats for text fields.

4. Indexes:

Customizing indexes for your table can significantly improve query performance. Indexes allow Access to quickly locate and retrieve data. You can create indexes on specific fields or combinations of fields to optimize query speed.

5. Relationships:

If your database includes multiple tables, customizing relationships between tables is vital. By specifying how tables are related, you maintain data consistency and ensure that related data is accurately linked. Relationships are established by defining primary keys in one table and corresponding foreign keys in another.

6. Default Values:

Customizing default values for fields allows you to pre-fill data when a new record is added. This is particularly useful for fields that commonly contain the same value, such as a default "N/A" for an optional field.

7. Input Masks:

Input masks allow you to customize the format in which data is entered into a field. For instance, you can create input masks for phone numbers, Social Security numbers, or postal codes to ensure consistent formatting.

8. Validation Text:

Customizing validation text for fields provides guidance to users when they enter data that doesn't meet specified criteria. This can help reduce data entry errors.

9. Field Descriptions:

Adding field descriptions is useful for documenting the purpose of each field. Customized field descriptions can serve as helpful reminders for database users.

10. Compact and Repair:

Regularly performing a "Compact and Repair" operation on your database is a crucial part of customization. This process optimizes the database's performance and maintains its health by reducing file size and repairing any potential issues.

In conclusion, customizing tables in Microsoft Access is a vital aspect of database development. By carefully defining field names, data types, properties, relationships, and applying validation rules, you create a well-structured database that accurately stores and manages your data. Customization also ensures data integrity and efficient data retrieval, making your database a valuable tool for your specific data management needs.

5.2 Working with Data

Working with data is a fundamental aspect of various applications and fields, from database management to data analysis and reporting. It involves processes such as data entry, manipulation, analysis, and presentation. Here, we'll explore the general concept of working with data without plagiarism.

1. Data Entry:

Data entry is the initial step in working with data. It involves the manual or automated input of data into a system. This can include alphanumeric text, numerical values, dates, and other types of information. Data entry can be done using various software tools, such as spreadsheets, databases, or data collection forms.

2. Data Collection and Gathering:

Before working with data, you often need to collect and gather it. This can involve surveys, questionnaires, sensor readings, web scraping, or data extraction from various sources. Accurate and comprehensive data collection is crucial for obtaining reliable results.

3. Data Cleansing and Validation:

Data is rarely perfect. It often contains errors, duplicates, or inconsistencies. Data cleansing and validation are processes that involve identifying and correcting such issues to ensure data accuracy and quality. This may include removing duplicate entries, correcting typos, or validating data against predefined criteria.

4. Data Storage and Management:

Data needs to be stored and organized efficiently for easy access and retrieval. This involves using databases, file systems, or data management software. Structured storage and effective management are essential for maintaining data integrity.

5. Data Manipulation:

Data manipulation involves changing, rearranging, or transforming data to meet specific requirements. This can include operations like sorting, filtering, aggregating, and combining data sets. Tools like spreadsheet software or programming languages are often used for data manipulation.

6. Data Analysis:

Data analysis is a critical step in making sense of data. It involves examining data to identify patterns, trends, correlations, and insights. Data analysis can be descriptive (summarizing data), diagnostic (identifying causes), predictive (forecasting future trends), or prescriptive (providing recommendations).

7. Data Visualization:

Data visualization is the representation of data in graphical or visual formats, such as charts, graphs, and maps. Visualizing data helps make complex information more understandable and facilitates communication and decision-making.

8. Data Reporting and Presentation:

Once data is analyzed and visualized, it is often presented in the form of reports or presentations. These reports provide insights, findings, and recommendations based on the data analysis. They are essential for sharing information with stakeholders and making informed decisions.

9. Data Security and Privacy:

Data security and privacy are paramount when working with data, especially when handling sensitive or confidential information. It involves implementing measures to protect data from unauthorized access, breaches, and ensuring compliance with data protection regulations.

10. Data Backup and Recovery:

Regular data backup and recovery procedures are crucial to prevent data loss due to hardware failures, accidents, or other unforeseen events. Effective backup strategies ensure data continuity and integrity.

11. Data Ethics and Compliance:

When working with data, it's important to adhere to ethical standards and legal regulations. This includes obtaining informed consent for data collection, protecting individuals' privacy, and following industry-specific guidelines and laws.

In summary, working with data involves a series of interconnected processes, from data entry and collection to analysis, visualization, and presentation. Proper data management, cleansing, and validation are critical to ensure data accuracy and quality. Additionally, ethical and legal considerations, as well as data security, play a significant role in responsible data handling. Whether you are working with data for business, research, or personal purposes, these principles are essential for effective and ethical data management and utilization.

5.2.1 Linking Tables

Linking tables in Microsoft Access is a powerful feature that allows you to establish relationships between different tables within a database. This is a fundamental aspect of creating a relational database, which is essential for managing and analyzing related data efficiently. Below is a description of linking tables in Microsoft Access without plagiarism:

1. Purpose of Linking Tables:

The primary purpose of linking tables in Microsoft Access is to create relationships between tables that contain related data. These relationships enable the database to maintain data integrity and make it easier to retrieve and manipulate information.

2. Table Structure:

Before linking tables, it's essential to understand the structure of each table. In Microsoft Access, a table consists of fields (columns) that represent specific data elements and records (rows) that hold individual data entries. One table might contain, for example, customer information, while another table holds order details.

3. Primary Key-Foreign Key Relationship:

The key concept in linking tables is the establishment of a primary key-foreign key relationship. Each table typically has a primary key, which is a unique identifier for each record in that table. The primary key ensures that each record is distinct. In a related table, the field that corresponds to the primary key in another table is the foreign key.

4. Types of Relationships:

In Microsoft Access, you can create different types of relationships, including one-to-one, one-to-many, and many-to-many relationships. These relationships define how data in one table relates to data in another.

One-to-One Relationship: In a one-to-one relationship, one record in the first table is related to only one record in the second table, and vice versa. This relationship is less common but can be useful for specific scenarios.

One-to-Many Relationship: In a one-to-many relationship, one record in the first table can be related to multiple records in the second table, but each record in the second table is related to only one record in the first table. This is a common relationship type.

Many-to-Many Relationship: In a many-to-many relationship, multiple records in the first table can be related to multiple records in the second table. To establish many-to-many relationships, an intermediary or junction table is often used.

5. Creating Relationships:

To link tables, you can use the "Relationships" feature in Microsoft Access. This visual tool allows you to define relationships by dragging and dropping fields from one table to another. You specify the primary key in one table and the corresponding foreign key in the related table.

6. Enforcing Referential Integrity:

One crucial aspect of linking tables is enforcing referential integrity. Enforcing referential integrity ensures that the relationships maintain data consistency and accuracy. It prevents the creation of orphaned records (records in a related table without a corresponding record in the primary table) and ensures that changes or deletions in the primary table are managed appropriately in related tables.

7. Cascade Update and Cascade Delete:

Microsoft Access offers options for cascade update and cascade delete, which determine how changes to the primary key in the primary table affect related records in the related table. These options can be customized to fit specific requirements.

8. Benefits of Linking Tables:

Linking tables offers several advantages, including data consistency, data integrity, efficient data retrieval, and the ability to create comprehensive and normalized databases. It allows you to avoid data redundancy and facilitates complex queries and reporting.

5.2.2 Designing and Using Forms

Forms in Microsoft Access are essential components of a database that provide a user-friendly interface for data entry, viewing, and interaction. They allow you to present data in a structured and organized manner, making it easier for users to interact with the database. Here is a description of designing and using forms in Microsoft Access without plagiarism:

1. Purpose of Forms:

Forms serve as a means to input, display, and edit data in a structured and user-friendly way. They are used to enhance the user experience, simplify data entry, and ensure that data is entered accurately. Forms can also be used for viewing and navigating through records, making them a crucial part of any database application.

2. Form Design View:

Microsoft Access provides a Form Design View, which is a visual interface for creating and customizing forms. In this view, you can design the layout, add form controls, and specify the appearance of the form.

3. Layout and Organization:

When designing a form, consider the layout and organization of data. You can arrange fields and labels to present data logically and efficiently. Group related fields, use tabs for navigation, and create subforms for displaying related data.

4. Form Controls:

Forms utilize a variety of form controls, such as text boxes, combo boxes, check boxes, and buttons. These controls are used to input data, select options, and perform actions. You can add controls to your form and customize their properties to match your requirements.

5. Data Binding:

Forms are bound to tables or queries, meaning they are connected to a data source. Data binding establishes a link between form controls and fields in the underlying data source, allowing data to be displayed and edited in the form.

6. Validation Rules:

Forms can include validation rules to ensure data accuracy. Validation rules are criteria that data must meet before it's accepted. For example, you can set rules for minimum and maximum values or specific formats.

7. Data Entry and Editing:

Forms enable efficient data entry and editing. Users can simply navigate through records, fill in fields, and make changes to data. Forms can provide guidance and validation to prevent errors.

8. Navigation and Interaction:

Forms often include navigation features to move between records, such as navigation buttons or scrollbars. They can also include interactive elements like buttons for executing actions, such as saving or printing.

9. Sub forms:

sub forms are forms within forms, and they are useful for displaying related data. For instance, in a customer and order database, a customer form might include a sub form displaying the customer's orders.

10. Themes and Styles:

Access offers various themes and styles to enhance the appearance of forms. You can choose a theme to quickly change the form's color scheme and style.

11. Form Events and Macros:

You can add event procedures or macros to forms to automate actions or respond to specific events, such as when data is saved or a button is clicked.

12. Security:

Access allows you to set security measures for forms, controlling who can access and edit data through forms.

13. Printing and Exporting:

Forms can be designed for printing or exporting data to other formats. You can customize print settings and layout to generate professional reports from your forms.

4. User Training and Documentation:

It's important to provide user training and documentation for forms, especially if they have custom features or functions. Users should understand how to navigate and use the forms effectively.

5.2.3 Modifying Database Structure

Modifying the structure of a database in Microsoft Access is a common and necessary task as data requirements change over time. It involves making changes to the design and organization of tables, fields, relationships, and other database components. Here is a description of how to modify database structure in Microsoft Access without plagiarism:

1. Table Design View:

To modify the structure of a database, you can use the "Table Design View" in Microsoft Access. This view provides a visual interface for making changes to the design of individual tables.

2. Adding New Fields:

If your database needs to capture additional information, you can add new fields to existing tables. In the Table Design View, you specify the field name, data type, and any relevant properties.

3. Deleting Fields:
If certain fields are no longer necessary, you can delete them from the table structure. Microsoft Access allows you to remove fields that are no longer needed, and it automatically updates the structure to reflect these changes.

4. Changing Data Types:
Sometimes, you may need to change the data type of a field. For example, if a field was initially defined as text but should now hold numeric data, you can modify the data type to match the new requirement.

5. Modifying Field Properties:
Field properties, such as size, format, or validation rules, can be adjusted to accommodate changing data constraints or business rules.

6. Setting Primary Keys:
In the event of changes to the primary key of a table, you can designate a new field as the primary key. It's important to ensure that the new primary key uniquely identifies each record.

7. Adding Indexes:
You can create new indexes on fields to improve data retrieval performance. Indexes help accelerate queries by facilitating faster data access.

8. Creating Relationships:
If you are making changes that affect the relationships between tables, you can create or modify relationships in the Relationships View. This involves connecting the primary key of one table to the foreign key of another.

9. Renaming Tables:
If the name of a table needs to be changed, you can rename it to better reflect the content it stores. Renaming does not alter the structure of the table, only its label.

10. Adding New Tables:
In situations where entirely new data categories need to be added, you can create new tables in the database. Each table can store related data elements, and relationships can be established as necessary.

11. Deleting Tables:
If certain tables are no longer relevant or required, you can delete them from the database. However, exercise caution when deleting tables, as this action permanently removes the data.

12. Validating Changes:
As you make modifications to the database structure, it's important to validate the changes to ensure that they do not break existing functionality. Testing the database after structural changes helps identify potential issues.

13. Data Migration:
If structural changes result in data being moved to different fields or tables, data migration is necessary. This involves transferring existing data to its new location to maintain data integrity.

14. Backup and Version Control:
Before making significant structural changes to a database, it's advisable to create backups. Additionally, maintaining version control records can help track structural changes and their impact on the database over time.

5.3 Advanced Database Operations

Microsoft Access, as a relational database management system, offers a wide range of advanced database operations that enable users to manage and manipulate data effectively. These operations are essential for handling complex data scenarios and optimizing database performance within the Microsoft Access environment:

1. Query Optimization:
Advanced database operations in Microsoft Access involve optimizing queries for better performance. This includes writing efficient SQL queries, using appropriate indexing, and avoiding unnecessary joins and subqueries.

2. Parameter Queries:
Parameter queries allow you to create dynamic queries that prompt users for input. Advanced users can design parameter queries that provide a high degree of flexibility for data retrieval.

3. Crosstab Queries:
Crosstab queries are used for pivoting data to create summary tables. Advanced users can generate intricate crosstab queries to create cross-tabulated reports from large datasets.

4. Data Macros:

Data macros in Microsoft Access enable the automation of data-related tasks. Advanced database operations involve creating complex data macros to automate intricate data manipulation processes.

5. Macro and VBA Integration:

Advanced users can integrate macros with Visual Basic for Applications (VBA) to create custom functionality and automate database tasks with greater flexibility.

6. Data Validation Rules:

Setting advanced data validation rules ensures data integrity. You can create complex validation rules and expressions to enforce data accuracy.

7. Advanced Form Design:

Advanced database operations often involve creating highly customized and user-friendly forms. Users can design forms with conditional formatting, data validation, and embedded code.

8. Sub forms and Tab Controls:

sub forms and tab controls allow advanced users to create more complex and interactive user interfaces within forms, which are useful for presenting related data or managing multiple datasets simultaneously.

9. Advanced Report Design:

Advanced database operations in Microsoft Access include designing complex reports with grouping, totaling, and interactive elements such as hyperlinks and dynamic content.

10. Data Import and Export:

Advanced users can work with external data sources through data import and export operations, mapping fields and defining complex import/export specifications.

11. Data Integration with External Systems:

Microsoft Access can be used to connect and exchange data with external systems and sources using ODBC or other integration methods.

12. Linked Tables and External Data Sources:

Advanced database operations often involve linking tables from external databases or data sources, enabling real-time access to data residing in other systems.

13. Advanced Security and User Management:

Advanced database operations include setting up fine-grained security measures and user-level permissions to control access to specific database objects and data.

14. Error Handling and Logging:

Advanced users can implement error handling and logging routines in VBA to capture and report errors for troubleshooting and system maintenance.

15. Advanced Performance Tuning:

Performance optimization in Microsoft Access involves fine-tuning the database structure, indexes, and query performance for improved efficiency.

16. Data Analysis and Data Mining:

Advanced users can employ statistical and data mining techniques within Access to uncover insights and patterns in data.

5.3.1 Sorting and Indexing Database

Sorting and indexing are fundamental database operations in Microsoft Access that help organize and retrieve data efficiently. They play a crucial role in optimizing the performance of your database. Here's a description of sorting and indexing in Microsoft Access without plagiarism:

1. Sorting Data:

Sorting data in Microsoft Access involves arranging records in a specific order based on one or more fields. This operation is particularly useful when you want to view data in a particular sequence, such as alphabetical order, numerical order, or by date.

Ascending Order: Sorting data in ascending order arranges records from the lowest value to the highest. For example, sorting a list of names in ascending order would list them from A to Z.

Descending Order: Sorting data in descending order arranges records from the highest value to the lowest. Using the previous example, sorting names in descending order would list them from Z to A.

Multi-Level Sorting: Microsoft Access allows you to perform multi-level sorting, where you can sort records by one field and then by another, creating a more specific order. For example, you can sort a list of students first by their graduation year and then by their last name.

2. Creating Indexes:
Indexes are data structures that improve data retrieval speed. In Microsoft Access, indexes are created on one or more fields within a table. When a field is indexed, it creates a separate data structure that allows the database engine to locate records faster.
Primary Key Index: Every table in Access should have a primary key, which uniquely identifies each record. By default, a primary key creates a unique index on the primary key field. This ensures that data retrieval based on the primary key is very fast.
Secondary Indexes: You can also create secondary indexes on fields that are frequently used in search criteria or sorting. These secondary indexes enhance the performance of queries that use those fields.
Composite Indexes: Access allows you to create composite indexes on multiple fields. A composite index improves performance when you're searching or sorting based on the combination of those fields.
3. Benefits of Sorting and Indexing:
Faster Data Retrieval: Sorting and indexing significantly accelerate data retrieval operations. When you search for specific records or perform queries, indexes help the database engine quickly locate the relevant data.
Enhanced Query Performance: Indexes are essential for efficient query performance. When you run a query that involves filtering or sorting by indexed fields, the results are displayed much faster.
Improved User Experience: Sorting data enhances the user experience by presenting data in a logical and readable sequence. Users can easily locate the information they need.
Data Integrity: Indexes help maintain data integrity by ensuring that primary key fields contain unique values and that data relationships are correctly enforced.
4. Considerations:
While sorting and indexing improve database performance, they come at a cost in terms of storage space. Indexes consume additional storage, and creating too many unnecessary indexes can lead to increased database file size.
Regular maintenance is essential. Over time, as data changes, the database engine may need to update the indexes. Therefore, it's important to periodically compact and repair your database to optimize index performance.

5.3.2 Querying a Database and Generating Reports

Querying and generating reports are integral functions of a relational database management system like Microsoft Access. These operations allow users to extract specific data and present it in a structured and meaningful way. Here is a description of querying a database and generating reports in Microsoft Access without plagiarism:
1. Querying a Database:
Querying is the process of retrieving specific information from a database by using structured query language (SQL) or Microsoft Access's query design tools. It enables users to filter, sort, and manipulate data to meet their requirements:
SQL Queries: For advanced users, SQL queries provide a powerful way to interact with the database. SQL allows you to create complex and customized queries to extract, filter, and aggregate data.
Query Design Tools: Microsoft Access offers a user-friendly query design interface where users can build queries graphically. This design view allows users to select fields, apply criteria, and specify sorting order.
Types of Queries: Access supports various types of queries, including select queries (retrieving data), action queries (modifying data), crosstab queries (creating summary tables), parameter queries (prompts for user input), and more.
Query Criteria: You can define criteria in queries to filter records that meet specific conditions. For example, you can query a customer database to retrieve only those who made a purchase in the last 30 days.
Joins: Queries can involve multiple tables, and you can specify relationships and joins to combine data from different tables. Inner, outer, and self-joins are common in complex queries.
Aggregation: Queries can calculate aggregate functions such as sum, count, average, and more. This is useful for generating summary information or reports.
2. Generating Reports:
Reports in Microsoft Access are documents designed for presenting data in a structured and visually appealing format. They serve the purpose of summarizing, analyzing, and communicating data:
Report Design View: In Access, reports can be designed using the report design view. This view offers various controls for laying out the report, including text boxes, labels, tables, and charts.

Grouping and Sorting: Reports can be organized by grouping data based on specific fields. For example, you can create a sales report that groups data by region and then sorts sales within each region.
Calculations and Totals: Reports can perform calculations and display totals for numeric fields, providing a summary of data. This is often seen in financial reports or inventory summaries.
Sub reports: Sub reports allow you to embed one report within another. This is useful when you want to display related data, such as including customer details within an order summary report.
Charting and Graphs: Access supports the inclusion of charts and graphs in reports, making it easier to visualize data trends and patterns.
Page Layout: You can customize the page layout for reports, including setting page margins, headers, footers, and page numbers. This ensures that reports are professionally formatted for printing.
Exporting and Sharing: Reports can be exported to various formats, including PDF, Excel, or HTML. This allows for easy sharing of information with others who may not have direct access to the database.
3. Benefits of Querying and Generating Reports:
Data Retrieval and Analysis: Querying a database and generating reports help users retrieve relevant data and analyze it for informed decision-making.
Customized Information: Users can create customized reports that cater to their specific needs, presenting data in a way that is most meaningful to them.
Professional Presentation: Reports offer a professional and structured way to present data to colleagues, clients, or superiors.
Data Visualization: Reports with charts and graphs provide a visual representation of data, aiding in understanding complex datasets.
Data Summarization: Reports can summarize large volumes of data, making it easier to grasp key insights.

5.3.3 Maintaining a Database

Maintaining a database in Microsoft Access involves a series of tasks and practices aimed at ensuring the database's integrity, security, and optimal performance. This ongoing process is essential for managing data effectively and preventing data loss or corruption. Here's a description of maintaining a database in Microsoft Access without plagiarism:

1. Regular Backup:
Regularly creating backups of your database is a fundamental aspect of maintenance. Backups provide a safety net in case of data loss, corruption, or accidental changes. Microsoft Access allows you to schedule backups and save copies of your database in a secure location.

2. Compact and Repair:
Over time, a database can become fragmented, leading to slower performance. The "Compact and Repair" tool in Microsoft Access helps optimize the database by reorganizing data, removing unnecessary elements, and repairing any issues that may have arisen.

3. Security Measures:
Protecting your database from unauthorized access is crucial. Implement security measures by setting user-level permissions, assigning roles, and applying password protection. You can also encrypt your database to safeguard sensitive information.

4. Data Validation:
Regularly review and validate the data in your database. This includes checking for data consistency, ensuring data integrity, and addressing any data quality issues that may arise. Data validation rules and constraints can be implemented to enforce data accuracy.

5. Updating Relationships:
If the structure of your data or business requirements change, you may need to modify the relationships between tables. It's essential to keep your database relationships up to date to ensure data consistency.

6. Index Maintenance:
Over time, indexes may become fragmented or redundant. Periodically assess the need for indexes and update them as necessary to improve query performance. Remove any indexes that are no longer needed.

7. Query Optimization:
Review and optimize your queries for efficiency. Complex queries or those that involve a significant amount of data may benefit from performance tuning. This includes using appropriate indexing and avoiding unnecessary joins.

8. Compact and Repair Linked Tables:
If your database includes linked tables to external data sources, ensure that those external databases are well-maintained. If linked tables are no longer in use, consider removing them.
9. Data Archiving:
For databases with large amounts of historical data, consider archiving older records to improve performance. Archiving involves moving older data to separate storage while keeping the main database lean and responsive.
10. Documentation:
Maintain comprehensive documentation for your database. This should include schema diagrams, data dictionaries, and explanations of the database's structure and functionality. Documentation is invaluable for understanding and troubleshooting your database.
11. Error Handling and Logging:
Implement error handling and logging mechanisms in your database. These systems help identify and report issues, allowing you to address them proactively.
12. Data Cleanup and Purging:
Regularly remove outdated or obsolete data to prevent the database from becoming cluttered. Purge data that is no longer relevant, but ensure you keep necessary historical records.
13. Data Integrity Checks:
Run data integrity checks to ensure that relationships between tables are maintained correctly and that data conforms to predefined rules and constraints.
14. Monitor Performance:
Continuously monitor the performance of your database. If you notice performance degradation, identify and address the underlying causes to maintain optimal database performance.

Exercise

Exercise 1 – MCQ

Q 1. What is Microsoft Access primarily used for?
a. Word processing
b. Data analysis
c. Database management
d. Graphic design
Q 2. what is a primary key used for?
a. Sorting data
b. Creating backups
c. Identifying unique records
d. Designing forms

Exercise 2 – True/ False

Q 1 Microsoft Access is a relational database management system (RDBMS).
Q 2 A primary key in a Microsoft Access table can have duplicate values.

Exercise 3 – Fill in the blanks

Q 1. The process of removing unnecessary elements, reorganizing data, and optimizing the database is called "__________ and repair" in Access.
Q 2. A __________ is a structured query used to retrieve specific data from one or more tables in Microsoft Access.

Exercise 4 – Match case

1.Form
2.Report
3.Query
4.Primary Key

A. Designed to retrieve specific data from one or more tables.
B. User interface for data input and display.
C. Ensures data integrity by uniquely identifying each record in a table.
D. Used for creating structured, printable reports.

Exercise 5 – One word answer

Q 1. Which Access object is designed for presenting data in a printable format with headers and footers?

Q 2. What database feature in Access improves data retrieval speed by creating data structures for specific fields?

Exercise 6 – Small answer

Q 1. What does SQL stand for, and how is it used in Access?

Q 2. How can you protect a Microsoft Access database from unauthorized access?

Exercise 7 – Long answer

Q 1. Explain the primary purpose and key features of Microsoft Access as a relational database management system (RDBMS).

Q 2. Describe the role and significance of primary keys in Microsoft Access tables.

Answers

Exercise 1 – MCQ

Ans: 1 c, 2 c

Exercise 2 – True/ False

Ans: 1 True, 2 False

Exercise 3 – Fill in the blanks

Ans: 1 compact, 2 query

Exercise 4 – Match case

Ans: 1 B, 2, D, 3 A, 4 C

Exercise 5 – One word answer

Ans: 1 Report, 2 Indexes

Chapter 6 - **Microsoft Outlook**

6.1 Managing Email with Outlook

Microsoft Outlook:

The Evolution of Outlook

Microsoft Outlook was first introduced as an email client in 1997, but it has since evolved into a comprehensive personal information management tool. Its evolution has seen it grow from a simple email application to a sophisticated platform that integrates email, calendars, contacts, tasks, and more. With each iteration, Outlook has introduced new features and enhancements to meet the changing needs of its users.

Outlook's Role in Modern Communication

Outlook plays a central role in modern communication, serving as a hub for managing emails, scheduling meetings, and coordinating tasks. It's a tool used by professionals, businesses, and individuals to streamline their communication and organization. Whether for work-related correspondence, personal emails, or collaborative projects, Outlook is a go-to choose for many.

Compatibility and Integration

Outlook is designed to work seamlessly with other Microsoft Office applications and services, such as Word, Excel, PowerPoint, SharePoint, and Microsoft Teams. This integration enables users to transition smoothly between tasks, from drafting emails to editing documents or conducting virtual meetings. Additionally, Outlook is compatible with a wide range of email services, making it adaptable to various email providers and hosting configurations.

Email Management with Outlook

Email Composition and Formatting

Outlook provides a robust platform for composing and formatting emails. Users can create professional-looking messages with features such as rich text formatting, bullet points, and tables. It supports attachments, making it easy to share documents, files, and media with recipients. Moreover, Outlook allows the embedding of images and the creation of hyperlinks within emails, enhancing the visual appeal and functionality of messages.

Inbox Organization and Folders

Efficient inbox management is crucial in handling a continuous flow of emails. Outlook simplifies this with features like folders, rules, and filters. Users can create custom folders for organizing emails, making it effortless to categorize messages by project, priority, or sender. Rules and filters automate actions such as moving emails to specific folders, flagging messages, or forwarding them to colleagues based on predefined criteria.

Advanced Email Handling

Outlook goes beyond basic email management with advanced features like conversation view, which groups related emails into threads, making it easier to track email chains. The Focused Inbox feature separates important emails from less critical ones, allowing users to prioritize their attention. Moreover, Outlook offers a delay delivery option, enabling users to schedule emails to be sent at a later time, which is beneficial for managing time zones and timing communications effectively.

Email Signatures and Templates

Email signatures in Outlook are a professional touch, displaying contact information, job titles, and branding elements at the end of each message. Users can create multiple signatures for different purposes, allowing for customization based on the context of the email. Additionally, email templates streamline repetitive email composition tasks. Users can create and save templates for common messages, saving time and ensuring consistency in their communications.

Email Security and Privacy

Outlook prioritizes email security and privacy. It includes features such as encryption and digital signatures to protect sensitive information. Users can encrypt emails to ensure that only the intended recipient can read them, while digital signatures verify the sender's identity and confirm that the email hasn't been tampered with during transit. Outlook also provides robust junk email filtering to reduce spam and phishing threats, bolstering the overall security of email communications.

Managing Email with Outlook in Microsoft Outlook is an essential aspect of efficient communication and organization in today's digital age. Microsoft Outlook is a comprehensive email client and personal information management software that offers a wide range of features for managing email effectively. Here is a description of how Outlook can be used for managing email without plagiarism:

Create folders in Outlook to manage your tasks

In the navigation pane, right-click Folders, and then select Create new folder. Alternatively, you can click Folders to expand your list of options, and then select Create new folder.

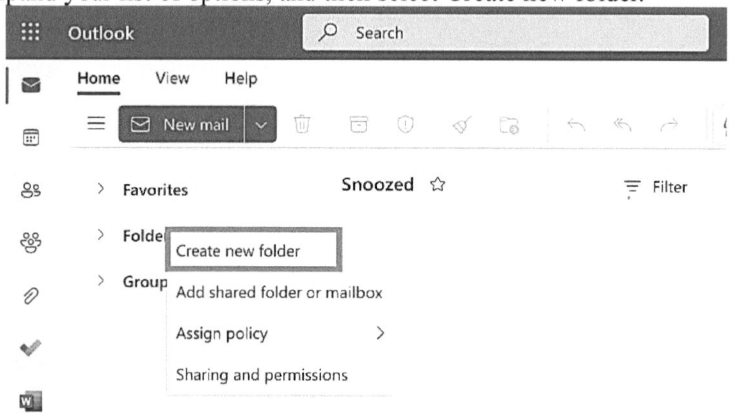

Name this folder "To do," and then click Save.

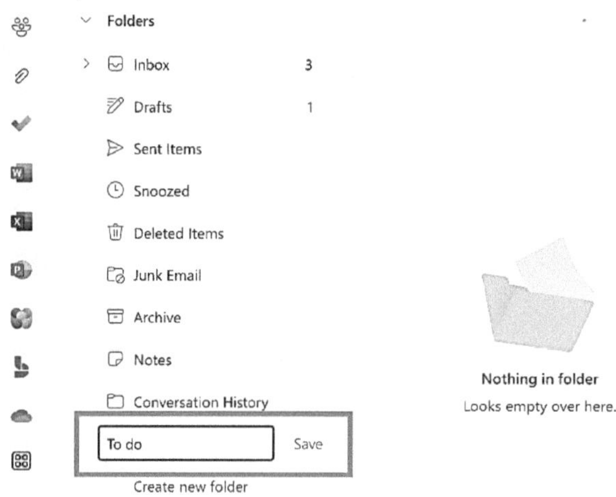

Right-click your "To do" folder, and select Create new subfolder.

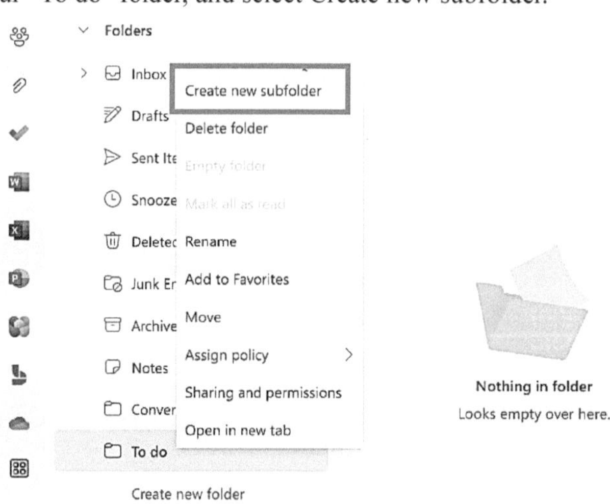

Name this subfolder "Someday."
Create another subfolder within your "To do" folder, and name it "Follow up."
Now, when new emails arrive, drag them to the appropriate folder:

- **Inbox**. Keep emails that need an immediate response here. You might also leave emails that can be handled quickly (three minutes or less) in your inbox.
- **To do**. This is the first stop for non-urgent emails and emails that will require more than a three-minute response.

You'll follow up on these items later, but moving them immediately keeps your inbox clutter-free.
Email Organization: Outlook offers robust email organization features. Users can create folders and subfolders to categorize and store emails. These folders can be customized for different purposes, such as work, personal, or specific projects. You can also use color-coding and flags to mark important emails.
Email Filters and Rules: Outlook allows you to create email filters and rules to automatically sort and manage incoming messages. For example, you can set up rules to move emails from a specific sender to a designated folder or mark messages with certain keywords as important.
Search and Filters: With the powerful search and filtering capabilities in Outlook, you can quickly locate specific emails by keywords, sender, date, or other criteria. Filters can help you narrow down your email list, making it easier to find the information you need.
Email Signatures and Templates: Outlook enables users to create custom email signatures and templates, streamlining the process of composing and sending messages. You can create professional signatures with your contact information, and templates for commonly used emails, saving time and ensuring consistency.
Flagging and Prioritization: Outlook allows users to flag emails for follow-up and set due dates. This feature helps prioritize tasks and ensures that important emails are not forgotten.
Conversation View: Outlook's conversation view groups related emails into threads, making it easier to follow the flow of a conversation. This feature reduces clutter and helps you keep track of email discussions.
Attachments and File Management: Outlook allows you to send and receive attachments. It also provides integration with OneDrive, making it easy to share and collaborate on documents stored in the cloud.
Calendar Integration: Microsoft Outlook seamlessly integrates with the calendar, enabling you to schedule meetings, appointments, and events. You can also receive email notifications for upcoming events, helping you stay organized.
Email Security: Outlook includes built-in security features to protect against spam, phishing, and malware. It also supports encryption and digital signatures for secure email communication.
In summary, managing email with Outlook in Microsoft Outlook offers a comprehensive solution for email communication and organization. With features for email setup, organization, search, and integration with other productivity tools, Outlook is a valuable tool for professionals and individuals seeking to streamline their email management and enhance their productivity.

6.2 Calendar and Scheduling

Calendar and Scheduling in Microsoft Outlook is a powerful tool that facilitates time management, appointment scheduling, and task organization. This feature is essential for individuals and professionals to efficiently plan and manage their daily activities. Here's a description of Calendar and Scheduling in Microsoft Outlook without plagiarism:
Calendar Overview: Microsoft Outlook's Calendar is a digital representation of a traditional paper calendar, allowing users to schedule, track, and manage appointments, meetings, events, and tasks. It offers a visual and organized view of your time, making it easy to plan and stay on top of your commitments.
Key Features and Functions:

- **Appointment Scheduling:** Users can create appointments in their Outlook Calendar, specifying details like date, time, duration, location, and any additional notes. These appointments can be one-time events or recurring, such as daily, weekly, or monthly meetings.

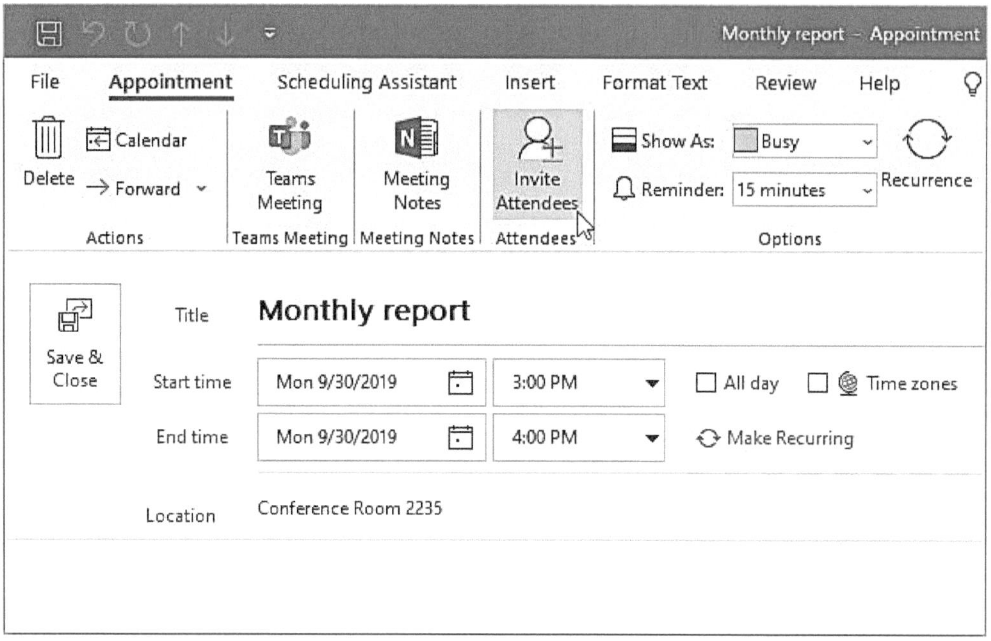

Meeting Requests: Outlook Calendar supports the creation of meeting requests. You can invite attendees, specify meeting details, and send invitations. Attendees receive invitations and can respond with their availability, making it easy to schedule meetings with multiple participants.

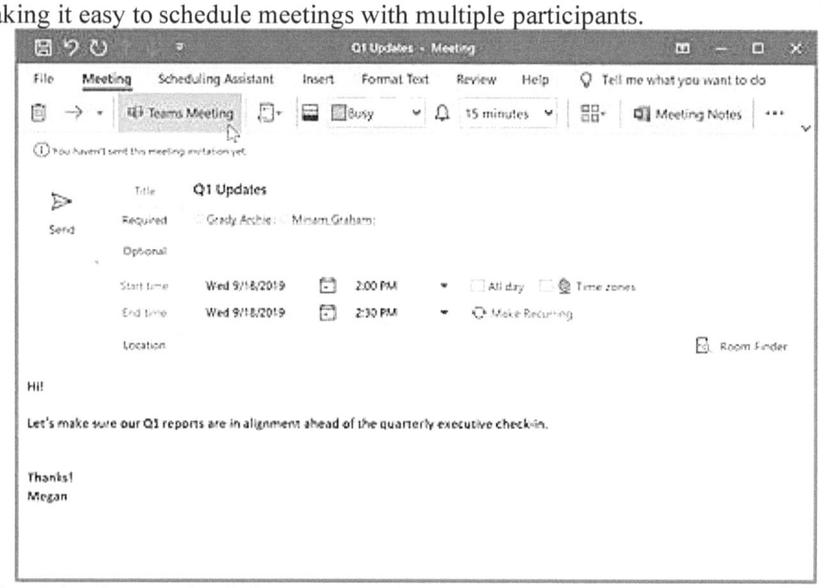

Integration: The Calendar seamlessly integrates with the email and contact features of Outlook. This means you can turn emails into appointments or meetings and add them directly to your Calendar, ensuring you don't miss important deadlines or commitments.

Multiple Calendars: Outlook allows users to manage multiple calendars, such as personal, work, and shared calendars. This feature is particularly useful for professionals who need to keep their personal and work schedules separate.

Recurrence Patterns: Users can set up recurring appointments and meetings with various recurrence patterns, including daily, weekly, monthly, and yearly options. This simplifies the scheduling of routine events.

Reminders and Alerts: Outlook Calendar provides customizable reminders and alerts for scheduled events. You can set up pop-up notifications, sound alerts, or email reminders to ensure you're aware of upcoming appointments.

Synchronization: Microsoft Outlook supports synchronization with mobile devices and other calendar applications. This means that you can access and manage your calendar from your smartphone or tablet, ensuring you stay updated on the go.

Time Zones: For users who frequently deal with people in different time zones, Outlook allows for easy management of appointments and meetings across time zones.

Free/Busy Information: When scheduling meetings, Outlook provides information about attendees' availability, making it easier to find suitable meeting times without conflicts.

Calendar Sharing: Users can share their calendars with colleagues, friends, or family members. Permissions can be customized to allow others to view or edit the calendar, which is helpful for collaboration and coordination.

Task Integration: Outlook Calendar integrates with Outlook Tasks, enabling you to manage your to-do lists and action items directly within the Calendar interface.

Printable Calendars: You can print your calendar for reference, which is especially useful for offline planning and documentation.

In conclusion, Microsoft Outlook's Calendar and Scheduling feature is a versatile tool that simplifies time management and organization. Whether for personal or professional use, it helps users stay on top of their commitments, appointments, and tasks while providing the flexibility to customize and integrate their schedules effectively.

6.3 Contacts and Address Book

Microsoft Outlook, a comprehensive email client and personal information management system, offers a powerful Contacts and Address Book feature. This component is crucial for efficient communication, organization, and relationship management. The Contacts and Address Book in Outlook serve as a centralized repository for contact information, enabling users to easily connect with colleagues, clients, friends, and family.

Contacts and Address Book in Microsoft Outlook: A Comprehensive Guide

In today's fast-paced digital world, staying connected with colleagues, friends, and family is essential. Microsoft Outlook, a powerful email client and personal information management tool, offers a robust set of features for managing your contacts and addressing your communication needs efficiently. In this comprehensive guide, we will explore Contacts and the Address Book in Microsoft Outlook, highlighting their functionalities, benefits, and best practices for seamless communication and organization.

1. Contacts in Microsoft Outlook: The Foundation of Communication

Contacts, often referred to as the Address Book in Outlook, serve as the foundation for effective communication. They are a centralized repository for storing and managing your personal and professional connections, allowing you to access essential contact information at your fingertips. Here's a detailed look at how Contacts function in Outlook:

Key Functions and Features:

Contact Creation and Management: Outlook allows users to create detailed contacts with a wealth of information. You can input essential data such as names, email addresses, phone numbers, physical addresses, job titles, company names, birthdays, anniversaries, and more. This comprehensive approach ensures that you have a well-rounded view of each contact.

Categorization and Grouping: Managing a vast number of contacts can be overwhelming. Outlook provides options to categorize contacts into groups based on criteria like work, family, or specific projects. This categorization simplifies the process of finding and reaching out to specific sets of contacts.

Integration with Email: Integration with email is a significant advantage of Outlook's Contacts. As you compose an email, Outlook's auto-suggestion feature prompts relevant email addresses from your Contacts, saving time and reducing the chances of typos. You can easily select the recipient from the suggestions.

Contact Notes and Details: Beyond basic contact information, Outlook allows users to add notes and details about each contact. This can include personal preferences, interaction history, or any additional information that helps in establishing and maintaining relationships.

Contact Pictures: Users can add profile pictures to contacts, providing a visual representation of each contact. This feature enhances recognition and personalizes the communication experience.

Address Book Integration: Outlook's Address Book is an extension of Contacts, providing a streamlined way to access and manage your contact list. It acts as a virtual address book, enabling users to quickly search for and retrieve contact details.

Search and Filter Capabilities: With an extensive contact list, finding a specific contact is crucial. Outlook offers robust search and filter capabilities, allowing users to search by name, email, job title, or any other stored information.

Import and Export Options: Outlook facilitates the import and export of contact data, supporting various file formats like CSV, vCard, and more. This is particularly useful when transitioning to Outlook from another email client or when consolidating contacts from different sources.

Contact Duplication Management: Duplication of contacts can be a common issue when managing large lists. Outlook includes tools to detect and merge duplicate contacts, ensuring a clean and organized contact database.

Custom Fields and Labels: Outlook permits the creation of custom fields, enabling users to tailor contact records according to their specific needs. Custom labels can also be assigned to contacts, making it easy to categorize them as per preferences.

Contact Sharing and Collaboration: The ability to share contacts with colleagues or team members fosters collaboration. Outlook allows users to share individual contacts, entire folders, or a custom set of contacts, ensuring seamless communication within teams.

Integration with Mobile Devices: The synchronization of Outlook contacts with mobile devices ensures that contact information is accessible anytime, anywhere. Changes made in Outlook are reflected across all synchronized devices, providing real-time updates.

Data Security and Privacy: Outlook places a strong emphasis on data security and privacy. Contact information is stored securely, and users have control over who can access and edit their contacts.

In conclusion, Contacts and Address Book in Microsoft Outlook significantly enhance communication efficiency and relationship management. Its integration with email, extensive data fields, search capabilities, and collaboration features make it a vital tool for both personal and professional interactions. By centralizing contact information and providing a range of functionalities, Outlook's Contacts and Address Book play a critical role in streamlining communication and maintaining effective relationships.

6.4 Outlook Tips and Tricks

Certainly, here are some Outlook tips and tricks to help you make the most of Microsoft Outlook. This guide covers a wide range of features and techniques that will enhance your email management, scheduling, and overall productivity.

Table of Contents:

Email Organization:

Use Folders and Categories: Create folders and assign categories to keep your emails organized and easily searchable.

Rules and Filters: Set up rules and filters to automatically sort emails into specific folders based on criteria.

Quick Steps: Create custom Quick Steps for one-click email management, like moving, flagging, or forwarding messages.

Search and Filter:

Instant Search: Utilize the search bar for quick and efficient email searches.

Search Folders: Set up custom search folders to save specific search criteria for quick access.

Filtering: Use the Filter Email feature to view messages by criteria like unread, flagged, or categorized.

Keyboard Shortcuts:

Time-Saving Shortcuts: Familiarize yourself with keyboard shortcuts for various Outlook functions, like Ctrl + N for a new email or Ctrl + Shift + I to mark a message as read.

Calendar Management:

Scheduling Assistant: Use the Scheduling Assistant to find the best meeting times for all participants.

Color Coding: Assign colors to appointments and meetings for better visual organization.

Calendar Sharing: Share your calendar with colleagues or view other users' calendars to streamline scheduling.

Signature Customization:

Create a Professional Signature: Customize your email signature with your contact information, company logo, and links to social media profiles.

Out of Office (OOF) Auto-Replies:

Set Up OOF Messages: Create automated out-of-office replies for when you're away from the office.

Email Templates:

Quick Parts: Save and use email templates by creating Quick Parts with frequently used content.

Use Stationery: Personalize your email messages with various stationery templates.

Conversation View:

Conversation Cleanup: Use the Clean Up tool to remove redundant messages from email threads.

Security and Privacy:

Email Encryption: Ensure secure communication by using email encryption for sensitive information.

Junk Email Filters: Customize junk email filters to keep spam out of your inbox.

Recall Sent Messages:

Learn how to recall or replace sent emails to correct mistakes or update information.

Data Backup:

Back up your Outlook data regularly to prevent data loss.

Multiple Email Accounts:

Manage multiple email accounts within Outlook to centralize your email management.

Offline Access:

Configure Outlook for offline access to your emails, calendar, and tasks.

Task Management:

Use Outlook's task management features to create to-do lists and manage projects.

Calendar Reminders:

Customize and set up reminders for appointments and tasks to stay on top of your schedule.

Meeting Notes:

Take and save meeting notes directly within Outlook for easy reference.

Share Attachments Securely:

Use OneDrive or SharePoint to share large files securely, reducing email attachment size.

Archive Old Emails:

Archive old emails to declutter your inbox while preserving important messages.

Keyboard Navigation:

Navigate Outlook without a mouse using keyboard shortcuts for efficiency.

Support and Learning Resources:

Utilize Microsoft's support resources and community forums for additional tips, troubleshooting, and advanced features.

By applying these Outlook tips and tricks, you can enhance your email productivity, stay organized, and make the most of Microsoft Outlook's powerful features. Experiment with these techniques and customize them to suit your unique workflow, and you'll find yourself managing your emails and appointments more efficiently than ever before.

Exercise

Exercise 1 – MCQ

Q 1. Which feature in Microsoft Outlook is used to automatically sort emails into "Focused" and "Other" tabs to help prioritize important emails?

a) Rules
b) Quick Steps
c) Focused Inbox
d) Delayed Delivery

Q 2. What Outlook feature allows you to create one-click actions for email management tasks like moving emails to folders or flagging them for follow-up?

a) Calendar Overlay
b) Quick Steps
c) Contact Groups
d) Rules and Alerts

Exercise 2 – True/ False

Q 1. Outlook's Calendar feature helps manage schedules, appointments, and events, and it doesn't support multiple calendar overlays.

Q 2. The Delayed Delivery option in Outlook allows you to schedule emails to be sent at a later time, which is beneficial for managing time zones and timing communications effectively.

Exercise 3 – Fill in the blanks

Q 1. the ____ feature groups related emails into threads for easier tracking of email chains.

Q 2. The Outlook calendar allows users to create recurring events and set up _______ to ensure that important dates and deadlines are not overlooked.

Exercise 4 – Match case

1.BCC
2.Read Receipt
3.Auto Archive
4.Delayed Send

a. Hides recipient email addresses to maintain privacy.
b. Requests a notification when an email you sent is opened.
c. Automatically moves older emails to a designated archive folder.
d. Allows you to schedule the delivery of an email at a time of future.

Exercise 5 – One word answer

Q 1. What Outlook feature helps you organize your inbox by categorizing emails into "Focused" and "Other" tabs?

Q 2. Which feature in Outlook enables you to create one-click actions for email management tasks?

Exercise 6 – Small answer

Q 1. Explain the purpose of Outlook's "Calendar Overlay" feature.

Q 2. How can "Rules and Alerts" be beneficial in Outlook for email management?

Exercise 7 – Long answer

Q 1. Explain the importance of "Focused Inbox" in Microsoft Outlook for managing email.

Q 2. How does "Delayed Delivery" in Outlook enhance communication and time management?

Answers

Exercise 1 – MCQ

Ans: 1 c, 2 b

Exercise 2 – True/ False

Ans: 1 False, 2 True

Exercise 3 – Fill in the blanks

Ans: 1 Conversation View, 2 Reminders

Exercise 4 – Match case

Ans: 1 A, 2 B, 3 C, 4 D

Exercise 5 – One word answer

Ans: 1 Focused Inbox, 2 Quick Steps

Chapter 7 - **Microsoft OneNote**

OneNote is an electronic notebook, It allows you to organize notes, files, articles, pictures, and more information in a single digital notebook. It is available approximately for all devices such as Mobile, Laptops, Desktops, and also for all the operating system (IOS, MAC, Windows, and Android).

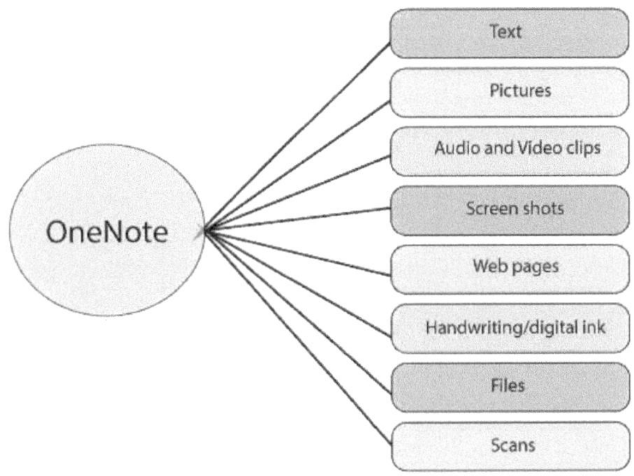

Features of OneNote

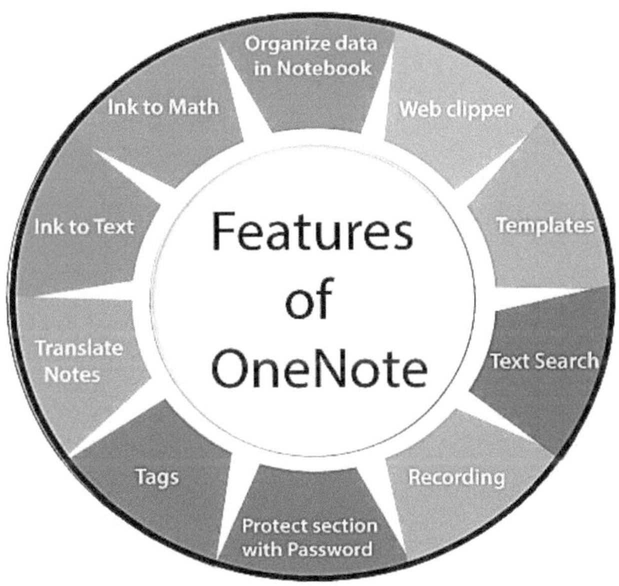

1. Organize data in Notebook
Organize data in Notebook is one of the best features of OneNote. It allows you to store data in the form of Notebook. A notebook is made up of one or more sections, and each section contains the individual pages or subpages. In Notebook, we store information in the form of **text, image, audio, and video**.
2. Web clipper
OneNote web clipper allows you to extract information from a web page to OneNote. You can access clipped webpages on any computer, tablets, or phones.
3. Templates
The template is a pre-designed layout of OneNote. OneNote 2016 contains several in-built templates, including **decorative page backgrounds, uniform appearance,** or a **consistent layout**.

4. Text Search
OneNote has an ability to search the particular text. You can simply press the **Ctrl+E** key to enable the search panel, and type what you want to search.
5. Recording
A recording is one of the important features of OneNote. In OneNote, you can record audio or video by clicking on **Insert -> Record Audio or video**. It helps you to record any interview, important notes on your own voice, etc.
6. Protect Sections with Password
OneNote provides password security for each section in a notebook. To make your section password protected, right-click on the section and select **Password-Protect this section**.
7. Tags
Tags in OneNote helps you to **organize content, remember tasks, or find content** based on the tags attached to it.
8. Translate Notes
OneNote allows you to translate the notes from one language to your preferred language, which is easily understandable by you.
9. Ink to Text
Ink to text is used to convert the handwritten notes into typed text. It helps you for writing the formal document, resume, and reports.
10. Ink to Math
Ink to Math is used to covert the equation to formatted equations.

Creating a Notebook
Creating a Notebook is a very simple task. When you open OneNote for the first time, a default notebook is created for you. You can also use this default notebook and add your own pages to it, or create a new blank notebook.
To create a notebook, follow the steps given below:
Step1: Open OneNote2016. Click on **File->New->provide the notebook name**. Then click on create Notebook.

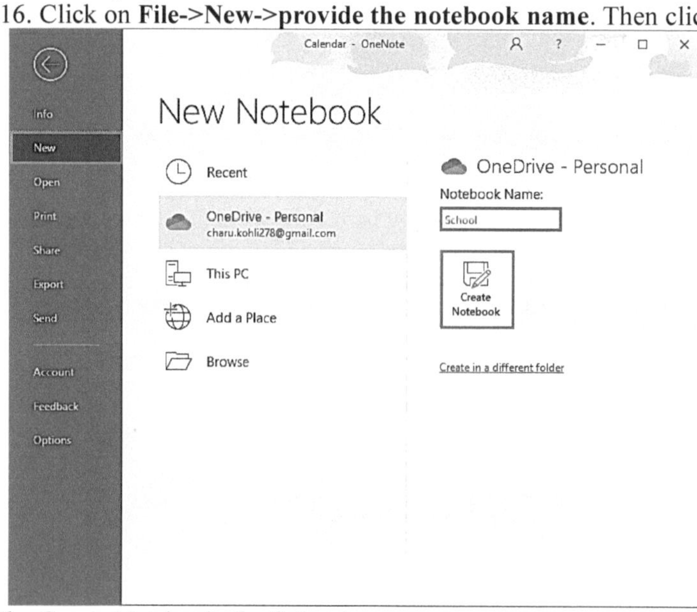

Step2: After clicking on the Create Notebook, the following screen appears.

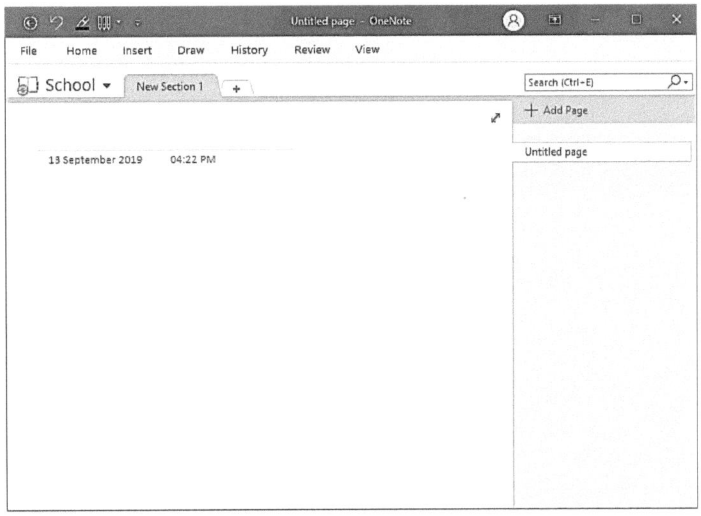

Rename the Section

To rename the Section, Right-click on the section then select Rename Section and provide a name that you want.

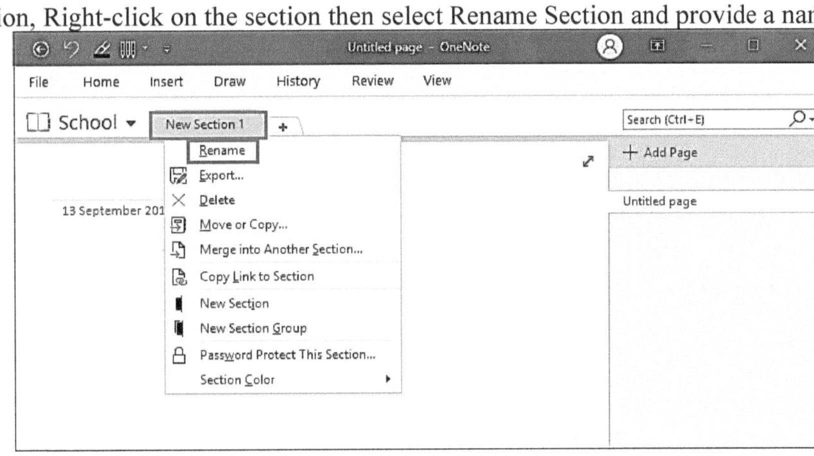

Adding the Section

To add the Section, Click on the + at the top of the screen. Then type a name of the section which you want to add.

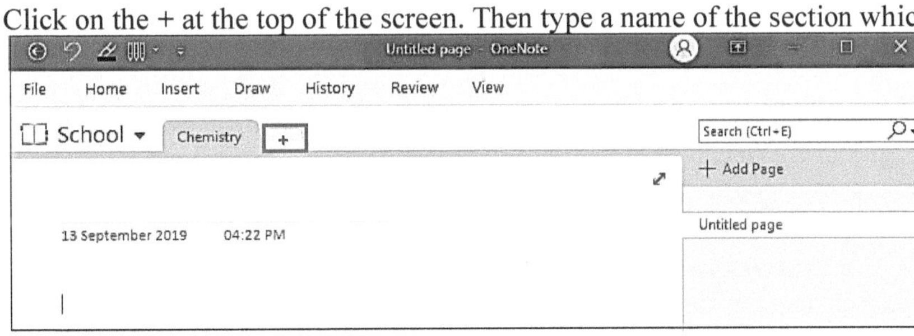

Similarly, you can add more sections according to your requirement.

Rename the page

To rename the Page, Right-click on the page then select Rename, provide the name that you want to add.

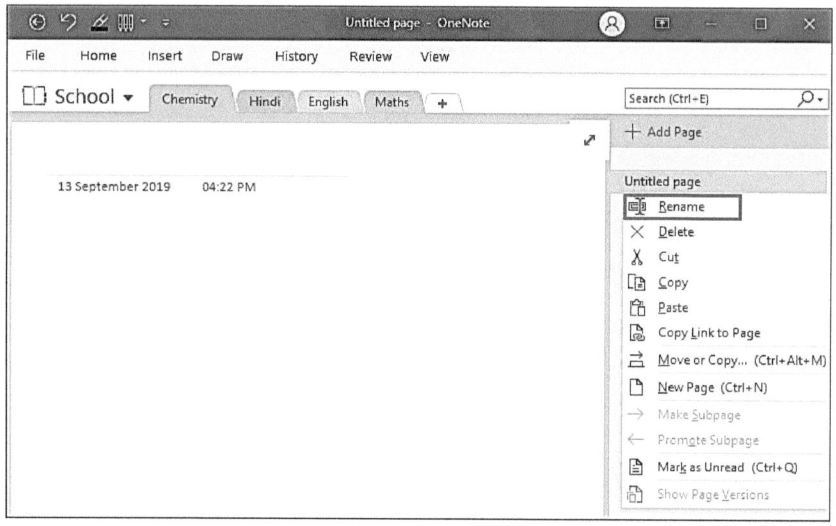

Adding the Page

To add the page, click on the **+Add page** at the Right panel of the screen. Then type a name of the page that you want to add.

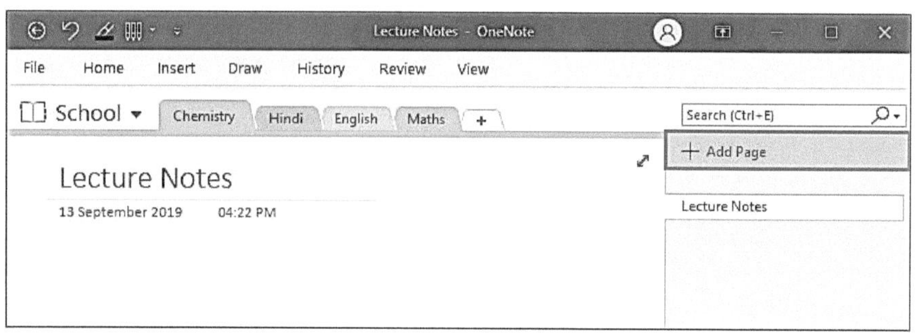

Similarly, you can add more pages according to your requirement.

7.1. Note-Taking and Organization

Microsoft OneNote is a versatile and powerful note-taking application that allows users to create and organize digital notebooks. Whether you're a student, professional, or anyone who needs to keep track of information, OneNote offers a robust platform for capturing, storing, and organizing notes, ideas, and content. In this description, we'll explore the key features and strategies for effective note-taking and organization in Microsoft OneNote.

Structure of OneNote Notebooks

OneNote is organized into notebooks, sections, and pages, mimicking the structure of a physical notebook. Understanding this hierarchy is crucial for efficient note-taking and organization:

Notebooks: These are like the binders that contain your notes. Each notebook can be dedicated to a specific subject, project, or category. For example, you might have separate notebooks for work, personal life, and education.

Sections: Within a notebook, you have sections, which are equivalent to the dividers in a physical binder. Sections help you further categorize your notes. For instance, in a "Work" notebook, you could have sections for different projects or departments.

Pages: Pages are where you write your notes. They are like the individual sheets of paper in your physical binder. You can create as many pages as you need in each section.

Note-Taking Tools

OneNote provides a variety of tools for taking and formatting notes. Here are some key features:

Text and Typing: You can type and format text just like in a word processor. Use different fonts, sizes, and styles to highlight important information.
Ink and Drawing: For touch-enabled devices or tablets, you can draw, sketch, or write with a stylus or your finger. OneNote recognizes handwritten text, making it searchable.
Inserting Content: OneNote allows you to insert various types of content, including images, audio, video, files, links, and tables. You can drag and drop files directly into your notes.
Tagging: Tags are a powerful way to categorize and organize your notes. You can add tags like "To-Do," "Important," or create custom tags. This makes it easy to find and filter notes later.
Audio and Video Recording: OneNote enables you to record audio or video directly into your notes. This is valuable for capturing lectures, meetings, or your own voice notes.

Effective Note-Taking Strategies

To make the most of OneNote, consider the following note-taking strategies:

Organize Your Notebooks: Create notebooks for different aspects of your life or work. For instance, have separate notebooks for work projects, personal goals, and hobbies.
Structure Your Sections: Within each notebook, use sections to categorize your notes. Name sections according to specific projects, subjects, or timeframes.
Use Templates: OneNote offers templates for different types of notes, such as meeting notes, to-do lists, or project planning. Templates can save you time and maintain consistency.
Searchable Notes: OneNote's powerful search feature lets you find notes quickly. It even recognizes handwritten text, making your notes fully searchable.
Tagging and Categories: Apply tags to your notes for easy categorization. Create a tagging system that suits your needs, such as tagging notes as "Action Items," "Ideas," or "Reference."
Cross-Linking: OneNote allows you to link pages or sections within your notebook. This is handy for creating relationships between related notes.
Sync and Accessibility: OneNote synchronizes your notes across devices, making them accessible from anywhere. You can work on your computer, tablet, or smartphone with ease.
Sharing and Collaboration: Share your notebooks or specific sections with others for collaborative work. OneNote supports real-time collaboration on shared notebooks.

In conclusion, Microsoft OneNote is a dynamic tool for note-taking and organization. By structuring your notebooks, using its versatile note-taking tools, and applying effective strategies, you can harness the full potential of OneNote to stay organized, capture ideas, and collaborate with others efficiently. Whether you're a student, professional, or creative thinker, OneNote empowers you to keep your digital notes and ideas in one place, accessible at your fingertips.

7.2. Collaborative Notebooks

Microsoft OneNote is not just a powerful tool for individual note-taking and organization; it also excels at fostering collaboration. One of its standout features is the ability to create collaborative notebooks, enabling multiple users to work together on shared projects, assignments, or any collective endeavor. In this description, we will explore the concept of collaborative notebooks in Microsoft OneNote and how they can enhance teamwork and productivity.

Shared Notebooks: A Collaborative Hub

OneNote's collaborative functionality revolves around shared notebooks. Unlike personal notebooks, which are accessible only to the owner, shared notebooks can be accessed and edited by multiple users. Here's how they work:

Creating a Shared Notebook

To initiate collaboration in OneNote, you start by creating a shared notebook. This notebook is stored in a location that allows authorized users to access it, such as on OneDrive, a shared network drive, or a SharePoint site. Once the notebook is created, you invite others to join and collaborate.

Access Control

OneNote provides robust access control, allowing you to specify who can view or edit the notebook. You can grant permissions to specific individuals or groups, ensuring that only the intended users have access.

Real-Time Collaboration

One of the remarkable aspects of collaborative notebooks is real-time collaboration. Multiple users can work in the same notebook simultaneously. Changes made by one user are instantly visible to others, making it ideal for projects that require immediate feedback and input.

Synchronization

Collaborative notebooks synchronize automatically. This means that changes made by one user are synchronized to the cloud or shared location, making them accessible to others instantly. Users can work on the notebook from various devices, ensuring everyone is always on the same page.

Use Cases for Collaborative Notebooks

Collaborative notebooks in OneNote find applications in various scenarios, including:

Team Projects

In a professional setting, collaborative notebooks are ideal for team projects. Multiple team members can collectively contribute to brainstorming sessions, document research findings, or develop project plans. With real-time collaboration, everyone stays updated on project progress.

Education

In the realm of education, collaborative notebooks are a game-changer. They allow students to work together on group assignments, take shared lecture notes, and compile research for group presentations. Educators can also provide feedback and monitor student contributions.

Group Brainstorming

For creative endeavors, collaborative notebooks are a creative space for group brainstorming. Teams can jot down ideas, sketches, or design concepts collectively. As changes are made, participants see the evolution of ideas in real time.

Meeting Notes

Collaborative notebooks are excellent for capturing meeting notes. Multiple attendees can add their insights, action items, and comments during the meeting. This eliminates the need for extensive post-meeting documentation and ensures that all stakeholders have the same information.

Research and Reference

In research and knowledge management, shared notebooks are a valuable resource. Researchers can pool resources, share findings, and curate references. This is especially useful for research groups working on collaborative projects.

Benefits of Collaborative Notebooks

Collaborative notebooks in OneNote offer a range of benefits:

- **Efficient Collaboration:** Real-time collaboration speeds up the decision-making process, making teams more agile and responsive.
- **Accessible from Anywhere:** Users can access collaborative notebooks from various devices, ensuring they can contribute even when on the go.
- **Version History:** OneNote keeps track of changes and offers version history, allowing users to revert to previous versions if needed.
- **Reduces Email Overload:** Instead of endless email threads, collaborative notebooks keep discussions, comments, and notes in a centralized location, reducing inbox clutter.
- **Enhanced Organization:** OneNote's organization features, such as sections, tags, and search capabilities, help teams manage content efficiently.

In conclusion, collaborative notebooks in Microsoft OneNote are a boon for teamwork and productivity. They provide a platform for multiple users to collaborate seamlessly on projects, share knowledge, and brainstorm ideas. With access control, real-time collaboration, and synchronization, OneNote's collaborative notebooks foster efficiency and facilitate teamwork in a wide range of settings, from business and education to creative endeavors and research projects.

7.3. Integrating OneNote with Other Office Apps

Microsoft OneNote, a versatile digital note-taking tool, seamlessly integrates with other Microsoft Office applications, enhancing productivity, organization, and collaboration. This integration ensures that you can harness the full power of the Office suite, such as Word, Excel, PowerPoint, and Outlook, to complement your note-taking and organizational efforts. In this description, we will explore the advantages and features of integrating OneNote with other Office apps.

Streamlined Note-Taking with Word

OneNote's integration with Microsoft Word simplifies the process of turning your notes into polished documents. Here's how it works:

Exporting Notes to Word

After you've taken notes in OneNote, you can export them directly to Word. This is particularly useful when you need to create reports, essays, or other structured documents.

Formatting Control

When you export notes to Word, you have control over the formatting. OneNote allows you to choose between various pre-defined styles and templates. You can also customize the formatting to match your preferences.

Collaboration with Word

Word is a standard tool for document collaboration. By exporting your OneNote notes to Word, you can leverage Word's collaboration features, such as track changes and comments, to work with others on your documents.

Data Analysis and Calculation with Excel

Integrating OneNote with Excel empowers you to work with data and perform calculations more efficiently:

Embedding Excel Spreadsheets

OneNote enables you to embed live Excel spreadsheets within your notes. This means you can input, edit, and update data directly in your notes. This feature is valuable for financial calculations, data analysis, and tracking expenses.

Linking to Excel

You can link to existing Excel files, ensuring that your OneNote notes are always connected to the most up-to-date data. This is especially beneficial when you need to reference data regularly.

Dynamic Presentations with PowerPoint

When it comes to creating and delivering presentations, OneNote and PowerPoint offer a seamless connection:

Creating Presentation Outlines

In OneNote, you can create presentation outlines with structured content and speaker notes. Once your outline is ready, you can export it to PowerPoint, where it will be transformed into a presentation with slides and accompanying notes.

Presenter Tools

OneNote provides tools for presenters, including a virtual laser pointer and a "Next Slide" view. These tools help you stay organized and focused during presentations.

Email Management with Outlook

OneNote and Outlook work together to enhance your email management:

Clipping Emails to OneNote

You can clip important emails and email content to OneNote for future reference. This is a practical way to keep track of important information without cluttering your inbox.

Task Management

OneNote's integration with Outlook tasks allows you to create to-do lists in OneNote and sync them with Outlook. This ensures that your tasks are centralized and easy to manage.

Calendar Integration

You can link your Outlook calendar with OneNote to keep track of meetings, appointments, and important dates alongside your notes. This integration ensures that you have all the information you need in one place.

Seamless Collaboration

One of the key benefits of integrating OneNote with other Office apps is the ability to collaborate seamlessly with others. Multiple users can work together on Word documents, Excel spreadsheets, or PowerPoint presentations, while keeping all relevant notes, ideas, and comments in OneNote. This streamlines communication and ensures that everyone has access to the same information.

Accessibility Across Devices

OneNote's integration with the Office suite means you can access your notes and integrated content across different devices. Whether you're using a computer, tablet, or smartphone, your notes are synchronized and accessible, ensuring that you can work and collaborate from anywhere.

In conclusion, integrating OneNote with other Microsoft Office applications is a game-changer for productivity, organization, and collaboration. The seamless flow of content between OneNote, Word, Excel, PowerPoint, and Outlook empowers users to work more efficiently and cohesively. Whether you're a student, professional, or creative thinker, this integration ensures that your notes and content are fully accessible, shareable, and ready for collaboration across the Office suite.

Exercise

Exercise 1 – MCQ

Q 1. what does the term "CC" stand for?
a) Carbon Copy
b) Copy Cat
c) Confidential Copy
d) Counter Check

Q 2. where can you store emails that are in-progress and not yet ready to be sent?
a) Inbox
b) Outbox
c) Sent Items
d) Drafts

Exercise 2 – True/ False

Q 1. The "BCC" (Blind Carbon Copy) feature in Microsoft Outlook reveals the email addresses of recipients to others.

Q 2. The "Drafts" folder in Microsoft Outlook is used to store emails that are ready to be sent.

Exercise 3 – Fill in the blanks

Q 1. The purpose of the "_____" feature in Microsoft Outlook is to mark an email for follow-up, often with a reminder date.

Q 2. you can use the "CC (Carbon Copy)" field to send a copy of the email to one or more recipients for their "_______."

Exercise 4 – Match case

1.Chat
2.Channels
3.Meetings
4.Files

A. Provides a space for real-time one-on-one or group conversations.
B. Dedicated areas within teams for organized discussions and collaboration.
C. Allows for scheduled or ad-hoc virtual gatherings, complete with video and screen sharing.
D. A central location for storing and sharing documents, spreadsheets.

Exercise 5 – One word answer

Q 1. Where are unfinished emails typically stored before they are sent?

Q 2. What is the primary purpose of the "Flag" feature in Microsoft Outlook?

Exercise 6 – Small answer

Q 1. What does the "Out of Office" feature in Outlook do?

Q 2. Where are emails that are in-progress and not yet ready to be sent typically stored in Outlook?

Exercise 7 – Long answer

Q 1. Can you explain the purpose and function of the "Out of Office" feature in Microsoft Outlook? How does it work, and why is it useful?

Q 2. Describe the key differences between the "CC" (Carbon Copy) and "BCC" (Blind Carbon Copy) fields in Microsoft Outlook. When and why would you use each of them in an email?

Answers

Exercise 1 – MCQ

Ans: 1 a, 2 d

Exercise 2 – True/ False

Ans: 1 False, 2 False

Exercise 3 – Fill in the blanks

Ans: 1 Flag, 2 information

Exercise 4 – Match case

Ans: 1 A,2 B, 3 C, 4 D

Exercise 5 – One word answer

Ans: 1 Drafts, 2 Follow-up

Chapter 8 - **Microsoft Teams**

Microsoft Teams is a powerful collaboration and communication platform that has revolutionized the way organizations and teams interact, especially in the era of remote and hybrid work. As part of the Microsoft 365 suite, Teams provides a hub for teamwork, integrating chat, video conferencing, file sharing, and application collaboration in one place. This description provides an overview of Microsoft Teams, highlighting its key features and benefits.

A Unified Hub for Teamwork

Microsoft Teams serves as a unified hub where teams and organizations can coordinate their efforts. Key features include:

Chat and Messaging

Teams offers chat and messaging capabilities, allowing team members to have real-time conversations, one-on-one or in groups. It's an efficient way to discuss projects, share updates, or ask quick questions without cluttering email inboxes.

Video Conferencing and Meetings

Teams provides video conferencing and meeting functionality. Users can schedule, host, or join video meetings, making it a valuable tool for remote work and virtual collaboration. Features like screen sharing and meeting recording enhance the meeting experience.

File Sharing and Collaboration

Teams integrates seamlessly with Microsoft 365 apps, making it easy to share, edit, and collaborate on documents, spreadsheets, and presentations in real time. Users can co-author documents, reducing version control issues.

Integration with Apps

One of the standout features of Teams is its integration with various third-party and custom applications. You can add apps like Trello, Asana, or custom tools to enhance productivity and streamline work processes.

Channels and Organizational Structure

Teams use a channel-based organization, which helps categorize discussions and content by topic or project. This structure ensures that content is organized and accessible to relevant team members.

Customization and Personalization

Teams allows for customization and personalization. You can tailor your workspace to suit your team's needs by adding tabs, connectors, and bots. This flexibility ensures that Teams adapts to your unique workflow.

Benefits of Microsoft Teams

Microsoft Teams offers several benefits that have made it a go-to platform for businesses and organizations:

- **Efficient Communication:** Teams reduces the need for lengthy email threads, improving communication efficiency through instant messaging and chat.
- **Enhanced Collaboration:** With real-time document editing, file sharing, and integrated apps, Teams streamlines collaboration and teamwork.
- **Remote Work Support:** Teams is well suited for remote work, providing the necessary tools for video meetings, document collaboration, and virtual team engagement.
- **Centralized Workspace:** Teams consolidates various tools into a single platform, minimizing the need to switch between different apps and reducing context switching.
- **Security and Compliance:** Teams meets robust security and compliance standards, making it a secure platform for sensitive business communications.
- **Scalability:** Teams is scalable, suitable for both small teams and large organizations, making it a versatile solution.
- **Integration with Microsoft 365:** Teams seamlessly integrates with other Microsoft 365 apps, providing a cohesive experience for users familiar with the suite.

In conclusion, Microsoft Teams has emerged as a vital tool for organizations seeking to streamline communication, collaboration, and teamwork. Its unified platform, integration with Microsoft 365, and customization options make it a versatile solution for a wide range of industries and team sizes. As remote and hybrid work continue to be a prominent aspect of the modern work landscape, Teams has become a cornerstone in ensuring seamless and efficient communication and collaboration.

1. Sign in to MS Teams

On Windows, click **Start > Microsoft Teams.** On Mac, go to the **Applications folder** and click **Microsoft Teams**. On mobile, tap the **Teams icon**.

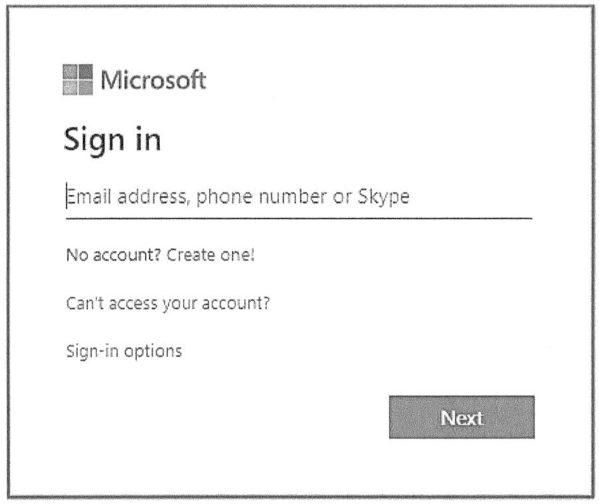

2. Pick a Team and Channel

A team is a collection of people, conversations, files, and tools—all in one place. A channel is a discussion in a team, dedicated to a department, project, or topic.

Go to **Teams** >>> And **choose a team** >>> **Pick a channel** to explore Posts, Files, and other tabs.

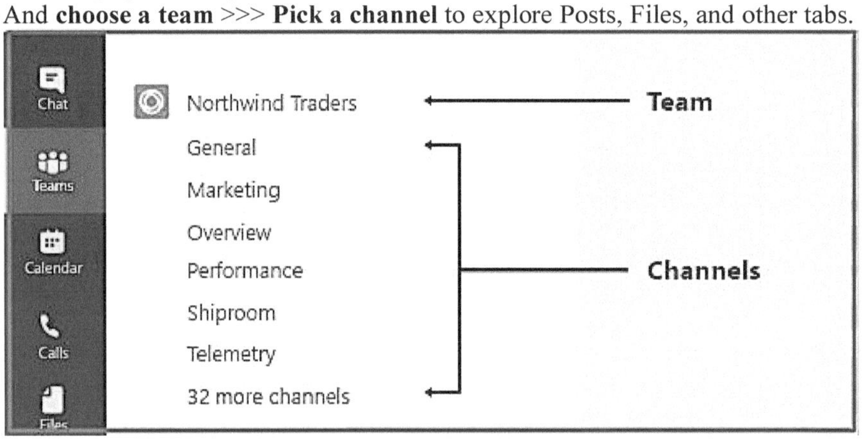

3. Set up your Teams mobile apps

Microsoft Teams is available as an iOS and Android app on mobile devices as well; you can download it from the App Store or Google Play Store.

Teams and Channels

4. Create a Team

First, click **Teams** on the left side of the app >>> Click **Join or create a team** at the bottom of your teams list >>> Then click **Create team** >>> Choose **Build a team from scratch** >>> Choose **Private** or **Public** >>> Enter details >>> Click **Create**.

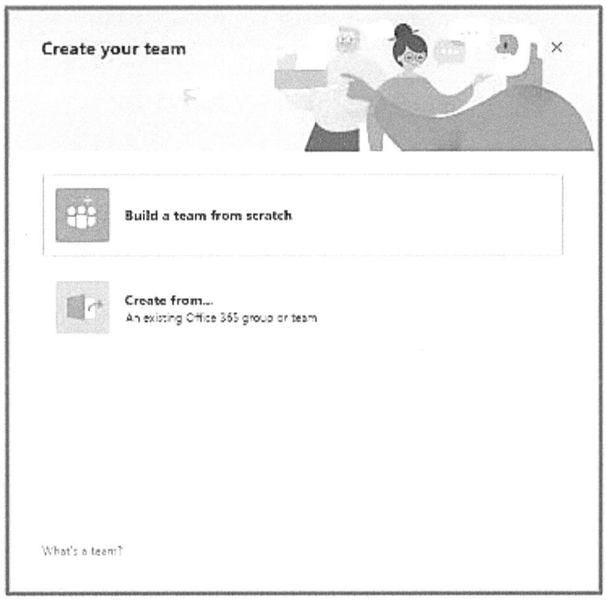

5. Create a team from an existing team

Click **Teams** on the left side of the app >>> Click Join or create a team >>> Then click **Create team** (first card, top left corner) >>> From here, select **Create from... >>>** then choose **Team** >>> You'll see a list of teams that you currently own >>> Choose the **team** you want to copy >>> Enter details >>> Click **Create.**

6. Join a Team

Go to **Teams** > **Join or create a team** at the bottom of the teams list >>> Use the **search box** to find a specific team and press Enter >>> Find the team you're looking for and select **Join team**.

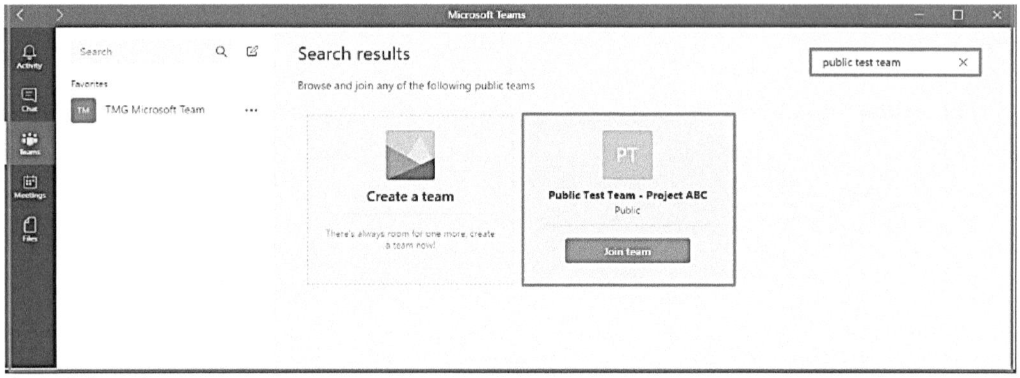

7. Use a code to join a team

Click **Teams** on the left side of the app >>> Then click **Join or create a team** at the bottom of your teams list >>> Go to **Join a team with a code** >>> **Paste the code** in the Enter code box >>> and click **Join**.

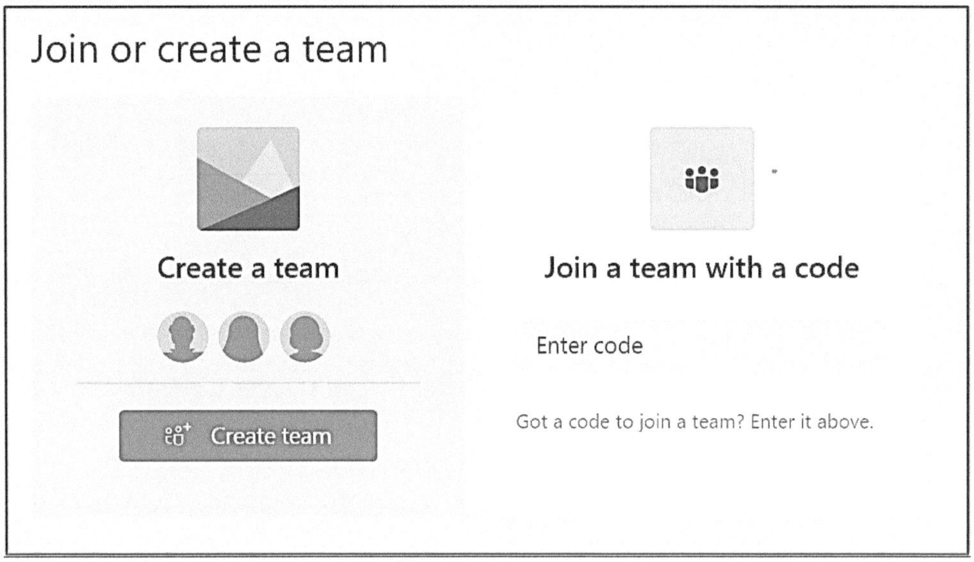

8. Add Team Picture to give your team personality

Select **More options** next to the team name >>> Select **Manage team** to find **Members**, **Channels**, **Settings**, and **Apps** for your team all in one place >>> Select **Settings** >>> **Team picture.**

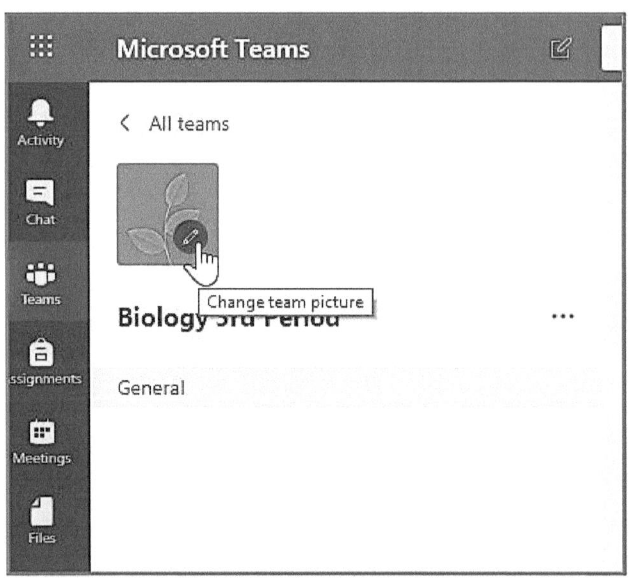

9. Add a member to a team

Go to the **team's name** in the teams list and click **More options** >>> **Add member**.

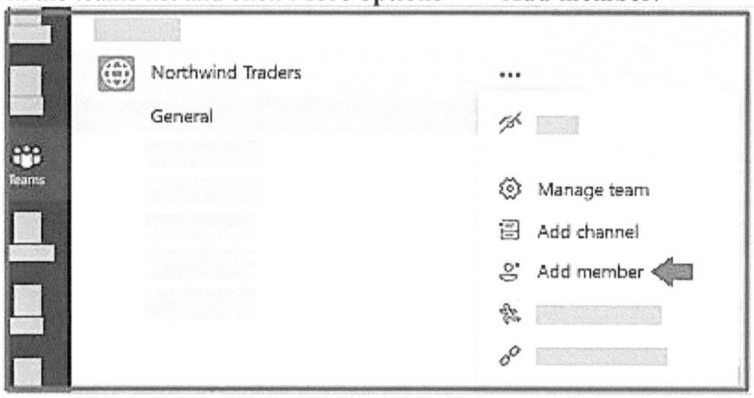

10. Manage your team settings and Permissions

Go to the team's name and click **More options** >>> **Manage team** >>> In the **Settings** tab, check or uncheck the options or permissions you want to use.

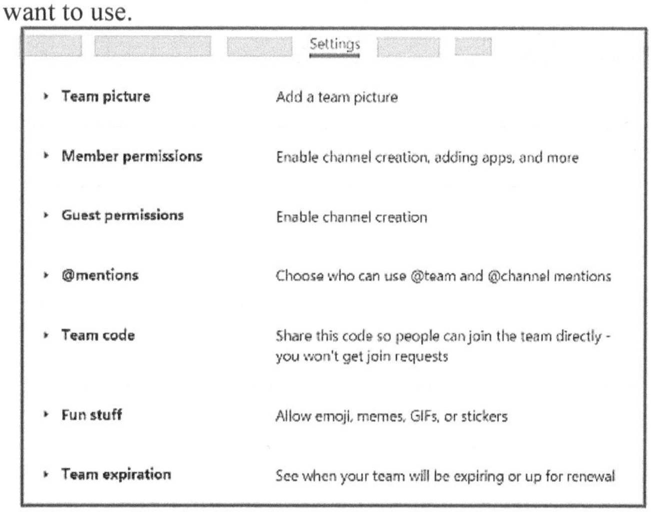

11. Check your Teams' Analytics

At the bottom of your teams list, next to **Join or create a team**, click **Manage teams** >>> On the **Analytics** tab, select a date range to show usage data for all teams.

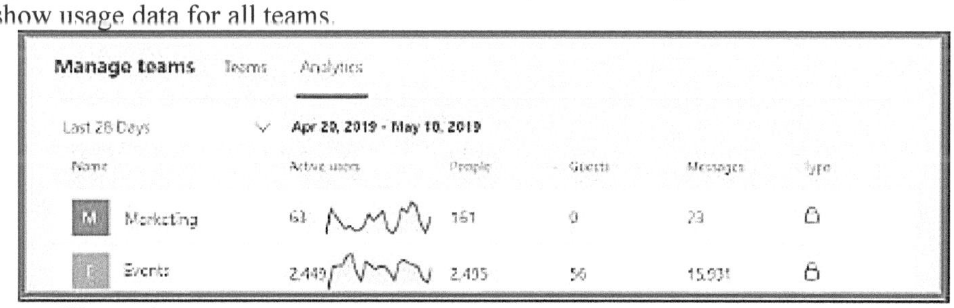

12. Hide a Team or Channel

Don't want a team or channel to show in your list? Head to a **team or channel name** >>> And select **More options** button >>> **Hide.**

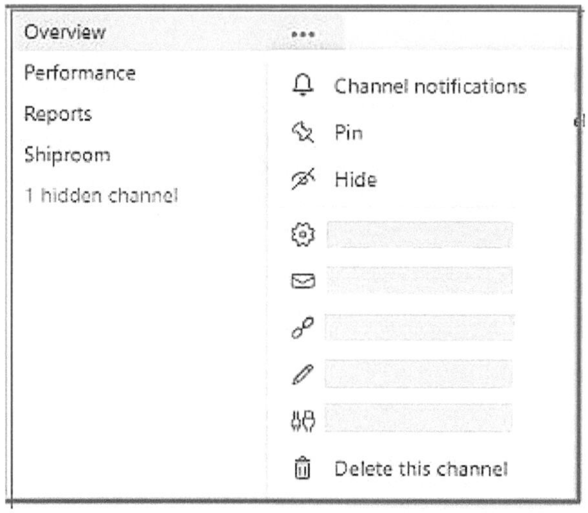

13. Create and Manage Tags in Teams

Select **Teams** on the left side of the app and find your team in the list >>> Then select **More options** >>> and choose **Manage tags** .

Here, you can create tags and assign them to people on your team.

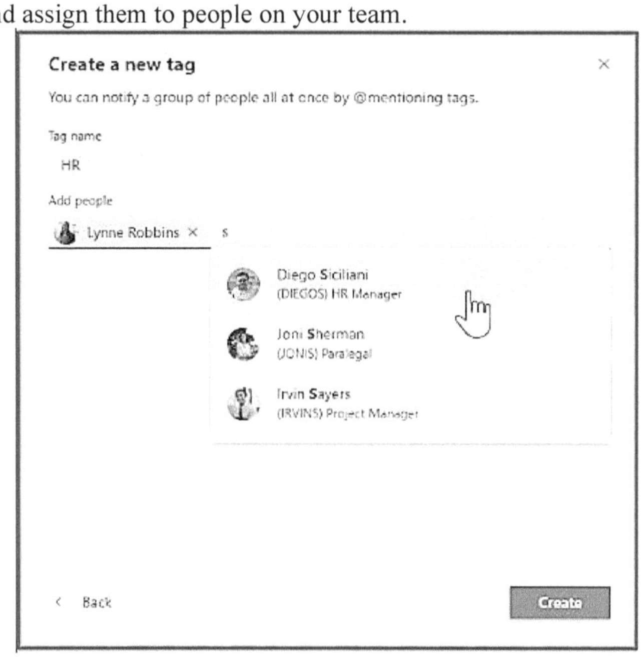

14. Arrange Your Team List

To reorder your teams, select **Teams** >>> Then click and drag the team name anywhere in your teams list.

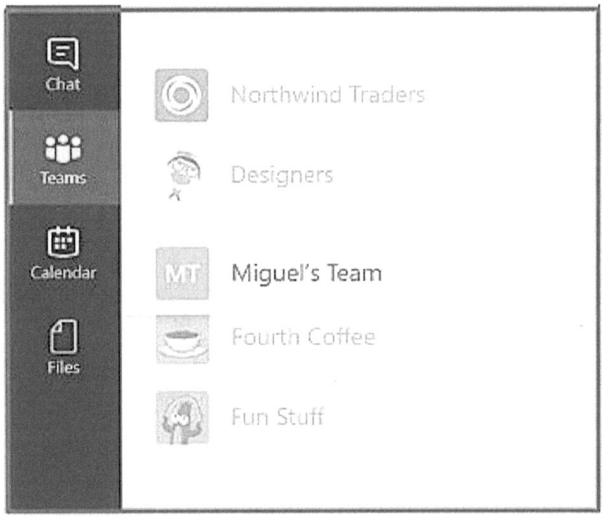

15. Add content and notes to a team

Just click **Files** at the top >>> Then click **Upload**. To create a new file, click **New**.

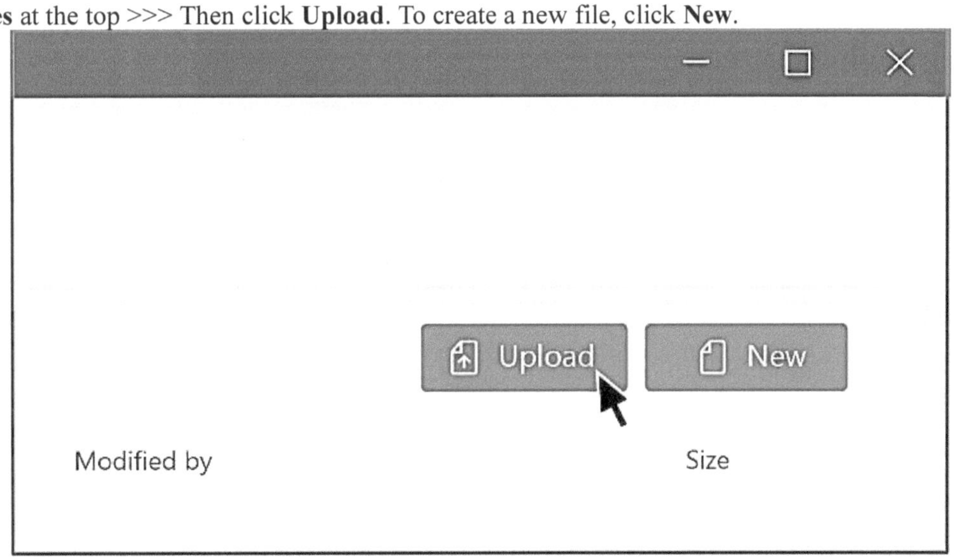

16. Add a guest to a team

Go to the **Team** >>> Select **more options icon** >>> **Add member** >>> Enter the guest's email address >>> **Edit guest information** and give a friendly name >>> Click **Add**. The guests will receive an email invitation.

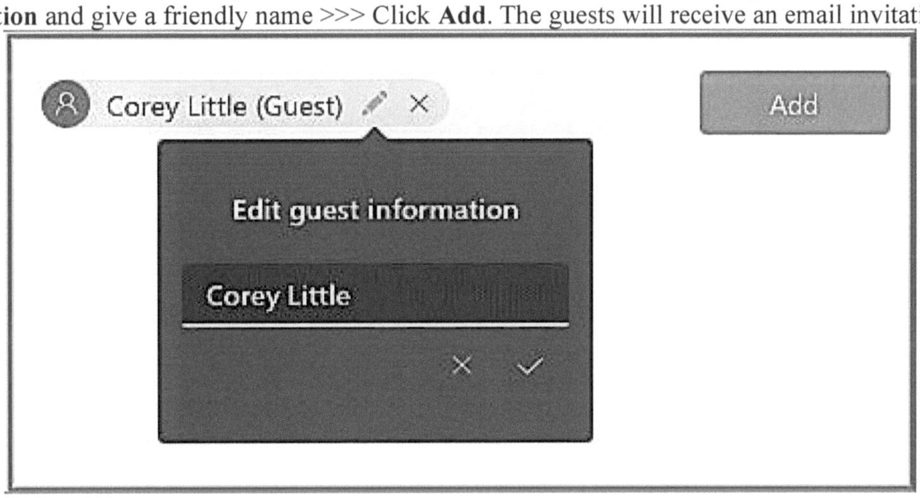

17. Leave a Team

You can leave a team at any time by going to the team name and clicking **More options** >>> **Leave the team**.

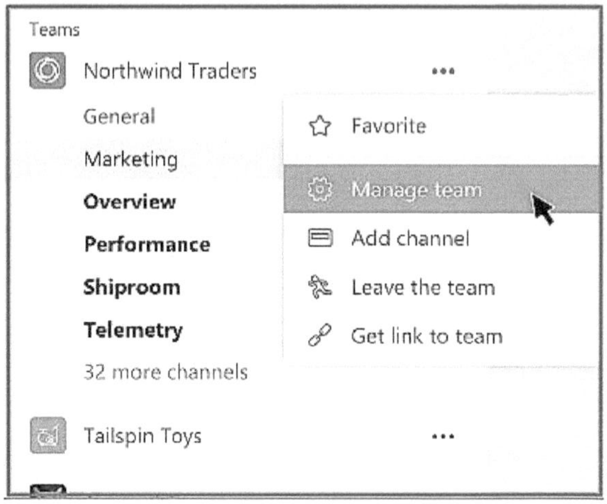

18. Create a Channel

Find the team's name and click **More options** >>> Add **channel**. You can also click the **Manage team**, and add a channel in the **Channels** tab.

19. Make a Channel Private

Go to the team you want to create the private channel for and choose **More options >>> Add channel** >>> Enter a **name and description** for your channel >>> Under **Privacy**, select the down arrow on the right, and then select **Private** – Accessible only to a specific group of people within the team >>> Select **Add**.

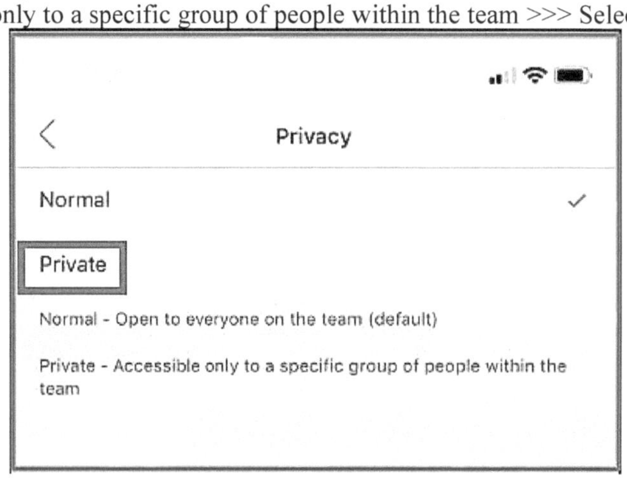

20. Send a message to a channel

Select the **channel** >>> Click **Reply** to respond to an existing thread or go to the compose box at the bottom of the Posts tab to start a new message >>> Next, **type your message** in the box >>> And select **Send.**

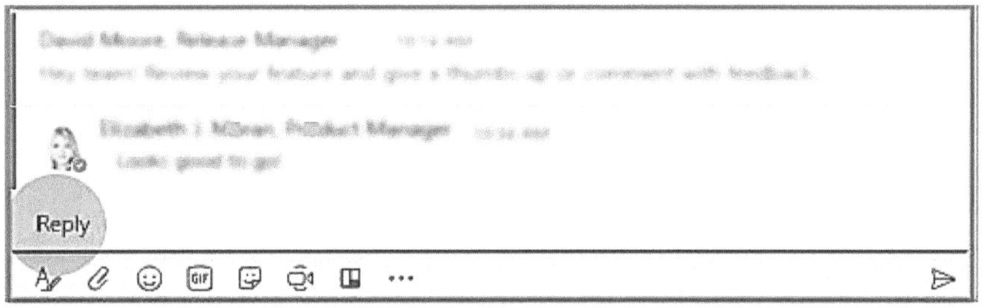

21. Create an announcement in a channel

Select **Format** under the message box >>> Click the arrow next to **New conversation** >>> **Announcement** >>> Type a headline, change its background color, or add an image >>> Type the topic of your announcement in the **Add a subhead** area >>> Then the body of your message >>> and click **Send**.

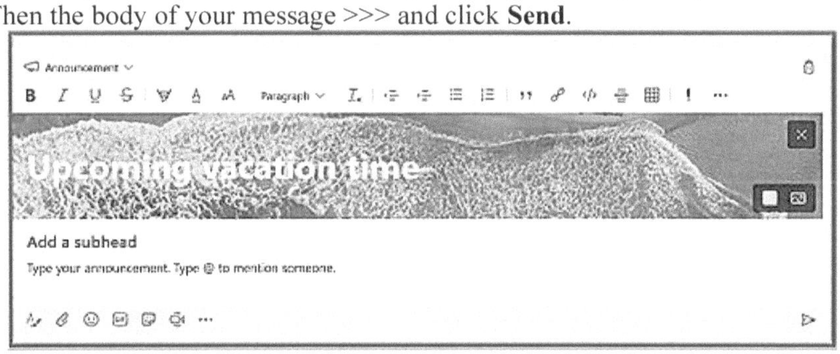

22. Forward Emails into a Channel

Go to the **channel name** >>> And click **More options three dotted icons** >>> **Get email address.**

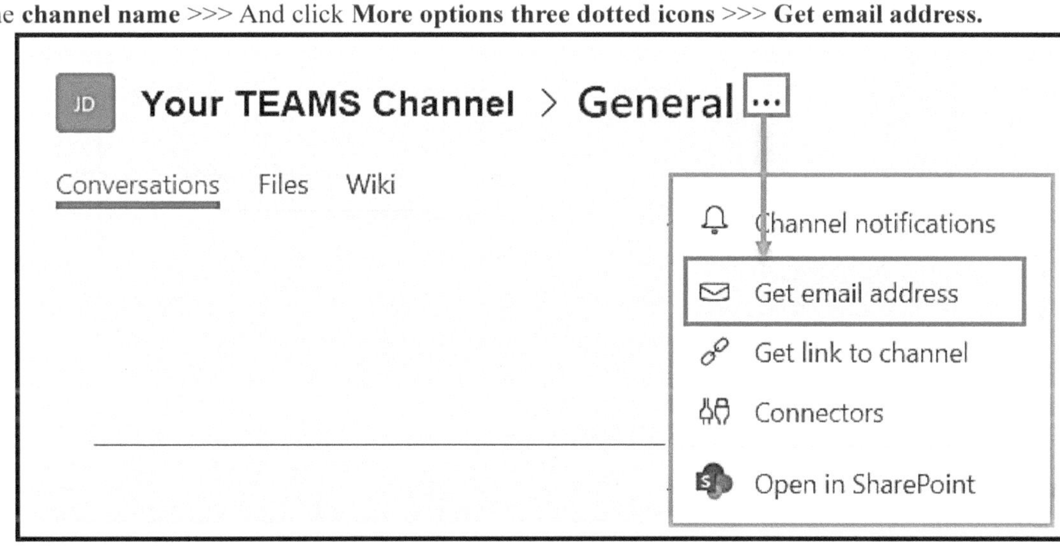

23. Cross-post a Channel Conversation

Select **Format** >>> Choose a **New Conversation** or **Announcement** >>> Select **Post in multiple channels** >>> Click Select **Channels** >>> Choose the Channels to post in >>> Select **Update** >>> Enter your messages >>> and click **Send**.

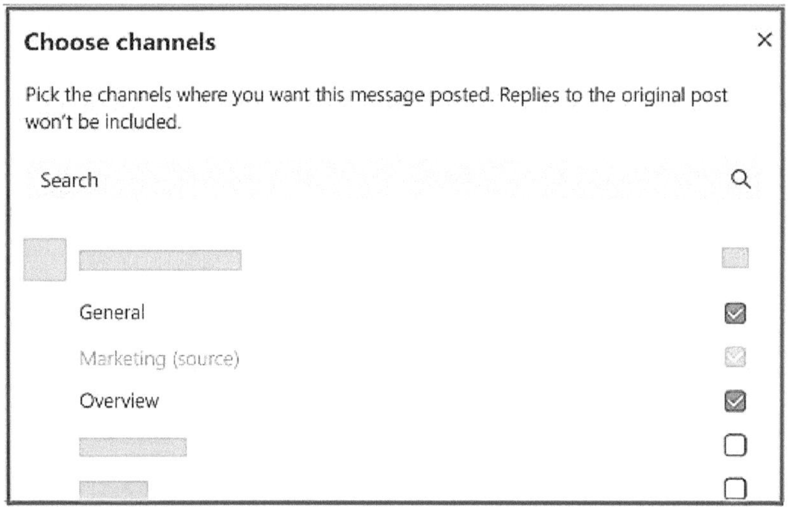

24. Customize Channel Notifications

Go to the channel name and select **More options icon** >> > Select **Channel notifications** >>> Choose what notifications you want to get and how. Here are different type of settings:

Banner and feeds.
All new posts.
Include all replies.
Channel mentions.

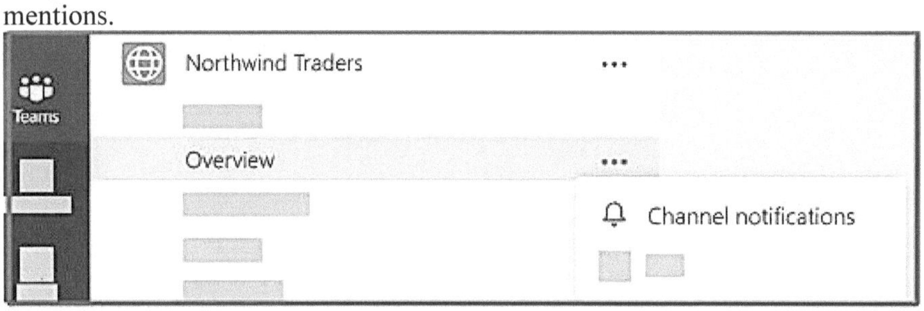

25. Set Guest Permissions In Channels

Select **Teams** >>> Go the team name >>> Click **More options icon** >>> Select **Manage team** >>> Choose **Settings** >>> Go to **Guest permissions** >>> Check or uncheck the permissions you want to use.

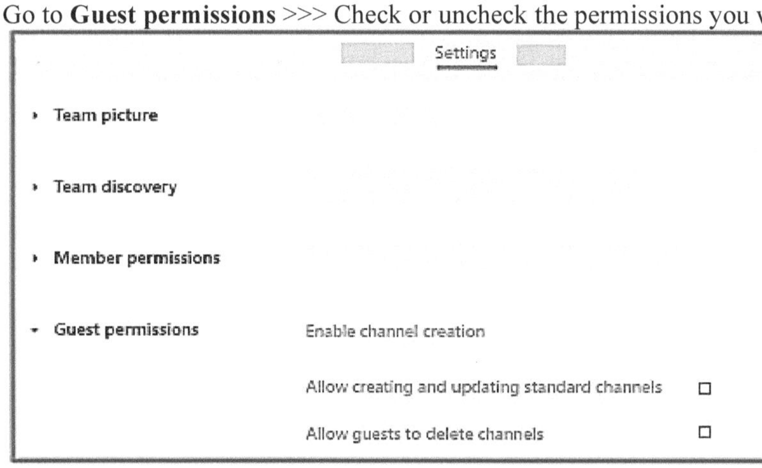

26. Pin a Channel

To pin a channel, go to a channel name and select **More options** >>> **Pin.**

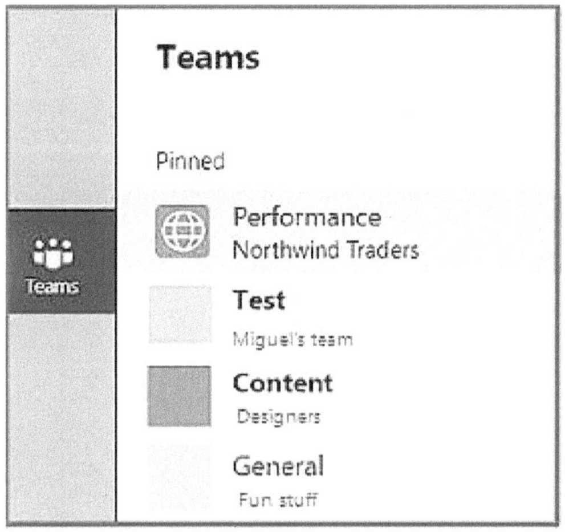

Notifications and Settings

27. Stop email notifications

Click on your **profile picture** in the top right >>> Then select **Settings >>> Notifications** >>> Here set the type of notifications you want for each type of activity on Teams.

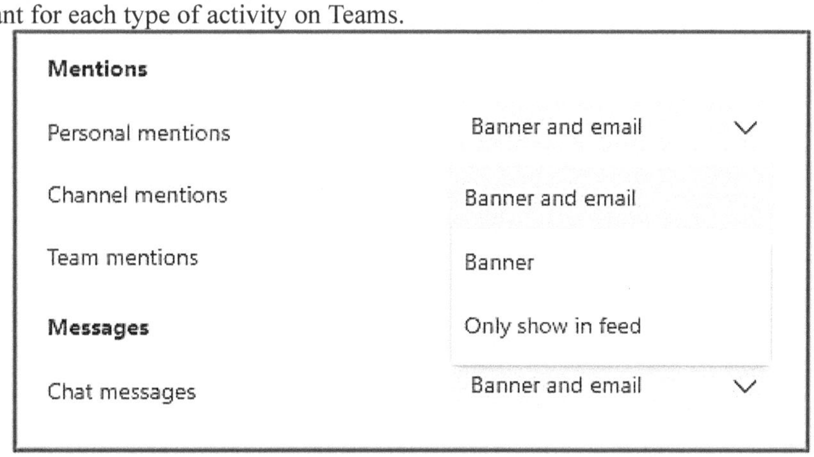

28. Turn off notifications for specific conversations

Go to the **top right corner of the message** >>> And select **More options button** >>> **Turn off notifications.**

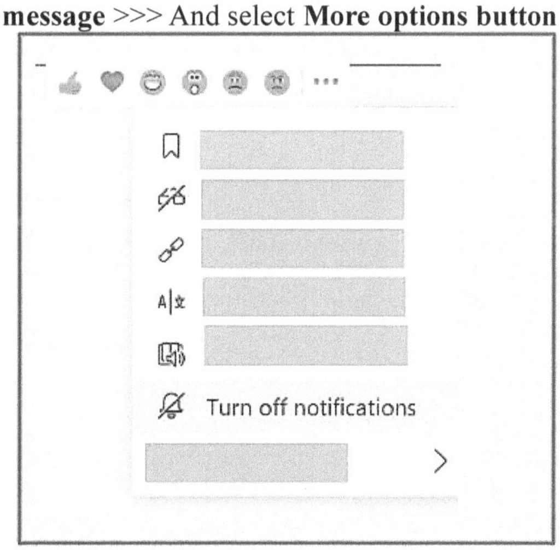

29. Change your profile picture

Click your current picture at the top right of the screen >>> And select **Change picture**.

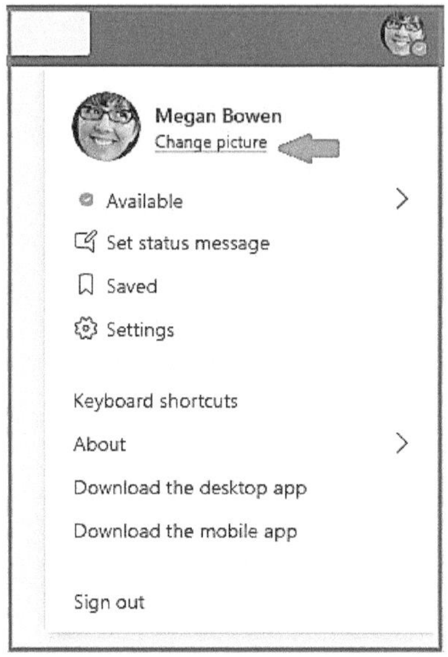

30. Change Themes

Click your profile picture at the top of the app, then select **Settings** >>> **General**. In the **Theme section** >>> click **High contrast** (You can also select the Dark or Default theme.)

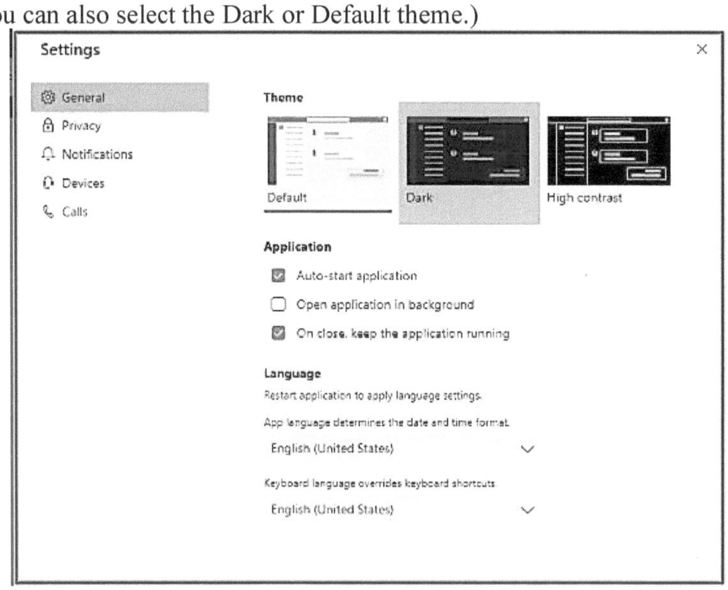

31. Change your status

To change your status, tap **Menu**. Then, tap your status to view your options.
Here are the options, you'll see: Available, Busy, Do Not Disturb, Be Right Back, and Appear Away.

32. Set your status message

Go to your profile pic at the top of Teams >>> and select **Set status message >>>** Type the message that you want to show other people in the box >>> select **Show when people message me** >>> Choose when you want the message to stop displaying >>> Select **Done**.

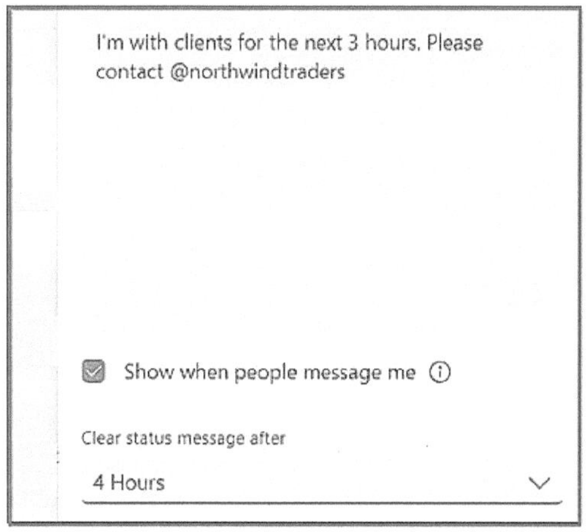

Chat and Files

33. Start a Conversation

Start one-on-one and group chats: Select New chat at the top of chat list >>> Enter the **person's or group's name** >>> **Compose your message** in the box >>> And Click **Send**.

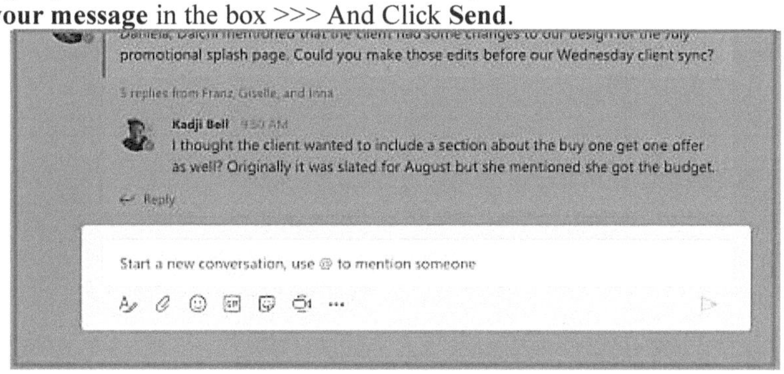

Want to send a message to the whole team.? Select **Teams >>>** Pick a **team and channel** >>> **Write your message** >>> and click **Send**.

34. Message Formatting

There are lots of formatting options for messages. Select **Format** beneath the box where compose your message >>> **Select the text** you want to format >>> Click **Send** once you're done.

35. Add Teammates to the Conversation

Click **Add people** (or **View and add participants** in group chat) in the top right corner of Teams >>> **Enter the names of the people** you'd like to chat with >> Select how much of the **chat history to include** >>> And click **Add**.

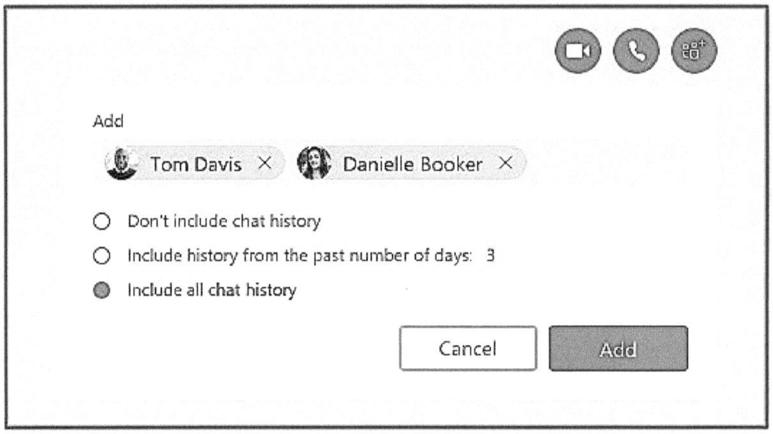

36. Mute a Chat

Select **Chat** to open the chat list. Find the name of the chat you want to mute. Then, select **More options** >>> **Mute**.

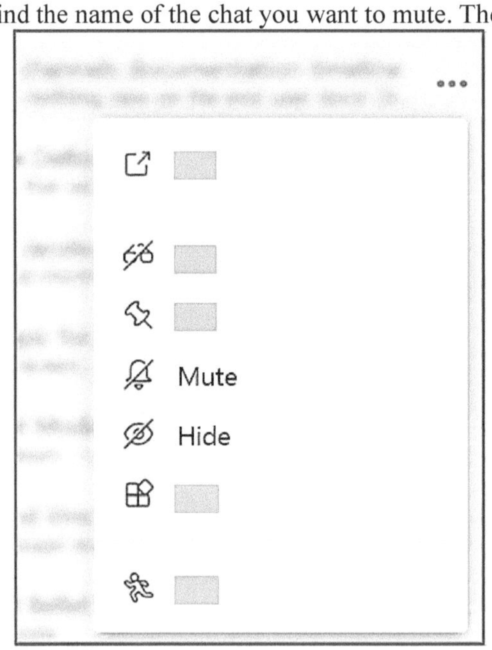

37. Pin a Chat

Select **Chat** to open the chat list. Find the name of the conversation you want to pin. Then, select **More options** >>> **Pin**.

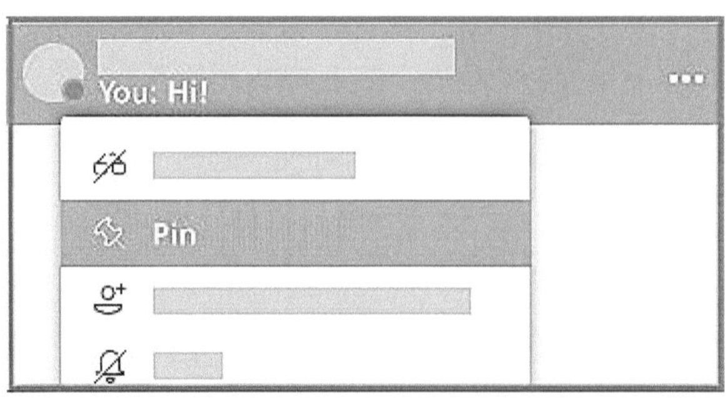

38. Pop-out a chat

Select **Chat** button on the left side of Teams to open the chat list >>> Find the name of the chat you want >>> Then, select **More options button** >>> **Pop-out chat** >>> Or, just double-click the chat name and you'll see a new pop-out chat window.

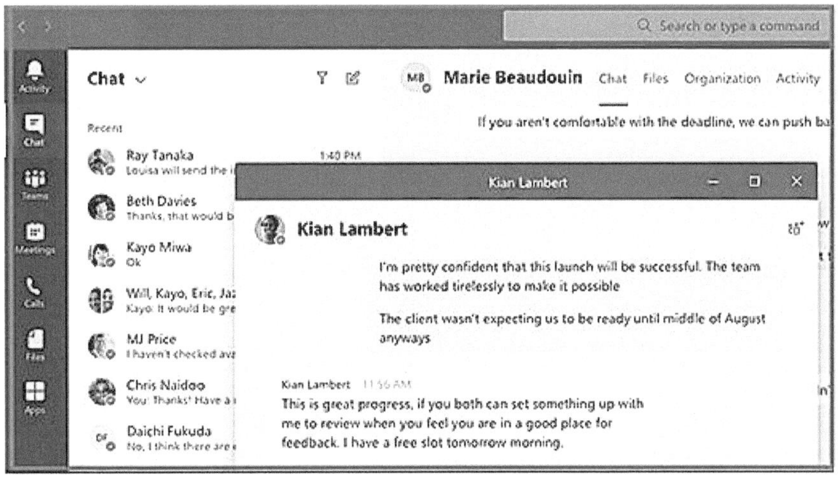

39. Reply to a Post

Channel posts are organized by date and then threaded. Find the thread you want to reply to >>> Click **Reply** >>> Add your thoughts and click **Send.**

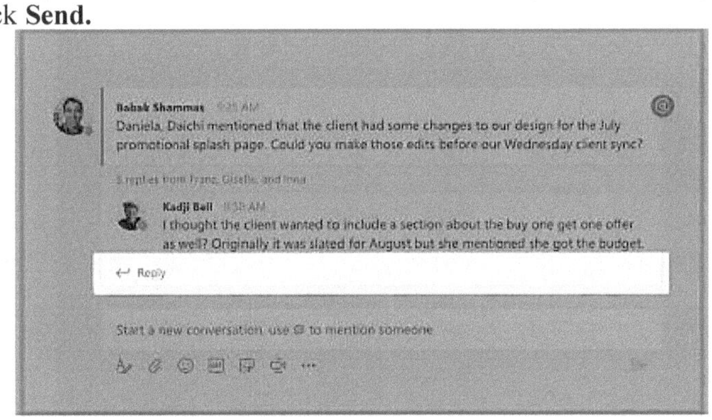

40. @mention Someone

To get someone's attention, type **@,** then their name (or pick them from the list that appears). Type **@team** to message everyone in a team or **@channel** to notify everyone who favorited that channel.

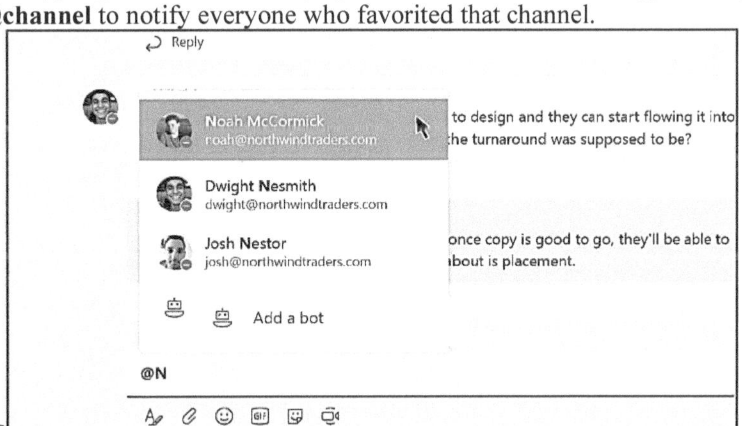

41. Send an emoji, GIF, or Sticker

Emoji, animated GIFs, and stickers add a fun element into your conversations!

To insert an emoji in a message, select **Emoji** beneath the message box >>> **Select the emoji** you want from the emoji gallery >>> Click **Send**.

To send a GIF: Just select **GIF** beneath the message box >>> **Use the search bar** to look for something specific (like "cats dancing") or browse the collection of popular GIFs.

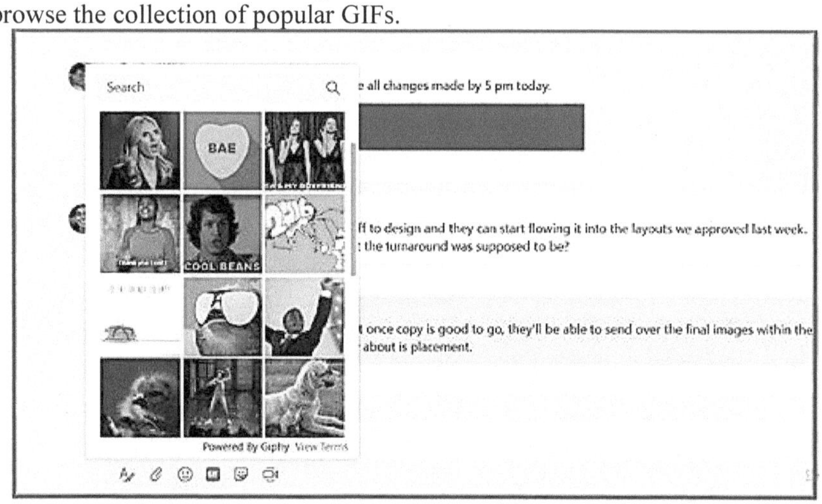

To send a meme or sticker: Click **Sticker** under the box where you type your message >>> Then **pick a meme or sticker** from one of the categories.

42. Translate Conversation

To translate a message to your preferred language, Tap the **ellipsis (three-dot) button** next to the text in the conversation >>> And select **Translate**.

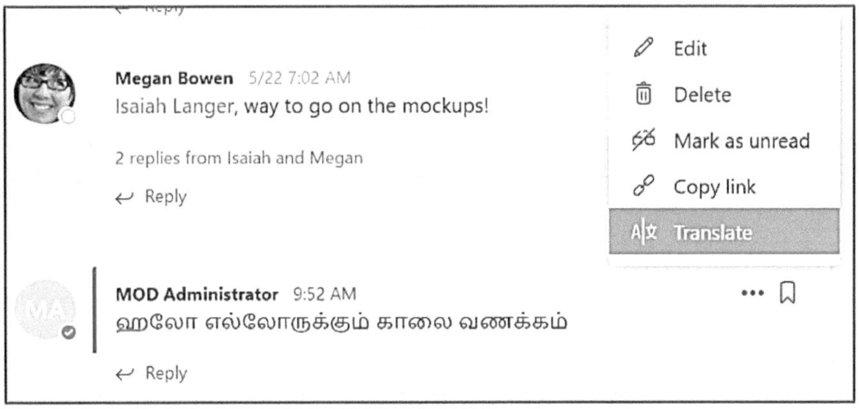

8.1 Collaboration and Communication

Microsoft Teams is a powerful platform that combines chat, video conferencing, document collaboration, and integration with various Microsoft 365 apps, all within a single environment. This makes it an ideal hub for collaboration and communication, especially for remote and hybrid teams. In this description, we will explore how Microsoft Teams enhances collaboration and communication, with a focus on its key features and benefits.

Real-Time Chat and Messaging

Microsoft Teams offers real-time chat and messaging capabilities that facilitate quick and efficient communication. Key features include:

Direct Messaging

Users can have one-on-one conversations or create group chats. This is perfect for quick questions, discussions, or sharing updates without the need for lengthy email threads.

Threaded Conversations

Conversations in Teams are threaded, making it easy to follow discussions and providing context to messages. Users can reply to specific messages, keeping conversations organized.

Rich Text Formatting

Teams supports rich text formatting, allowing users to emphasize messages, insert links, or attach files directly in the chat. This enhances the quality of communication.

Video Conferencing and Meetings

Microsoft Teams is equipped with a robust video conferencing and meeting platform that simplifies virtual collaboration. Features include:

Schedule and Host Meetings

Users can schedule and host video meetings with team members, clients, or external partners. This is especially valuable for remote work and maintaining virtual connections.

Screen Sharing

Teams offers screen sharing capabilities, enabling participants to share their screens, which is useful for presentations, collaboration on documents, and troubleshooting.

Meeting Recording

Meetings in Teams can be recorded for reference or for those who couldn't attend. This ensures that important discussions are not lost.

Document Collaboration

One of the standout features of Microsoft Teams is its integration with Microsoft 365 apps, which facilitates document collaboration:

Real-Time Document Editing

Users can work on documents, spreadsheets, and presentations in real time. Multiple team members can co-author files, eliminating version control issues.

File Storage and Sharing

Teams integrates with SharePoint and OneDrive for file storage and sharing. Documents and files can be easily accessed and collaborated on by authorized users.

Integration with Apps

Microsoft Teams supports integration with a wide range of third-party and custom applications, extending its functionality:

Tabs

Users can add tabs to their Teams channels, bringing in applications like project management tools, Trello boards, and custom apps, ensuring all the necessary tools are within reach.

Connectors

Teams allows the integration of connectors to receive updates and notifications from external services, such as news alerts, social media feeds, or task reminders.

Channels and Organizational Structure

Teams use a channel-based organizational structure. Channels are dedicated spaces for discussions and collaboration, which helps keep content organized and accessible to relevant team members.

Benefits of Microsoft Teams

Microsoft Teams offers numerous benefits, making it an essential tool for modern organizations:

- **Streamlined Communication:** Teams reduces the need for scattered email communication, enhancing collaboration and ensuring that important messages are not lost.
- **Improved Collaboration:** The integration with Microsoft 365 apps simplifies document collaboration, making it easy for team members to work together in real time.
- **Enhanced Productivity:** Teams streamlines workflows, reducing the time wasted on context switching between various apps and tools.
- **Remote and Hybrid Work Support:** Teams is tailor-made for remote and hybrid work, providing all the necessary tools for virtual collaboration.
- **Security and Compliance:** Teams meets robust security and compliance standards, making it a secure platform for sensitive business communication.
- **Scalability:** Teams is scalable and can accommodate teams of varying sizes, from small groups to large enterprises.

In conclusion, Microsoft Teams is a game-changing platform for collaboration and communication. Its unified environment, integration with Microsoft 365 apps, and support for third-party applications make it a versatile solution for a wide range of industries and team sizes. As remote and hybrid work continue to be a significant aspect of the modern work landscape, Teams has become an indispensable tool for seamless and efficient communication and collaboration.

8.2 Meetings and Video Conferencing

In the age of remote and hybrid work, effective meetings and video conferencing have become integral to keeping teams connected and productive. Microsoft Teams, a leading collaboration platform, offers a robust suite of features for conducting meetings and video conferences. In this description, we'll explore how Teams simplifies these essential activities and enhances the way teams communicate and collaborate.

Meeting Scheduling and Management

Microsoft Teams streamlines the entire meeting lifecycle, from scheduling to post-meeting follow-up:

Meeting Scheduling

Users can schedule meetings directly within Teams, with options to set date and time, recurring meetings, and invite participants. Integration with Outlook ensures that meetings appear in calendars seamlessly.

Meeting Invitations

Teams generates meeting invitations that include details like the meeting link, agenda, and participant list. Users can send invitations via Teams or email.

Real-Time Meeting Chat

Before, during, and after meetings, participants can use the meeting chat for discussions, sharing links, and notes. This chat persists after the meeting, providing a record of the conversation.

Video Conferencing

Video conferencing is a core feature of Microsoft Teams, offering several advantages:

High-Quality Video and Audio

Teams provides high-quality video and audio, ensuring that participants can see and hear each other clearly. This is essential for effective communication.

Screen Sharing

Users can share their screens during meetings, making it easy to present documents, slideshows, or demonstrate software. Screen sharing is valuable for presentations and collaborative work.

Meeting Recording

Meetings can be recorded, and the recordings are stored in Teams or OneDrive. This is useful for participants who couldn't attend the meeting or for reference purposes.

Live Captions and Transcription

Teams offers live captions during meetings, enhancing accessibility. Additionally, automatic transcription of the meeting's audio provides a written record of discussions.

Meeting Security and Control

Security is a top priority in Teams, with features such as:

Meeting Lock

Meeting organizers have the option to lock a meeting once it has started, preventing additional participants from joining. This is particularly important for secure or confidential meetings.

Participant Controls

Meeting organizers can control participant interactions, muting or removing participants if necessary. They can also designate presenters to share content.

Meeting Lobby

Meetings can be configured with a lobby, where participants wait until admitted by the organizer. This ensures that only authorized attendees enter the meeting.

Integration with Microsoft 365 Apps

Teams integrates seamlessly with other Microsoft 365 apps, enhancing the meeting experience:

Document Collaboration

During meetings, users can collaborate on documents in real time using apps like Word, Excel, and PowerPoint, ensuring that discussions translate into action.

Calendar Integration

Teams integrates with Outlook and Exchange calendars, providing a unified view of appointments, making scheduling meetings more efficient.

App Integration

Third-party and custom apps can be added to Teams channels and meetings, providing additional tools and functionalities to enhance collaboration.

Benefits of Microsoft Teams Meetings and Video Conferencing

Microsoft Teams offers a multitude of benefits for meetings and video conferencing:

- **Global Reach:** Teams allows for meetings with participants from around the world, making it easy to connect and collaborate globally.
- **Seamless Collaboration:** The integration of document collaboration within meetings ensures that discussions lead to concrete actions.
- **Productivity:** Meetings and video conferencing in Teams save time and increase productivity by minimizing the need for physical meetings.
- **Enhanced Communication:** High-quality video, audio, and chat features facilitate effective communication, even in remote work scenarios.
- **Security:** Teams' robust security features, including meeting locks and participant controls, ensure secure and confidential meetings.
- **Accessibility:** Features like live captions and automatic transcription improve accessibility for all participants.

In conclusion, Microsoft Teams' meeting and video conferencing capabilities make it a versatile and indispensable platform for organizations and teams. The platform's integrated features, security measures, and seamless communication tools ensure that meetings and video conferences are productive, efficient, and accessible, whether teams are working in the office or remotely. As the landscape of work continues to evolve, Teams remains a vital tool for keeping teams connected and achieving their goals.

8.3 Integrating Teams with Office Apps

Microsoft Teams, as part of the Microsoft 365 suite, offers a dynamic and cohesive environment for teamwork, communication, and collaboration. A fundamental strength of Teams is its seamless integration with a range of

Office apps, which significantly enhances productivity and collaboration. In this description, we will explore how this integration empowers users to work more efficiently and effectively.

Office Apps Integration in Microsoft Teams

Microsoft Word

Collaborative Document Editing: Teams enables real-time collaborative editing of Word documents. Multiple team members can work on a document simultaneously, with changes visible to all participants.

Direct File Sharing: Users can share Word documents within Teams channels or chat conversations, ensuring that everyone has access to the most recent version.

Microsoft Excel

Shared Spreadsheets: Teams allows for shared spreadsheets, fostering collaboration on data analysis, budgeting, and other tasks. Multiple users can edit Excel files at once.

Data Visualizations: Charts and graphs created in Excel can be shared directly in Teams conversations, making it easy to convey complex data.

Microsoft PowerPoint

Co-Authoring Presentations: Teams supports co-authoring of PowerPoint presentations. Team members can work on slides together, making it easier to create polished and impactful presentations.

Presentation Sharing: Users can share PowerPoint slides in meetings or chat conversations for real-time discussions and feedback.

Microsoft OneNote

Collaborative Note-Taking: Teams integrates with OneNote, enabling teams to take notes collaboratively during meetings or brainstorming sessions. These shared notebooks keep everyone on the same page.

Idea Sharing: Users can share OneNote pages or sections with team members, making it simple to collect and develop ideas together.

Microsoft Planner

Task Management: Teams users can create tasks and manage projects with Planner. Integration allows team members to track progress and assignments directly within Teams.

Visual Task Boards: Planner's visual task boards can be added to Teams channels, helping teams visualize progress and manage work more efficiently.

SharePoint

Document Repositories: Teams' integration with SharePoint enables easy access to SharePoint document libraries, ensuring that critical files are always within reach.

Structured Information: Users can pin SharePoint pages or lists to Teams channels, making it simple to access structured information.

OneDrive

File Storage and Sharing: Teams integrates with OneDrive for secure file storage and sharing. Users can access and share files from OneDrive directly within Teams.

Offline Access: OneDrive files can be made available for offline access within Teams, allowing users to work on documents without an internet connection.

Benefits of Integrating Office Apps in Microsoft Teams

The integration of Office apps within Microsoft Teams offers several advantages:

Streamlined Collaboration: Collaborative editing, real-time sharing, and seamless access to Office apps eliminate the need to switch between applications, streamlining workflows.

Consistency and Version Control: Integration ensures that all team members are working on the same version of documents, reducing version control issues.

Enhanced Productivity: The ability to create, edit, and share Office documents directly within Teams improves productivity by minimizing context switching.

Centralized Communication: Teams serves as a centralized hub for communication and document collaboration, ensuring that important information and files are easily accessible.

Security and Compliance: Microsoft's robust security and compliance standards apply to documents shared and edited within Teams, ensuring data safety.

Scalability: Integration benefits organizations of all sizes, from small teams to large enterprises.

In conclusion, the integration of Office apps within Microsoft Teams transforms the platform into a one-stop hub for productivity, communication, and collaboration. This feature-rich environment allows teams to work more efficiently, fosters consistency, and ensures that important documents and information are readily available. As remote and hybrid work continue to shape the modern workplace, the integration of Office apps in Teams plays a pivotal role in enhancing the way teams connect and collaborate.

Exercise

Exercise 1 – MCQ

Q 1. Which feature is used for instant messaging, file sharing, and audio/video calls within a team or group?
a) Teams Chat
b) Teams Connect
c) Teams Share
d) Teams Meet

Q 2. What is the primary purpose of the "Teams Meetings" feature in Microsoft Teams?
a) To create a group chat
b) To organize and conduct online meetings and video conferences
c) To share files with team members
d) To send email messages

Exercise 2 – True/ False

Q 1. Microsoft Teams allows real-time collaboration on documents, similar to Google Docs.

Q 2. You need to have a Microsoft 365 subscription to use Microsoft Teams.

Exercise 3 – Fill in the blanks

Q 1. you can create different "_____" to organize your communication and collaboration, such as project teams, departments, or interest groups.

Q 2. Teams Meetings can include features like screen sharing, "_____" controls, and meeting recording.

Exercise 4 – Match case

1. Teams Channels
2. Chat
3. Teams Meetings
4. Files Tab

A. Allows you to communicate one-on-one or in small groups with text, voice, or video.
B. Dedicated spaces for team collaboration, discussions, and file sharing.
C. Scheduled or ad-hoc virtual meetings for team members to join and collaborate.
D. A place to store, share, and collaborate on documents and files within a team.

Exercise 5 – One word answer

Q 1. What is the primary purpose of Teams Channels in Microsoft Teams?

Q 2. What is the primary function of "Teams Calendar"?

Exercise 6 – Small answer

Q 1. What is Microsoft Teams?

Q 2. How can you start a chat in Microsoft Teams?

Exercise 7 – Long answer

Q 1. How can you initiate a video call or virtual meeting using Microsoft Teams, and what are the benefits of these features?

Q 2. Explain the concept of Teams Channels in Microsoft Teams and how they facilitate collaboration within a team.

Answers

Exercise 1 – MCQ

Ans: 1 a, 2 b

Exercise 2 – True/ False

Ans: 1 True, 2 True

Exercise 3 – Fill in the blanks

Ans: 1 Teams, 2 Participant

Exercise 4 – Match case

Ans: 1 B, 2 A, 3 C, 4 D

Exercise 5 – One word answer

Ans: 1 Organization, 2 Scheduling

Chapter 9 - **Microsoft SharePoint**

SharePoint is a web-based platform that provides the powerful tools for organizing content of sites, sharing knowledge, provides collaboration, managing documents, and finding information.
The social functionality of SharePoint is that it is accessible anywhere in the world via an internet connection, which helps users to easily access data, documents, and information that they need.
SharePoint is a web-based platform developed by **Microsoft** and first launched in the year 2001. It provides an **enterprise collaboration** and **content management portal**, which enables users to connect with each other and share the information across the organization. Since it is a content management portal, so it also allows the non-technical users to easily create and manage their own web sites.
SharePoint provides sufficient space to store and share data, information, and documents.

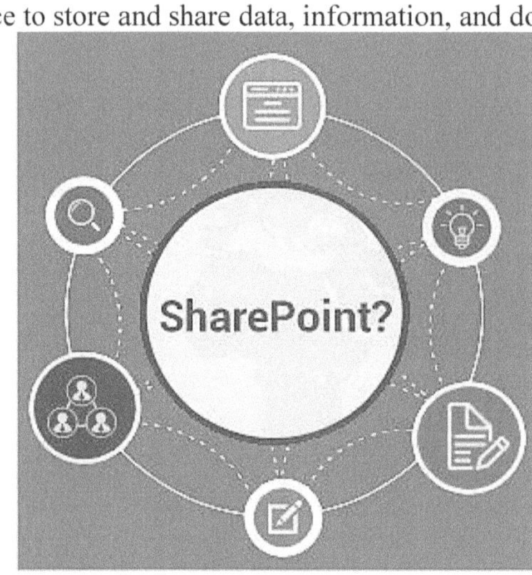

Microsoft SharePoint has 6 different areas, which are:

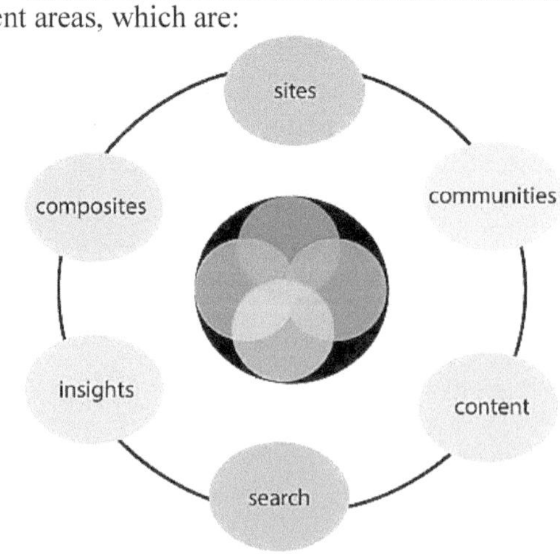

1) Sites: Building and managing Websites
SharePoint sites provide a set of tools that helps you to create your own websites, which can be your personal site, a website for your company, and the website for the world.
2) Communities: Creating a social Collaboration Environment
SharePoint Online provides modern approaches that help you to work, collaborate, organize, and communicate with multiple people at the same time. SharePoint 2013 and the above versions have an ability to create detailed user profiles, shared calendars, document libraries, and discussion boards.
3) Content: Managing your Documents, Information, and Records
SharePoint provides a place to store your content on the SharePoint rather than saving it in the local folder or network share device. SharePoint also provides a tool for managing all your organization's documents, information including that who can read and update them, and make content lock for further changes.
4) Search: The Google for your Organization's Private Info

SharePoint provides a complex search engine that allows you to search your content and people in a very easy and secure way.

Search in SharePoint includes the ability to:

- Enhance the search results with filters like the site, Author, Result Type, and more.
- Previews of the content within the result set
- Enhance search results based on the metadata.

5) Insights: Digging for Business intelligence

SharePoint allows you to bring all your information together, understand it, organize the content into different places such as spreadsheets, blogs, business intelligence systems, and present it in a way to make sense. It is also used to create dashboards, Visio diagrams, and scorecards.

6) Composites: Integrating your Business System

Composites in SharePoint combines data, documents, and business process in a "**do-it-yourself**" business solution. The main advantages of composites are that it provides better utilization of investment, Solutions do not depend on the coding, Rapid deployment, prototyping, and modifications.

Collaboration

The word Collaboration means "**working together**." It enables individual people to work together for a common purpose i.e., achieve business benefits.

A good collaboration includes the following:

- A shared sense of purpose
- A sense of shared responsibility
- Mutual trust

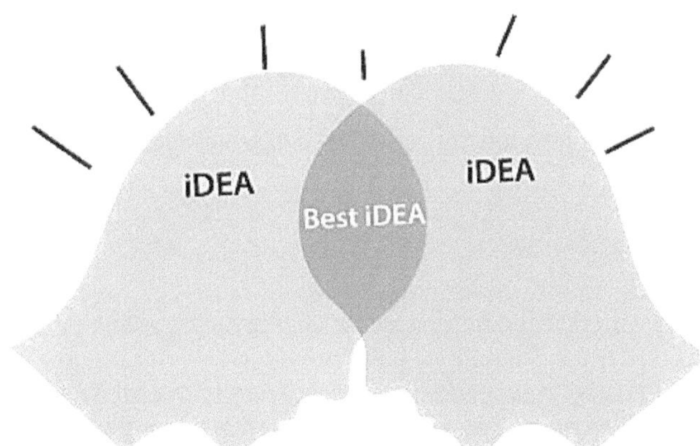

Features of SharePoint

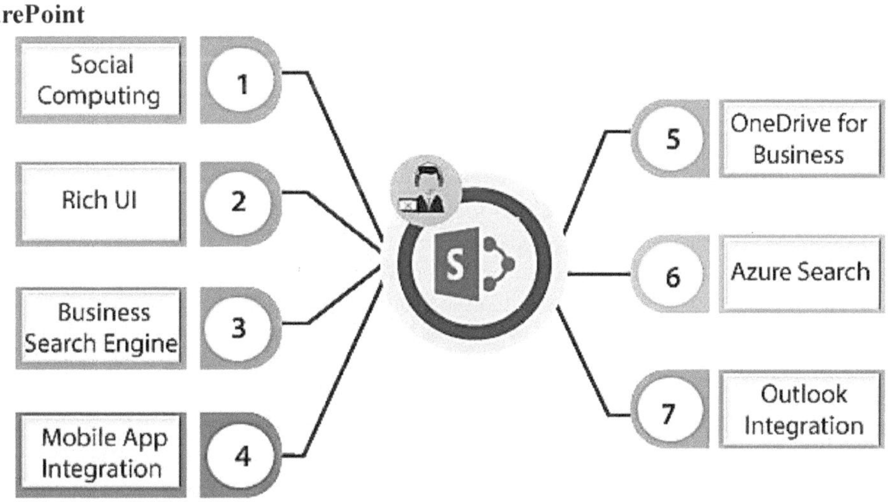

A list of features of SharePoint is given below -

Social Computing

Enables advanced collaboration within the SharePoint environment supports such as wikis, Blogs, Forums, etc.

For example, SharePoint integrates with skype, which allows employees to easily communicate with their business partners.

Rich UI

SharePoint offers automatically built the user interface for your websites in which you can easily edit, customize user interface according to your requirement.

Business Search Engine

SharePoint provides a business search engine that helps you to search relevant content based on your query, for example- Google.

Mobile App Integration

SharePoint integrates with the mobile app to carry your company intranet with you and all this is done by using SharePoint's mobile app. SharePoint mobile app allows you to use a mobile device for quick access to team sites, recent files, and more.

OneDrive for Business

Previously OneDrive is known as SkyDrive. It allows the employees to store files in one location for easily share and collaboration.

Azure Search

Azure Search uses the advanced search functionality with a customized application.

Outlook Integration

Outlook Integration with SharePoint extend capabilities using a folder hierarchy that can be accessed in both online and offline mode. It helps users to synchronize folders with SharePoint and use drag-drop or copy-paste to move emails to the folder.

9.1 Getting Started with SharePoint

SharePoint is a powerful platform for collaboration, document management, and communication. To get started with SharePoint, you need to understand how to set up a SharePoint site, its structure, and how to navigate the interface effectively.

1. Setting Up a SharePoint Site:

To set up a SharePoint site, follow these steps:

- **Access SharePoint:** Depending on your organization's setup, you can access SharePoint through a web browser. Enter the SharePoint URL provided by your organization.
- **Sign In:** Log in using your credentials. If you don't have an account, you will need to create one.
- **Site Creation:** Depending on your role and permissions, you may have the option to create a new SharePoint site or be directed to an existing site.

2. SharePoint Site Structure:

SharePoint organizes content within a hierarchical structure that includes key elements:

- **Site Collection:** This is the top-level container that can include multiple subsites, each serving specific functions or teams.
- **Subsites:** Subsites are created within site collections and cater to specific departments or projects. They have their own settings and permissions.
- **Libraries:** Libraries are where documents and files are stored. SharePoint includes default document libraries, and you can create custom libraries as needed.
- **Lists:** Lists are used for tracking and managing data, such as tasks, calendars, or issues.
- **Web Parts:** Web Parts are customizable components that can be added to pages, offering specific functionalities like document views, calendars, and more.
- **Permissions:** SharePoint allows you to set granular permissions, controlling who can view, edit, or delete content.

3. Navigating the SharePoint Interface:

Once you've set up a SharePoint site, navigating the interface is essential:

- **Home Page:** The home page typically provides an overview of the site's content, including news, recent documents, and links to important areas.
- **Top Navigation:** Use the top navigation bar to move between different areas of your site, such as lists, libraries, and subsites.
- **Left Navigation:** The left navigation pane displays a quick launch menu with links to important content and tools.

Document Libraries: When accessing document libraries, you can browse files, upload new documents, or create new folders.
Lists: Lists display data in a tabular format. You can filter, sort, and edit list items.
Search: Use the search bar to find specific content or documents within your SharePoint site.
Settings: Access site settings to configure permissions, manage site features, and customize the site's appearance.

SharePoint's interface is designed to make it easy for users to find, manage, and collaborate on content. As you become more familiar with SharePoint, you'll discover additional features for effective collaboration, document management, and automation of business processes.

9.2 Document Management in SharePoint

Document management in SharePoint is a fundamental aspect of the platform, allowing organizations to efficiently store, organize, and collaborate on various types of documents. Key components include document libraries, uploading and editing files, and implementing version control, as well as metadata and tagging.

1. Document Libraries:

Document libraries are the primary repositories for storing files and documents in SharePoint. They serve as organized containers where users can upload, manage, and share documents. Key features of document libraries include:

Templates: Document libraries often come with predefined templates that make it easy to create new documents based on standardized formats.
Permissions: You can set specific permissions to control who can access, edit, or delete documents within a library.
Metadata: Document libraries allow the use of metadata to categorize and describe documents for easier search and retrieval.

Creating a document library

A document library provides a secure place to store files, so that you and your team members can find those files easily, and can access from any device at any time.
There are the following steps to create a document library -
Step 1: Go to the home page of your site.

Step 2: Click on the + **New** and select **Document Library** from the drop-down menu.

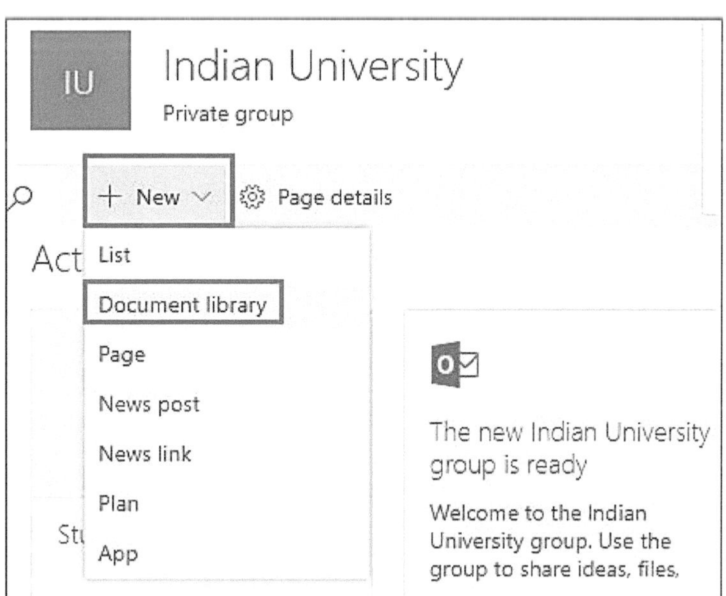

Step 3: Enter a name for the document library that you want to create and enter the Description about the library (Description is optional), then click on the **Create**.

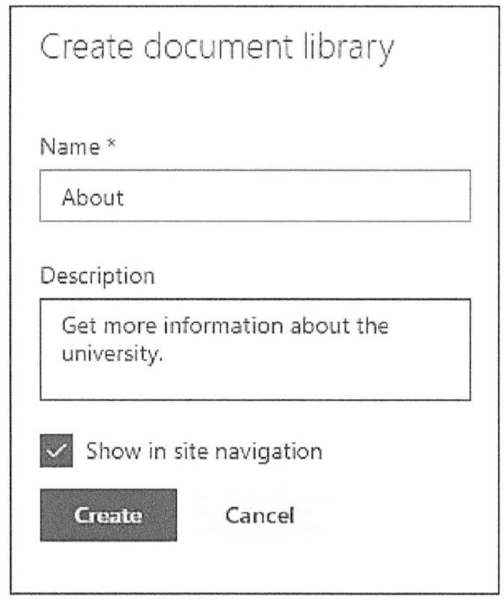

Now, you see that a document library "**About**" is created.

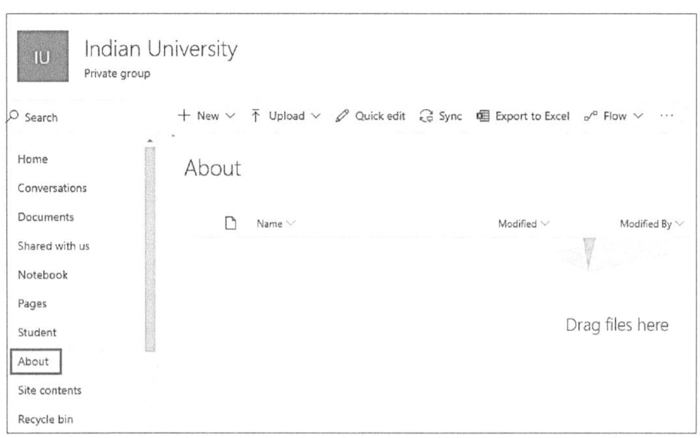

2. Uploading, Editing, and Version Control:

SharePoint streamlines the process of uploading, editing, and maintaining document versions.

Uploading: Users can easily upload documents to a library directly from their local devices. SharePoint supports a wide range of document formats.

Editing: Documents can be edited within SharePoint, allowing for real-time collaboration. Multiple users can work on a document simultaneously, with changes tracked to prevent conflicts.

Version Control: SharePoint maintains a history of document versions. This feature allows you to track changes over time and revert to previous versions if necessary. It's especially helpful for regulatory compliance and preventing data loss.

3. Metadata and Tagging:

Metadata and tagging are essential for effective document management and search capabilities in SharePoint.

Metadata: Metadata refers to additional information about a document, such as author, creation date, or document type. SharePoint allows you to create custom metadata fields to suit your organization's needs.

Tagging: Users can tag documents with relevant keywords or labels, making it easier to find documents through search or filtering. Tags enhance document discoverability and organization.

By leveraging document libraries, version control, and metadata/tagging, SharePoint ensures that documents are well-organized, accessible, and efficiently managed. This not only improves productivity but also enhances document security and compliance with organizational standards.

9.3 Collaboration and Communication

Collaboration and communication are at the core of Microsoft SharePoint's capabilities, enabling teams and organizations to work together seamlessly. Key features include Team Sites and Communication Sites, as well as using Lists and Libraries for collaboration, and co-authoring with real-time editing.

1. Team Sites and Communication Sites:

Team Sites: Team Sites are designed for collaboration within specific teams or departments. They provide a dedicated space where team members can work on projects, share documents, and communicate effectively. Team Sites often include features such as:

Document Libraries: Central repositories for storing team-related documents.

Calendars: To schedule events and deadlines.

Task Lists: For tracking tasks and project progress.

Discussion Boards: For team discussions and updates.

Communication Sites: Communication Sites are geared toward sharing information with a broader audience. They are often used for company-wide announcements, news, and branding. Communication Sites include:

News Web Parts: To post and share news articles.

Hero Web Parts: To showcase important content.

Quick Links: For easy navigation.

2. Lists and Libraries for Collaboration:

SharePoint includes Lists and Libraries to facilitate collaboration in various ways:

Lists: Lists in SharePoint are versatile and can be customized for various purposes, such as task tracking, issue tracking, contact lists, and more. They support features like version history and can be linked to Outlook for easy integration.

Libraries: Document Libraries are particularly useful for collaboration. They allow users to upload, edit, and share documents. Libraries support check-in/check-out functionality to prevent conflicting edits and maintain version history.

3. Co-Authoring and Real-Time Editing:

SharePoint offers co-authoring features that allow multiple users to simultaneously edit documents within a document library. This real-time editing capability greatly enhances collaboration and teamwork.

Real-Time Editing: When a document is opened for editing, SharePoint enables multiple users to make changes and see those changes reflected in real-time. This eliminates the need to wait for others to finish editing before making your own changes.

Version Control: SharePoint's version control keeps track of document revisions, making it easy to revert to previous versions if needed. This feature ensures data integrity and simplifies compliance and auditing.

Co-authoring and real-time editing enhance productivity, reduce bottlenecks, and foster efficient collaboration within teams and across the organization. SharePoint's versatile capabilities empower users to work together seamlessly and communicate effectively, driving better results and outcomes.

9.4 SharePoint Workflows

SharePoint workflows are a powerful tool for automating business processes, streamlining tasks, and ensuring efficient collaboration within an organization. In this context, we will explore the introduction to workflows, building custom workflows, and automating business processes within SharePoint.

1. **Introduction to Workflows:**
A workflow in SharePoint represents a defined series of tasks, steps, or actions that need to be completed in a specific order to achieve a particular business goal or process. Workflows are commonly used to automate repetitive tasks, facilitate approvals, and improve the efficiency of business processes. Key aspects of workflows include:
   - **Trigger Events:** Workflows are initiated by specific events, such as document approval, task assignment, or form submission.
   - **Workflow Actions:** Each workflow consists of actions or steps that define what needs to be done. Actions can include sending emails, updating documents, creating tasks, or initiating other processes.
   - **Workflow Templates:** SharePoint provides pre-built templates for common workflows, but custom workflows can also be created to meet specific business needs.
2. **Building Custom Workflows:**
Custom workflows are designed to address unique business requirements. Building custom workflows typically involves the following steps:
   - **Planning:** Define the objectives and requirements of the workflow, including the trigger event and the sequence of actions.
   - **Workflow Creation:** Use SharePoint Designer, Power Automate (formerly known as Flow), or other workflow development tools to create the workflow.
   - **Defining Actions:** Specify the actions that need to be performed, such as sending notifications, updating data, creating tasks, or initiating sub-workflows.
   - **Testing:** Thoroughly test the workflow to ensure it functions as intended and addresses the business need.
   - **Deployment:** Once the custom workflow is tested and approved, it can be deployed to SharePoint sites, lists, or libraries.
3. **Automating Business Processes:**
SharePoint workflows play a vital role in automating a wide range of business processes, such as:
   - **Document Approval:** Automate the approval process for documents, ensuring that they are reviewed and accepted by the appropriate personnel.
   - **Task Assignment:** Automatically assign tasks to team members based on predefined criteria or event triggers.
   - **Issue Tracking:** Use workflows to manage and track issues, including notifications, escalations, and resolutions.
   - **Onboarding/Offboarding:** Streamline employee onboarding and offboarding processes, ensuring consistency and compliance.
   - **Content Publishing:** Automate the process of content publication, from creation to approval to publication.

By automating business processes through SharePoint workflows, organizations can reduce manual intervention, minimize errors, enhance accountability, and improve overall operational efficiency. This results in cost savings, faster decision-making, and increased productivity, ultimately benefiting the organization's bottom line.

9.5 Use Cases for SharePoint

SharePoint is a versatile platform that serves numerous use cases across different organizations, each tailored to meet specific needs and objectives. Here, we explore some common use cases for SharePoint, including document repositories, intranet portals, project management, knowledge management, compliance and records management, as well as forms and workflow automation.

1. **Document Repositories:**

Document repositories in SharePoint are dedicated spaces within the platform designed to efficiently store, manage, and organize documents. These repositories offer a comprehensive solution for document management, ensuring easy access, version control, security, and collaboration. Here's a detailed description of document repositories in SharePoint:

1. Centralized Storage: SharePoint document repositories provide a centralized and secure location to store documents of various types, including text documents, spreadsheets, presentations, images, and more. This centralization ensures that documents are not scattered across individual users' computers or file servers, reducing the risk of data loss and improving accessibility.

2. Version Control: SharePoint offers robust version control features. Each time a document is edited or updated, a new version is automatically generated and stored. This ensures that previous versions are preserved, allowing users to track changes and revert to earlier iterations if necessary. Version history is crucial for auditing, compliance, and maintaining data integrity.

3. Metadata Tagging: SharePoint allows for the use of metadata, which involves attaching additional information to documents. Metadata can include details such as document author, creation date, document type, and keywords. This metadata enhances search and categorization, making it easier to find and organize documents efficiently.

4. Security and Permissions: Document repositories in SharePoint offer granular control over document access. Users can set specific permissions for each document or folder, specifying who can view, edit, or delete content. This feature is invaluable for maintaining data security and ensuring that sensitive information is only accessible to authorized personnel.

5. Collaboration: SharePoint is renowned for its collaboration capabilities. Users can collaboratively work on documents within document libraries, making real-time edits and comments. Co-authoring features are particularly useful for teams working on documents simultaneously, preventing conflicts and enhancing productivity.

6. Check-In and Check-Out: SharePoint includes a "check-in/check-out" system to prevent concurrent editing conflicts. When a user checks out a document, it becomes read-only for others, ensuring that no one else can make changes until it's checked back in. This feature is particularly helpful when detailed editing is required.

7. Accessibility and Mobile Support: Document repositories are accessible from various devices and platforms, including mobile devices. This ensures that team members can access and collaborate on documents even when working remotely, enhancing flexibility and efficiency.

8. Integration: SharePoint can be integrated with other Microsoft applications, making it easy to access and collaborate on documents directly from tools like Microsoft Word, Excel, and PowerPoint. This integration streamlines document management and collaboration further.

2. Intranet Portals:

Internal portals in Microsoft SharePoint are web-based platforms that serve as centralized hubs for enhancing communication, collaboration, and knowledge sharing within an organization. These portals are designed to create a unified digital workspace that connects employees, departments, and teams. Here's a detailed description of internal portals in Microsoft SharePoint:

1. Centralized Information Hub: SharePoint internal portals serve as centralized information hubs, consolidating various resources, documents, news, and announcements. This centralization ensures that employees have a single point of access for all essential organizational information.

2. Company News and Announcements: Internal portals often feature dedicated sections for company news and announcements. This is where organizations can share important updates, events, and corporate news, ensuring that employees are well-informed about the latest developments within the organization.

3. Employee Directories: SharePoint portals typically include employee directories, making it easy for staff to find and connect with their colleagues. These directories often provide contact information, job roles, and department details, fostering better interdepartmental communication and collaboration.

4. Collaborative Spaces: Internal portals create collaborative spaces where teams and departments can share documents, collaborate on projects, and engage in discussions. These collaborative spaces are typically built using SharePoint Team Sites, allowing teams to work together effectively.

5. Integration with Business Applications: SharePoint's flexibility enables integration with various business applications and tools. This integration allows employees to access critical business applications directly from the portal, streamlining workflows and enhancing productivity.

6. Departmental Sites: Internal portals can be organized into departmental sites, creating dedicated areas for each department within the organization. This segmentation allows departments to have their own spaces for documents, communication, and project management.

7. Announcements and Updates: SharePoint internal portals often include features like news web parts, where announcements and updates can be posted and easily viewed by employees. This ensures that employees are up-to-date on important information and events.

8. Quick Links: Quick links or navigation menus make it easy for employees to access different sections and resources within the portal. These links provide efficient navigation, ensuring that employees can quickly find the information they need.

9. Document Management: SharePoint's robust document management capabilities are integrated into internal portals. This means that documents can be uploaded, shared, and collaborated on within the portal, enhancing document management and version control.
10. Security and Access Control: SharePoint provides granular control over access permissions. Internal portals enable organizations to control who can view, edit, and contribute to the portal's content, ensuring that sensitive information is protected.
11. Mobile Access: Internal portals are designed to be accessible from various devices, including mobile phones and tablets. This ensures that employees can stay connected and access important information even when working remotely.

3. Project Management:

Project management in Microsoft SharePoint involves the utilization of the platform's collaborative and document management features to plan, execute, monitor, and control projects effectively. SharePoint provides tools and functionalities that enhance project coordination, task assignment, document sharing, and communication among project teams. Here's a detailed description of project management in Microsoft **SharePoint:**
1. Task Lists and Timelines: SharePoint offers task lists and timelines to help project managers and team members track project progress. Task lists enable the creation of tasks, assignment of responsibilities, and setting of due dates. Timelines provide a visual representation of project schedules and dependencies, aiding in project planning and tracking.
2. Document Management: SharePoint's robust document management capabilities are essential for project management. Project teams can create document libraries to store project-related documents, including project plans, reports, status updates, and other project artifacts. Version control ensures that project documents remain organized and current.
3. Collaboration: Collaboration is at the core of successful project management. SharePoint Team Sites and collaborative workspaces allow project teams to work together efficiently. Team members can co-author documents, share updates, and engage in discussions related to project tasks and milestones.
4. Gantt Charts: Gantt charts are instrumental in visualizing project schedules and timelines. SharePoint provides the option to create Gantt charts that display task dependencies and milestones, helping project managers and team members better understand the project's structure and critical path.
5. Notifications and Alerts: SharePoint allows project teams to set up notifications and alerts for specific events, such as task assignments, document updates, or changes in project status. This ensures that team members stay informed and can respond promptly to project-related activities.
6. Task Assignment and Tracking: Task assignment features in SharePoint make it easy to assign project tasks to team members and track their progress. Each task can have an assigned owner, due date, and status, enabling project managers to monitor task completion and identify any bottlenecks.
7. Reporting and Dashboards: SharePoint enables the creation of project-related reports and dashboards. Project managers can generate visual reports to provide an overview of project status, resource allocation, and potential risks. Dashboards can be customized to display key performance indicators (KPIs) and project metrics.
8. Issue and Risk Tracking: SharePoint is equipped to handle issue tracking and risk management within projects. Teams can document and monitor project issues and risks, assign responsibilities for resolution, and track the mitigation of risks and resolution of issues.
9. Integration: SharePoint integrates with various Microsoft applications, such as Microsoft Project and Microsoft Planner, to extend project management capabilities. These integrations allow project managers to use specialized project management tools while keeping the team's collaborative work within SharePoint.
10. Security and Access Control: SharePoint provides granular control over document and site access. Project managers can define who has access to project documents and data, ensuring that sensitive project information is protected.
11. Mobile Access: Project teams can access SharePoint project management features from various devices, including mobile phones and tablets. This mobility enables teams to stay connected and make updates on the go, facilitating remote work and flexibility.

4. Knowledge Management:

Knowledge management in Microsoft SharePoint revolves around the systematic process of capturing, organizing, and sharing the collective knowledge and expertise within an organization. SharePoint provides a platform to facilitate this process, enabling companies to harness and disseminate their institutional wisdom. Here's a detailed description of knowledge management in Microsoft SharePoint:

1. Centralized Knowledge Repository: SharePoint serves as a centralized repository for storing and managing knowledge assets. These assets can include documents, presentations, reports, best practice guides, policies, templates, research findings, and more. By centralizing this information, SharePoint ensures that it's readily accessible to employees across the organization.

2. Document Management: SharePoint's document management capabilities are at the heart of knowledge management. Organizations can create document libraries dedicated to various categories of knowledge. Version control ensures that documents are current and that past versions are preserved for reference or auditing purposes.

3. Wikis and Knowledge Bases: SharePoint offers the creation of wikis and knowledge bases, providing a structured platform for documenting and sharing information. These resources are valuable for creating comprehensive knowledge articles, FAQs, and reference materials.

4. Collaboration and Authoring: SharePoint's collaborative features enable team members to author and edit knowledge documents collectively. Co-authoring ensures that multiple contributors can work on the same document simultaneously, making the knowledge management process more efficient.

5. Expertise Location: SharePoint helps organizations identify internal experts and subject matter specialists. Employee profiles can include areas of expertise, and the platform can facilitate searching for experts within the organization. This feature streamlines knowledge sharing and ensures that employees can connect with experts when needed.

6. Taxonomy and Tagging: SharePoint allows the use of metadata and tagging, making it easier to categorize and search for knowledge resources. This feature ensures that documents are well-organized and easy to find, improving knowledge accessibility.

7. Knowledge Repositories: Organizations can create dedicated knowledge repositories within SharePoint to house specialized knowledge areas. These repositories might focus on specific domains such as IT solutions, customer support, product information, or industry insights.

8. Best Practice Sharing: SharePoint facilitates the sharing of best practices and lessons learned. Teams and departments can document their successful strategies and experiences, making this knowledge available to others for replication and improvement.

9. Search and Discovery: SharePoint provides powerful search functionality, enabling employees to locate knowledge resources quickly. Enterprise search features ensure that employees can find the information they need efficiently, even in large repositories.

10. Compliance and Records Management: SharePoint ensures that knowledge resources adhere to compliance standards and records management policies. This feature is crucial for regulatory compliance and maintaining a record of knowledge assets over time.

11. Mobile Access: Knowledge management in SharePoint is accessible from various devices, including mobile phones and tablets. This flexibility ensures that employees can access knowledge resources whenever and wherever they need them.

5. Compliance and Records Management:

Compliance and records management in Microsoft SharePoint involves the implementation of policies and tools to ensure that organizations adhere to regulatory requirements, maintain data integrity, and effectively manage their records throughout their lifecycle. Here's a detailed description of compliance and records management in Microsoft SharePoint:

1. Regulatory Compliance: SharePoint offers features and capabilities to help organizations comply with various industry regulations and legal requirements. Whether it's data protection regulations, industry-specific compliance standards, or international data privacy laws, SharePoint provides tools to meet these obligations.

2. Document Retention Policies: SharePoint enables organizations to establish document retention policies, specifying how long documents should be retained and when they can be safely disposed of. These policies are crucial for ensuring data compliance and managing the document lifecycle efficiently.

3. Records Management: SharePoint supports records management, which involves identifying, classifying, and managing records within the organization. Records can include important documents, contracts, financial reports, legal agreements, and more. SharePoint helps in declaring documents as records, which ensures their preservation and protection.

4. Audit Trails and Logging: SharePoint includes auditing and logging features that allow organizations to track document and data activities. This includes monitoring who accessed, edited, or deleted documents. Audit trails are valuable for regulatory compliance and maintaining data security.

5. Secure Document Storage: SharePoint provides secure document storage and access control. Organizations can define permissions and access levels to ensure that only authorized personnel can view, edit, or delete sensitive documents. This security is essential for compliance with data protection and confidentiality requirements.

6. **Legal Holds:** SharePoint supports the implementation of legal holds on documents and records. Legal holds ensure that certain records are not deleted, altered, or tampered with during legal proceedings, investigations, or audits. This is critical for litigation and compliance purposes.

7. **Metadata and Tagging:** SharePoint's metadata and tagging features enhance the organization of records. Metadata allows documents to be categorized and indexed for easier search and retrieval. Proper tagging ensures that records are easily findable and well-organized.

8. **Archiving:** SharePoint includes archiving capabilities for storing records that are no longer actively used but must be retained for compliance or historical purposes. Archiving ensures that records are preserved while reducing clutter in active document libraries.

9. **Data Encryption:** SharePoint supports data encryption, which is vital for protecting sensitive information from unauthorized access. Data encryption is crucial for organizations that handle personally identifiable information (PII) and financial data.

10. **Records Disposition:** SharePoint helps organizations define records disposition schedules, which determine how records are managed, whether they are retained, archived, or disposed of. This process ensures that records are handled according to legal and regulatory requirements.

11. **Compliance Reporting:** SharePoint provides reporting capabilities to track compliance efforts and demonstrate adherence to regulations. Organizations can generate reports showing document histories, audit trails, access logs, and adherence to compliance policies.

6. **Forms and Workflow Automation**:

Forms and workflow automation in Microsoft SharePoint involves the creation, management, and automation of business processes to improve efficiency and productivity within an organization. SharePoint provides a powerful platform for designing custom forms, creating automated workflows, and streamlining various business processes. Here's a detailed description of forms and workflow automation in Microsoft SharePoint:

1. **Custom Forms Creation:** SharePoint allows users to design custom forms for data entry and information collection. These forms can be tailored to meet specific business requirements, such as employee onboarding, customer surveys, or expense approvals. Custom forms help ensure consistency and accuracy in data capture.

2. **Integration with SharePoint Lists and Libraries:** Custom forms are often integrated with SharePoint lists and libraries, enabling organizations to manage and track data more effectively. For example, a custom form for expense reports can feed data directly into a SharePoint list for finance tracking and approval.

3. **Workflow Design:** SharePoint offers a visual workflow designer that allows users to create automated workflows without extensive coding. Workflows are designed to automate sequential and parallel processes, such as document approval, task assignment, or issue escalation.

4. **Workflow Triggers:** Workflows can be triggered by specific events or actions. SharePoint provides various triggers, including item creation, item modification, or specific date and time events. This ensures that workflows are initiated at the right moment in the business process.

5. **Approval Workflows:** Approval workflows are common in SharePoint and are used for document review and approval processes. When a document is submitted, the workflow routes it to designated approvers who can review, approve, or request changes.

6. **Notifications and Alerts:** SharePoint workflows can generate notifications and alerts to keep relevant stakeholders informed about the progress of a workflow. This includes email notifications, task assignments, and updates on workflow status.

7. **Document Management Workflows:** SharePoint includes document management workflows for tasks such as document review, version control, and archiving. These workflows help organizations maintain document integrity and adherence to document management policies.

8. **Business Process Automation:** Organizations can automate entire business processes using SharePoint workflows. For instance, employee onboarding can be automated, with workflows that generate tasks for HR, IT, and managers, ensuring a seamless onboarding experience.

9. **Data Validation and Business Rules:** SharePoint workflows can include data validation and business rules to enforce compliance with established guidelines. For example, a purchase order workflow can verify that expenses are within budget limits.

10. **Integration with External Systems:** SharePoint can integrate with external systems and services to further streamline business processes. For example, a customer order workflow may interact with an external inventory management system to check product availability.

11. **Reporting and Analytics:** SharePoint provides reporting and analytics features to monitor the performance of workflows and identify areas for optimization. Organizations can generate reports to track workflow efficiency, bottlenecks, and completion times.

12. Mobile Access: Users can initiate, participate in, and monitor workflows through mobile devices. Mobile access ensures that employees can interact with business processes even when they are not in the office.

Exercise

Exercise 1 – MCQ

Q 1. What is Microsoft SharePoint primarily used for?
a) Graphic design
b) Document management and collaboration
c) Video editing
d) Web development

Q 2. Which feature in SharePoint allows for the automation of business processes?
a) SharePoint Forms
b) SharePoint Lists
c) SharePoint Workflows
d) SharePoint Document Libraries

Exercise 2 – True/ False

Q 1. SharePoint is primarily used for graphic design and image editing.
Q 2. SharePoint offers version control, allowing users to manage different versions of documents.

Exercise 3 – Fill in the blanks

Q 1. SharePoint is primarily used for document management and _______________.
Q 2. a _______________ is a repository for documents and files.

Exercise 4 – Match case

1.Read
2.Contribute
3.Edit
4.Full Control

A. Can view and download documents, but cannot edit or delete them.
B. Can view, add, update, and delete items and documents.
C. Can make changes to content, add, edit, and delete items.
D. Has full control over the site, including permissions management and configuration changes

Exercise 5 – One word answer

Q 1. What SharePoint feature manages different versions of documents?
Q 2. Which SharePoint feature automates business processes?

Exercise 6 – Small answer

Q 1. What does version control in SharePoint help manage?
Q 2. How can SharePoint Permissions be utilized?

Exercise 7 – Long answer

Q 1. What are the primary functions and use cases of Microsoft SharePoint within an organization, and how does it facilitate document management and collaboration among teams and departments?
Q 2. Describe how SharePoint Permissions work, their significance in controlling document access, and the different access levels that can be assigned to users.

Answers

Exercise 1 – MCQ

Ans: 1 b, 2 c

Exercise 2 – True/ False

Ans: 1 True, 2 True

Exercise 3 – Fill in the blanks

Ans: 1 Collaboration, 2 Document Library

Exercise 4 – Match case

Ans: 1 A, 2 B, 3 C, 4 D

Exercise 5 – One word answer

Ans: 1 Version Control, 2 Workflows

Chapter 10 - **Microsoft Visio**

Microsoft Visio is one of the most popular diagramming software that empowers diagramming, data visualization, and process modelling in a familiar interface. Visio comes with an array of templates and built-in shapes that allow creating virtually any diagram of any complexity. Visio also allows users to define their own shapes and import them into the drawing. Visio has been more of an enterprise-class software as home users rarely would need to use the advanced diagramming functions in Visio. However, many home users are purchasing the Standard edition of Visio to better visualize simple diagrams such as family trees or floor layout plans. Visio owes its success in the enterprise due to its tight integration with other Microsoft Office products such as Word, Excel, and Access. Data can be directly imported from this software and converted into meaningful diagrams, which change in real-time in accordance with the data. For example, an Excel spreadsheet might have information about current flows through an electrical line. Visio can be used to diagrammatically represent this and whenever the Excel data gets updated, the same will be reflected in the Visio diagram as well.

10.1 Getting Started with Visio

Start Screen:

The user interface of Visio is similar to that of other programs in the Office suite. You will be greeted with a Start page that lists some of the recent documents you have opened along with featured templates for creating common diagram types.

You can also search for templates on the Microsoft website right from the Start screen.

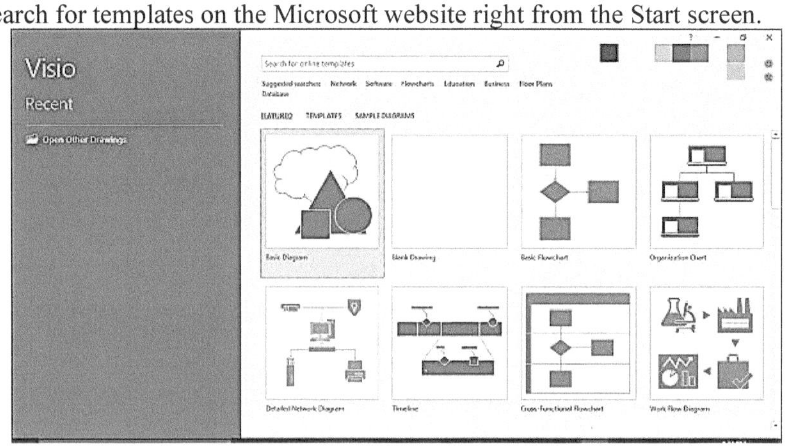

The top right corner shows the Microsoft account you are connected to, if you are an Office 365 subscriber. Apart from the featured templates, you can also click Templates to browse through the template categories.

Document Interface:

Clicking any of the above templates opens the template document.

The document interface of Visio is similar to other Office programs such as Word or Excel. On the top, you have the Quick Access toolbar, which contains common commands, such as Save, Undo, and Redo. This can be customized as needed.

Below the Quick Access toolbar is the familiar Office Ribbon. The Home tab lists common commands for working with the document. We will learn more about other tabs as we go along.

On the left-hand pane, there is Shapes, which lists the common shapes that go well with the template. To insert a shape, just click and drag the shape onto the canvas. There are many shapes available in Visio and we will get more familiar with them as we move ahead.

Of course, you can also search for more shapes, if needed online, using the built-in search tool.

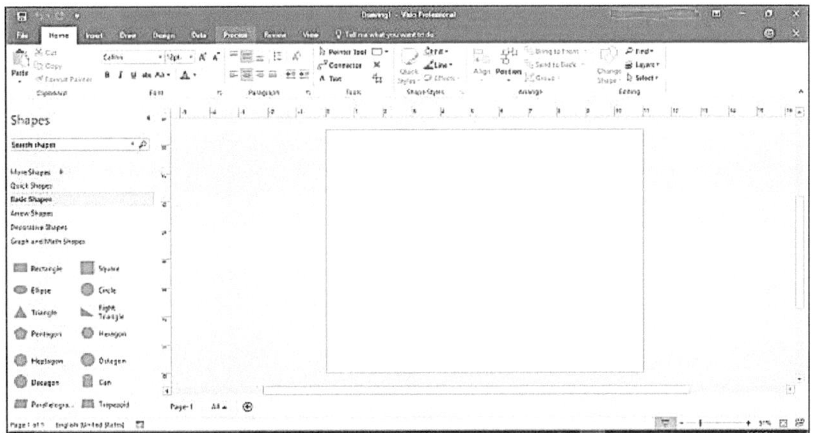

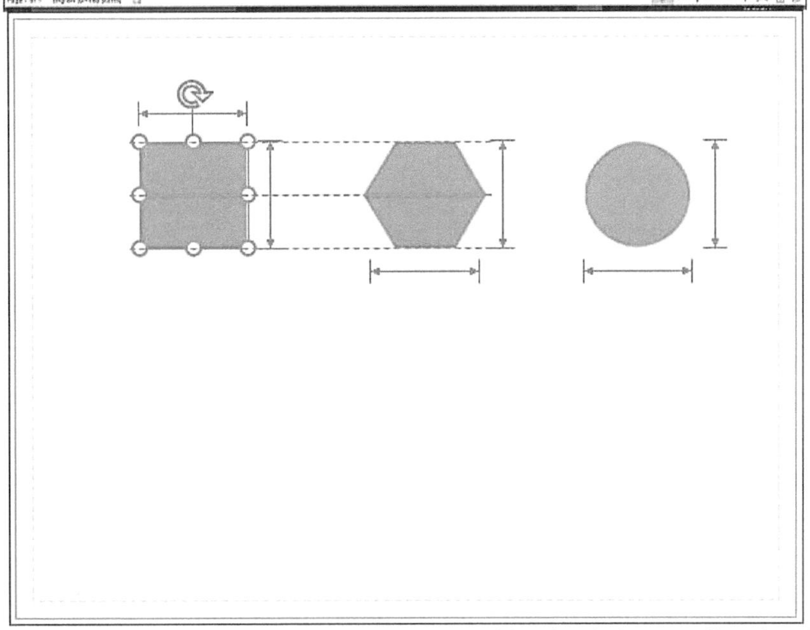

When you place shapes onto the canvas, you will see guides that help you align the shapes with respect to the objects already on the canvas. You also have a ruler on the top and left of the canvas. This gives a sense of perspective and lets you create perfectly aligned diagrams.

Shapes in Visio are basically vector graphics and as such you can enlarge or shrink the size as needed without loss of quality. You also get an idea of the relative dimensions of all the other shapes (indicated by green arrows) when you try to change the dimensions of any shape.

10.2 Working with Shapes

Smart Shapes provide contextual shapes which relate to the selected shape. Smart Shapes are connected to the original shape and the connector also moves whenever the Smart Shape is moved.

Creating a Smart Shape

Start with a blank document (in this case a flowchart diagram). You will notice that the Shapes pane has different shapes that are applicable to flowcharts. Click and drag a shape onto the empty canvas. You can resize or rotate the shape as desired. You can even align the shape with the help of the alignment guides.

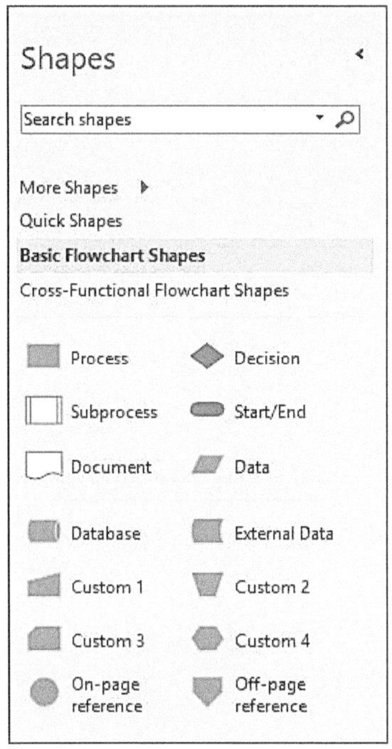

When you drag a shape onto the canvas, you will notice that there are four arrows along the shape. Hovering over any of these arrows will show possible shapes that can be created and linked to this shape.

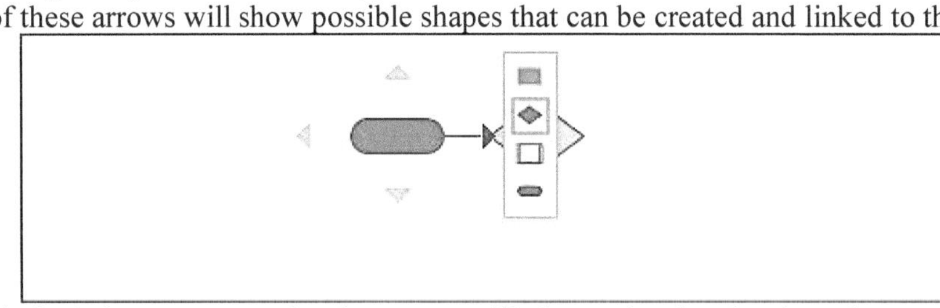

Click the desired shape to create the shape. You will also notice that the shape is automatically connected to the initial shape. If you were to drag the shape manually, you will need to connect it manually as well. The connections between the shapes are dynamic and they will move in relation to the placement of the shape.

Arranging Smart Shapes

The SmartShape arrow lists the first four shapes for the diagram that are seen in the Shapes pane. You might want to customize which shapes appear in the four SmartShape options depending on your workflow. To set the shapes that you prefer as SmartShapes, first select the desired shape in the Shapes pane and drag it to one of the first four shapes within the pane.

In this example, let us assume that the Database shape needs to be in the first four. Click and drag the Database shape into one of the first four positions.

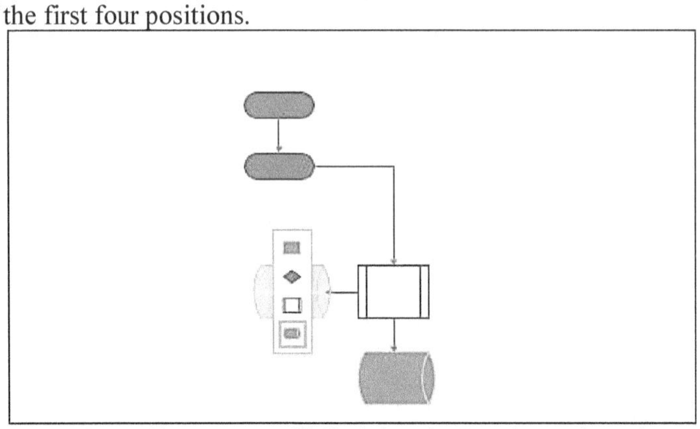

Now, when you create a SmartShape, you will find that the Database shape is made available.

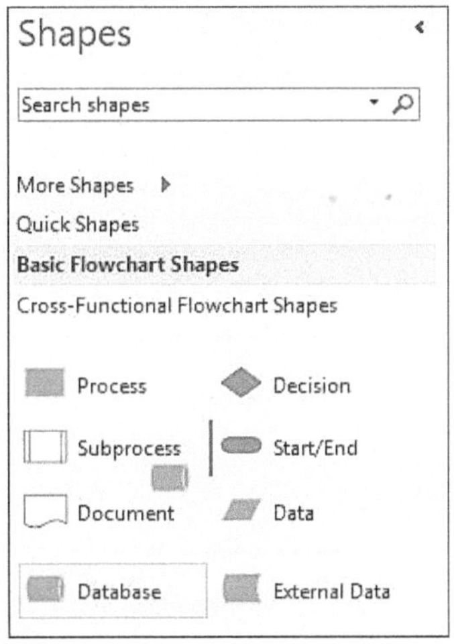

SmartShapes allows to automatically connect shapes. If you want to connect shapes that are not directly related, you can manually connect them.

To manually connect shapes, click the Connector tool in the Tools section of the Home tab. The mouse pointer now changes into a connector.

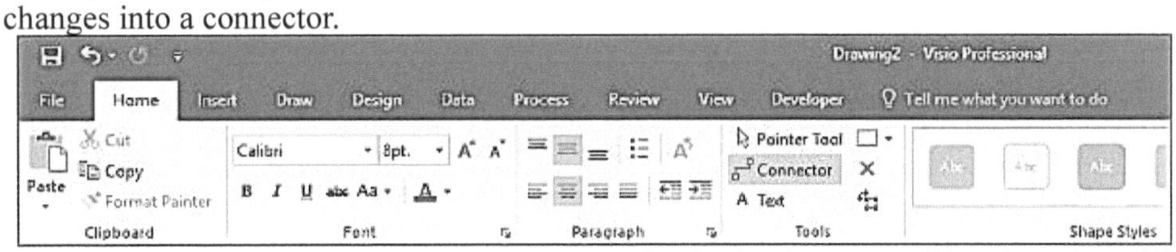

Draw a connecting line from the originating shape to the destination. You will notice a dotted line representing the connector. You can either glue this connector to the connection point or glue it to the destination shape. Gluing it to the shape will enable you to move the shape to a different location on the canvas along with the connector.

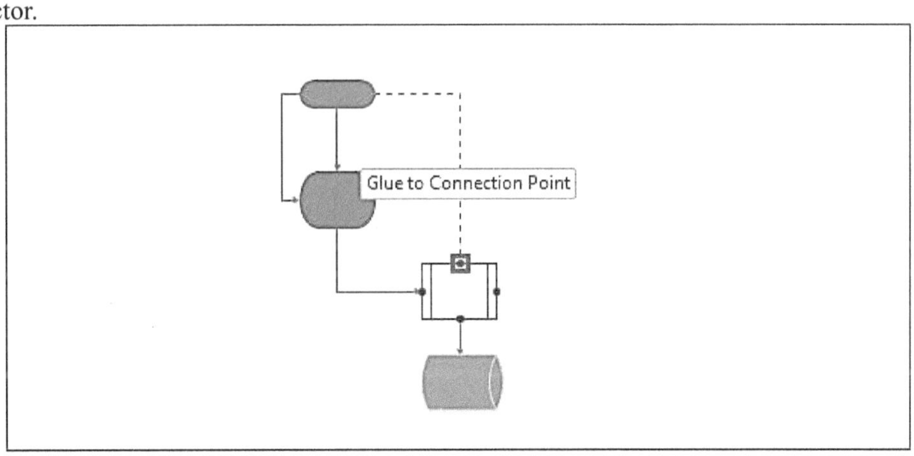

Click the Pointer Tool in the Tools section of the Home tab to return the mouse pointer back to normal.

Newer versions of Visio have built-in intelligence to help you place shapes between other shapes. Visio automatically adds the required spacing and connectors to ensure that the new shape is inserted in the correct position.

To insert a shape between two shapes, drag the new shape in between the desired shapes, till you see green squares on the connectors and release the mouse. The new shape will be inserted with equal spacing and appropriate connections.

If you delete the inserted shape, the connector extends all the way till the next shape.

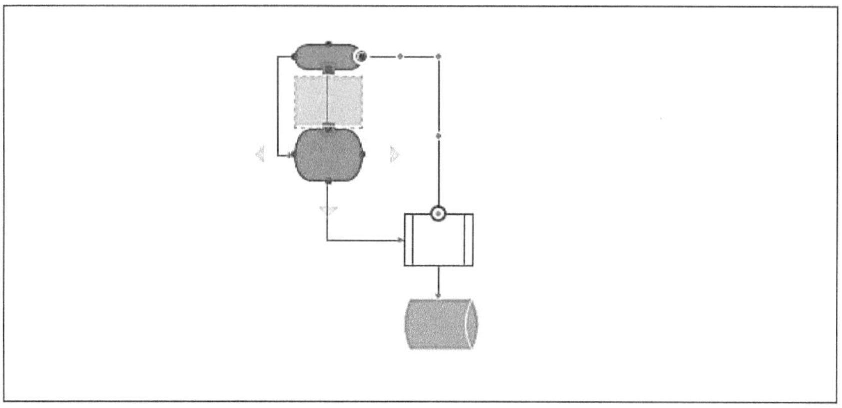

Align and Space Shapes

To automatically align and space shapes in a diagram, go to the Position dropdown menu in the Arrange section of the Home tab. Click either Auto Space or Auto Align & Space depending on the requirement. You can also hover the mouse on these commands to preview how the diagram would look after alignment.

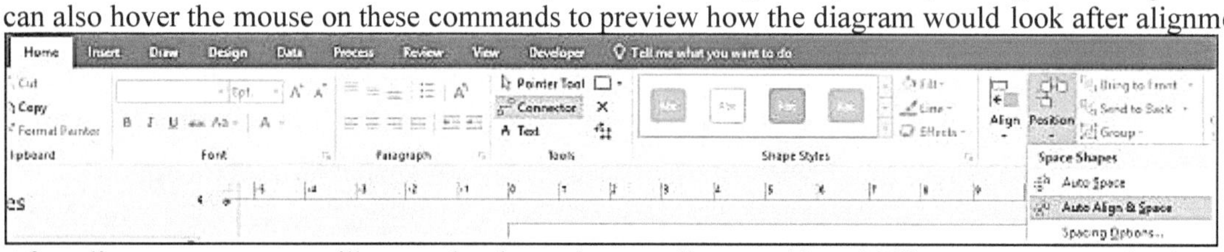

After alignment, you can still move the shapes in your diagram, if you'd like a more customized appearance.

10.3 Diagram Layout and Design

Visio provides options for automatically changing the layout of the diagram with the ReLayout Page command. The Re-Layout Page command provides commonly used layouts. You can also customize some of the aspects of the layout as needed.

Changing the Diagram Layout

Open the diagram and navigate to the Design tab on the Ribbon. Click the Re-Layout Page dropdown menu and select a layout as needed. You will see that the diagram now changes to the selected layout. You can also preview the look before clicking by hovering the mouse over the layout style.

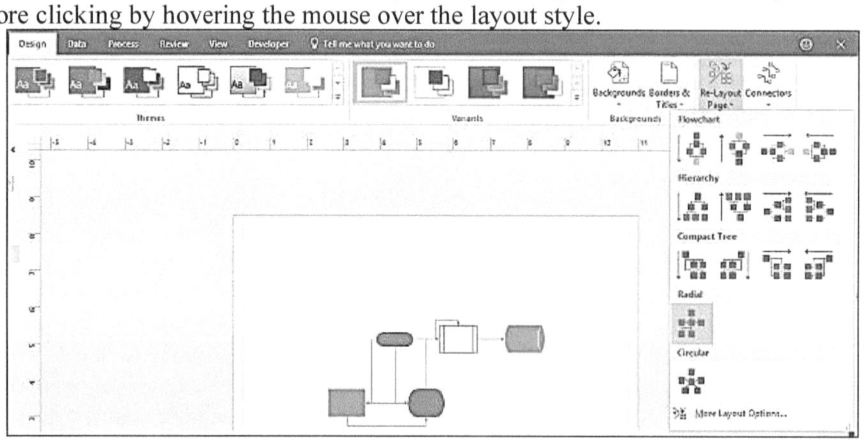

Customizing the Layout

You can further customize the layout by clicking More Layout Options… in the Re-Layout Page dropdown menu. This opens a dialog box in which you can configure the layout properties.

You can change the spacing between the shapes by manually changing the values in the Spacing field.

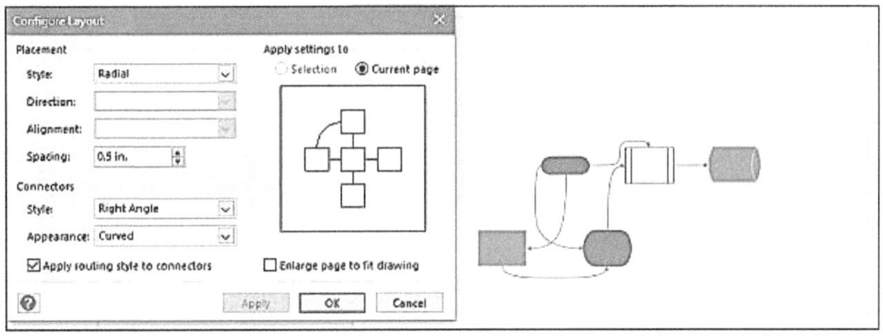

You can also change the appearance of the connectors to curved by selecting Curved in the Appearance dropdown menu. Remember to select the Apply routing style to connectors checkbox to be able to change the appearance of the connectors.

10.4 Adding Text and Data

Visio allows inserting text either within the shapes or in the document. You also get to do text formatting just like any other text editor.

Inserting Text in a Shape

It is easy to insert text within a shape. Just double-click within a shape to type the text. The text automatically wraps according to the shape, however, you can also press hard returns if you'd like to have your own wrapping. Notice that Visio automatically zooms into the shape to enable typing and zooms out when you click outside the shape.

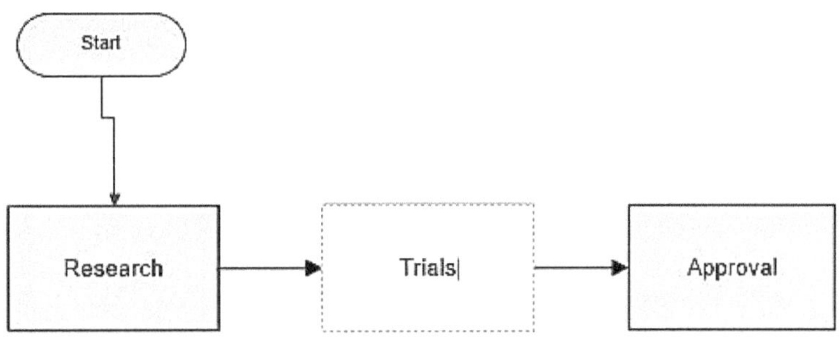

Inserting Text in a Document

To insert a text in a document such as a heading for the chart, click the Text Box dropdown menu in the Insert tab on the Ribbon and select either horizontal or vertical text box.

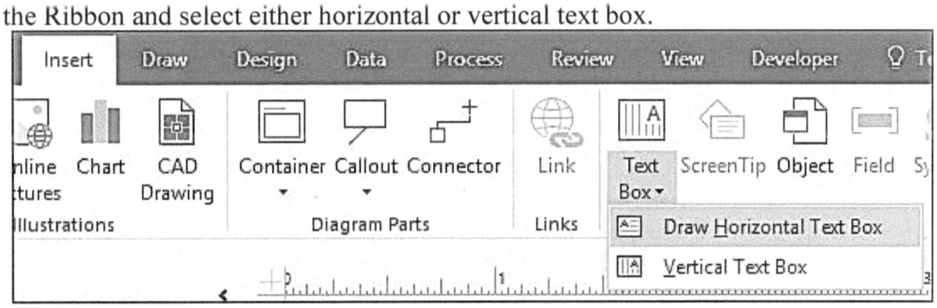

Then place the cursor on the document and draw a text box to start typing.

If you are familiar with Microsoft Word, you should be right at home in Visio with respect to formatting text. You can format titles and text within shapes. You can also use the Format Painter command to copy formatting and paste it into another shape or text box.

To format the text, select the text box containing the text or highlight the text itself. Then, choose from the options available in the Font and Paragraph sections of the Home tab.

You can change the font, size, color, and paragraph alignment. If you want to change the font styles in a shape, just double-click the shape to select the text within the shape and change the font styles as desired.

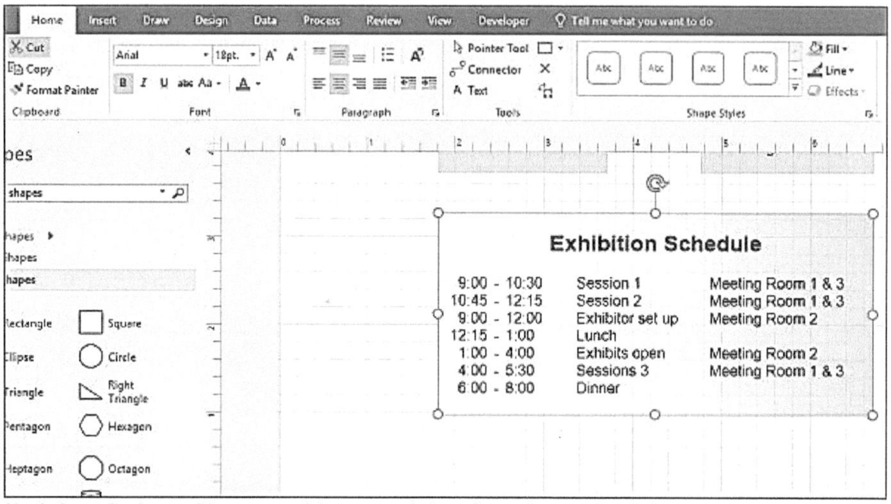

Here's a detailed description of how to add text and data in Microsoft Visio:

Text Boxes: Text is a primary element in any Visio diagram. To add text to a shape, select the shape, right-click, and choose "Add Text" or simply click on the shape and start typing. You can resize and reposition the text box as needed. Text boxes can be used to label shapes, provide descriptions, or add important information.

Shape Data: In addition to simple text labels, Visio allows you to associate data with shapes. This data can be in the form of custom properties or predefined fields. For example, in an organizational chart, you can associate each employee shape with data like name, title, department, and contact information. To add shape data, select a shape, right-click, and choose "Shape Data." You can then define data fields and enter relevant information.

Data Graphics: Data graphics are a powerful feature in Visio for visualizing shape data. They allow you to display shape data as text, data bars, color by value, or icons within the shape. To apply data graphics, go to the "Data" tab, select the shape, and choose a data graphic. You can customize the data graphic's appearance to match your specific needs.

Callouts: Callouts are text labels that are linked to shapes to provide additional information. They are especially useful in diagrams with complex relationships or when you want to avoid cluttering the main diagram. To add a callout, select the "Callout" tool, click the shape you want to link it to, and start typing your text. Callouts can be moved and connected to the appropriate shape.

Text Formatting: Visio provides various options for formatting text, including font style, size, color, and alignment. You can use these formatting tools to make your text more visually appealing and easier to read. Additionally, you can apply themes and styles to maintain consistency across your diagram.

Data Linking: For more advanced diagrams, Visio supports data linking to external data sources like Excel, Access, or SharePoint. This feature allows you to create dynamic diagrams that update automatically when data changes. To link data, go to the "Data" tab, choose "Link Data to Shapes," and follow the steps in the Data Selector wizard.

Review and Proofreading: Before finalizing your diagram, it's essential to review and proofread the text and data. Check for spelling errors, ensure data accuracy, and verify that the text provides a clear and concise explanation of the shapes and their relationships.

In summary, adding text and data in Microsoft Visio is a versatile and critical aspect of creating effective visual representations. Whether you're designing simple flowcharts or complex network diagrams, text and data elements enhance the clarity and value of your diagrams. With the right tools and techniques, Visio enables you to create diagrams that are not only visually appealing but also rich in information and insights.

Exercise

Exercise 1 – MCQ

Q 1. What is the primary purpose of Microsoft Visio?

a) Video editing

b) Graphic design

c) Document management

d) Data analysis
Q 2. Which tool in Microsoft Visio is used for adding text and data to shapes?
a) Data Graphics
b) Callouts
c) Data Linking
d) Font Styler

Exercise 2 – True/ False

Q 1. Microsoft Visio is primarily a video editing software.
Q 2. Callouts in Microsoft Visio are used to add linked text labels to shapes.

Exercise 3 – Fill in the blanks

Q 1. Callouts are used to add linked _______________ labels to shapes.
Q 2. Microsoft Visio allows users to create dynamic diagrams that update automatically when data changes through the feature of _______________.

Exercise 4 – Match case

1. VSSX
2. VSDX
3. VSTX

A. Visio Template
B. Visio Stencil
C. Visio Drawing

Exercise 5 – One word answer

Q 1. What is the primary purpose of Microsoft Visio?
Q 2. What is used in Visio to display shape data as text, data bars, and icons?

Exercise 6 – Small answer

Q 1. What is the significance of Data Graphics in Visio?
Q 2. How does Data Linking in Visio enhance diagram flexibility?

Exercise 7 – Long answer

Q 1. Can you explain the primary purpose of Microsoft Visio and how it benefits users in creating diagrams?
Q 2. How does the feature of Data Linking in Microsoft Visio work, and what are its practical applications?

Answers

Exercise 1 – MCQ

Ans: 1b, 2 b

Exercise 2 – True/ False

Ans: 1 False, 2 True

Exercise 3 – Fill in the blanks

Ans: 1 text, 2 text

Exercise 4 – Match case

Ans: 1 B, 2 C, 3 A

Exercise 5 – One word answer

Ans: 1 Diagramming, 2 Data Graphics

Chapter 11 - **Microsoft Yammer**

Microsoft Yammer is a powerful enterprise social networking platform designed to facilitate communication and collaboration within organizations. Yammer provides a private, secure space where employees can connect, share information, and engage in conversations, similar to popular social media platforms, but within a corporate context.
Unlike traditional email communication, which can often lead to information silos and overloaded inboxes, Yammer offers a dynamic and transparent way for employees to interact, bridging the gap between departments, locations, and hierarchies. It's a hub for open communication, knowledge sharing, and networking, fostering a more connected and engaged workplace.
Yammer's core features include posting updates, sharing files, liking and commenting on posts, and joining groups and communities. These features create a vibrant online environment that encourages employees to connect, collaborate, and stay informed. Yammer is not just a communication tool; it's a platform that can transform the way your organization works.

Key Features and Benefits

Let's delve into some of the key features and benefits that Microsoft Yammer brings to the table:

Open and Transparent Communication: Yammer breaks down communication barriers by providing a platform where employees can openly communicate, share ideas, and discuss matters without the restrictions of email. It encourages open dialogue and fosters transparency within the organization.

Ease of Collaboration: Yammer enables users to share documents, files, and ideas with colleagues effortlessly. Collaborative features such as file sharing and co-authoring make working on projects as a team more efficient.

Community Building: Yammer allows the creation of groups, making it easy for like-minded individuals or project teams to come together and collaborate. Communities can be formed around projects, departments, or common interests, fostering a sense of belonging and shared objectives.

Real-time Updates: The platform provides a live feed where users can see real-time updates from colleagues, groups, and topics they follow. This feature ensures that you are always in the loop and can respond promptly to important developments.

Enhanced Employee Engagement: By creating a space where employees can voice their thoughts and ideas, Yammer contributes to improved employee engagement. It empowers individuals to have their voices heard and recognized, leading to a more involved and satisfied workforce.

Mobile Accessibility: Yammer offers mobile apps for iOS and Android devices, ensuring that you can stay connected and participate in discussions even when you're on the go.

Integration with Microsoft 365: Yammer integrates seamlessly with other Microsoft 365 applications like SharePoint and Teams, providing a holistic collaboration experience and a unified digital workplace.

Improved Knowledge Sharing: The platform serves as a repository of knowledge, allowing users to search for information, discover experts, and share best practices, which can be especially valuable for onboarding new employees and solving common challenges.

In summary, Microsoft Yammer is a versatile and valuable tool for modern organizations. It promotes communication, collaboration, and knowledge sharing, ultimately leading to enhanced productivity, innovation, and employee satisfaction. It's an integral part of the modern digital workplace, connecting employees and breaking down communication barriers in a secure and controlled environment.

11.1 Getting Started with Yammer

Creating a Yammer Account

Creating a Yammer account is the first step to enter the world of enterprise social networking and collaboration. Here's a step-by-step guide on how to do it:

Access the Yammer Website: To create a Yammer account, navigate to the Yammer website (www.yammer.com) using your web browser.

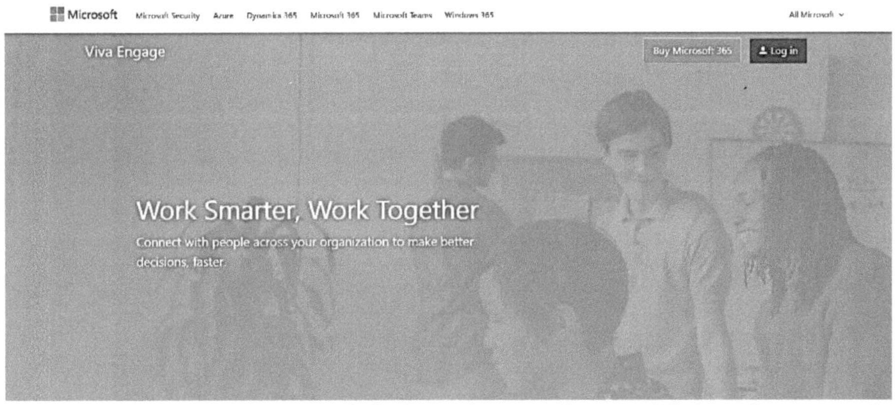

Sign Up: On the Yammer homepage, you'll find a "Sign Up" button. Click on it to start the registration process.

Use Your Work Email: Yammer is designed for business use. Sign up using your work email address to ensure that you are connected to your organization's network.

Account Information: Enter your work email address, your first and last name, and choose a strong password. Make sure to follow any password requirements set by your organization for security.

Join Your Network: After providing your account information, you may be prompted to join your organization's network. Click "Join" or "Sign Up" to complete the process.

Confirmation Email: You'll receive a confirmation email at the provided work email address. Open it and click on the confirmation link to verify your account.

Start Exploring: Once your account is confirmed, you can start exploring Yammer and connecting with colleagues.

Navigating the Yammer Interface

After creating your Yammer account, it's important to understand the interface to make the most of this collaborative platform:

Home Feed: The home feed is your central dashboard in Yammer. It displays posts and updates from colleagues, groups, and topics you follow. You can like, comment, or share posts from here.

Notifications: The notifications bell icon keeps you updated on mentions, likes, comments, and other activities related to your posts and interactions.

Messages: Clicking on the envelope icon takes you to your private messages, where you can engage in one-on-one or group chats with colleagues.

Groups: Explore and join groups relevant to your projects or interests. Groups provide spaces for focused discussions and collaboration.

Discover: The discover feature helps you find and connect with colleagues and content. It's a great way to expand your network within your organization.

Search: Use the search bar to look for specific posts, colleagues, or topics. It's a powerful tool to quickly find information and experts within your organization.

Profile: Click on your profile picture to access your profile. Here, you can edit your profile information, including your profile picture, job title, and contact details.

Setting Up Your Profile

A complete and well-maintained Yammer profile helps colleagues and peers identify and connect with you. Here's how to set up your profile:

Profile Picture: Add a professional profile picture. This helps others recognize you and promotes a sense of familiarity within the network.

Contact Information: Update your contact information, including your job title, department, and work location. Accurate information makes it easier for colleagues to find and connect with you.

Bio and Skills: Write a brief bio that introduces yourself and your expertise. Include your skills to make it easier for others to discover your areas of knowledge.

Contact Details: Ensure your contact details are up-to-date. This includes your email address, phone number, and any other contact information your colleagues might need.

Privacy Settings: Review and adjust your privacy settings to control who can see your profile and contact you. Yammer allows you to customize your privacy preferences.

Notifications: Set your notification preferences to receive updates and alerts relevant to your role and responsibilities.

A well-configured profile not only helps colleagues find and connect with you but also enhances your presence within the organization's Yammer network. It's an essential step to becoming an active and engaged participant in your enterprise's social network.

11.2 Joining and Creating Yammer Networks

Joining Existing Yammer Networks

Yammer networks are virtual spaces where communication and collaboration happen. These networks are often organized by organizations, departments, or teams. Joining existing Yammer networks can be a great way to connect with colleagues and stay informed. Here's how to do it:

Login to Your Yammer Account: To join an existing Yammer network, you need to be logged into your Yammer account. If you're not already logged in, do so using your work email and password.

Navigate to the Network Directory: Once logged in, look for the "Networks" tab or a similar option on your Yammer dashboard. This will take you to the network directory.

Search for Networks: In the network directory, you can search for specific networks by name, keywords, or by exploring categories. If you know the name of the network you want to join, you can search for it directly.

Request to Join: When you find a network you want to join, click on it to access the network's page. Here, you'll typically find an option to "Request to Join." Click on it, and your request will be sent to the network's administrators.

Approval and Access: Network administrators will review your request. Once approved, you'll gain access to the network. You'll start seeing posts, updates, and conversations from members of that network on your Yammer feed.

Engage and Connect: After joining a network, engage with the members and start connecting with colleagues who share your interests or work on similar projects. Participate in group discussions, share your insights, and collaborate with fellow network members.

Creating Your Own Yammer Network

Creating your own Yammer network can be beneficial when you want to foster communication and collaboration around a specific project, department, or interest group. Here's how to create a new Yammer network:

Log In and Access Networks: Begin by logging into your Yammer account. On the Yammer dashboard, look for the "Networks" tab or a similar option.

Create a New Network: In the networks section, you should find an option to "Create a Network" or "Start a New Network." Click on this option to begin the network creation process.

Network Details: You'll be prompted to provide details about your new network. This includes the network's name, description, and privacy settings. You can choose to make it a public network, where anyone in your organization can join, or a private network, where you invite specific members.

Admins and Members: You can specify network administrators who will have management privileges. These administrators can moderate the network and control its settings.

Invite Members: If your network is private, you'll need to invite members to join. You can do this by entering their email addresses or selecting colleagues from your Yammer contacts.

Create and Customize: Once your network is created, you can customize it with a profile picture, cover photo, and additional details to make it appealing and relevant to potential members.

Start Engaging: Start posting updates, sharing files, and engaging with members in your newly created network. Encourage discussions, and facilitate collaboration around the network's theme or purpose.

Creating a Yammer network gives you control over the communication and collaboration space, making it a valuable tool for project management, departmental discussions, or special interest groups. It's a great way to tailor the Yammer experience to your organization's specific needs.

11.3 Yammer Groups and Conversations

Understanding Yammer Groups

Yammer groups are the building blocks of collaboration within the platform. They provide dedicated spaces for focused discussions, document sharing, and collaboration around specific topics, projects, or teams.

Understanding Yammer groups is key to efficient communication and collaboration. Here's what you need to know:

- **Purpose of Groups**: Yammer groups serve as virtual meeting rooms where members with common interests or roles can interact, share information, and collaborate. They are ideal for departments, project teams, or any group that wants to stay connected and aligned.
- **Privacy Options**: You can create public or private groups. Public groups are open to anyone in your organization, while private groups require an invitation to join. This flexibility allows you to choose the level of access and participation that suits your group's purpose.
- **Group Feed**: Each group has its own feed where members can post updates, share files, and engage in discussions specific to the group's focus. This helps keep conversations organized and relevant.
- **Group Members**: Group members are colleagues who join the group to participate in discussions. Members can also be assigned different roles, such as group administrators, who manage group settings.
- **Discovering Groups**: You can find and join groups that interest you by exploring the Groups section on Yammer or by searching for specific groups. Joining relevant groups is a great way to stay informed and collaborate.

Creating and Managing Groups

Creating and managing Yammer groups is a straightforward process. Here's how you can create and manage your own groups:

Creating a Group:

- **Login to Yammer**: Start by logging into your Yammer account.
- **Access Groups**: Click on the "Groups" section on your Yammer dashboard.
- **Create a Group**: Look for an option to "Create a Group" or a similar option. Click on it.
- **Group Details**: Fill in the necessary details, including the group name, description, privacy settings (public or private), and the members you want to invite to the group.
- **Customize**: You can customize the group by adding a profile picture and cover photo, as well as setting additional details like group tags.
- **Create**: Once you've entered all the necessary information, click "Create." Your group is now ready for use.

Managing a Group:

- **Administer Roles**: As the group creator or administrator, you can manage roles, assign other members as administrators, and moderate discussions within the group.
- **Engagement**: Encourage group members to post updates, share relevant documents, and participate in discussions. The more active the group, the more valuable it becomes.
- **Group Settings**: You can access group settings to change the group's description, privacy settings, and other details at any time.
- **Managing Members**: You have control over group membership. You can invite new members or remove members as needed.

Participating in Group Conversations

Participating in group conversations in Yammer is a fundamental part of collaboration. Here's how to engage effectively:

- **Posting Updates**: Share updates, thoughts, questions, or relevant news within the group. This keeps the group informed and fosters discussions.
- **Liking and Commenting**: Show your engagement by liking posts and adding comments to contribute to ongoing discussions.
- **Sharing Files**: Upload and share documents, files, or links that are relevant to the group's topic or project.
- **@Mentions**: Use the "@" symbol to mention specific group members or tag them in posts. This notifies them and ensures they see your message.
- **Starting Discussions**: Initiate discussions on topics that are important to the group. This can be a question, a project update, or a piece of news.
- **Being Respectful**: Maintain a professional and respectful tone in all group interactions. Remember that group conversations are a part of your organization's professional environment.

Effective participation in group conversations not only keeps everyone informed but also contributes to productive collaboration and knowledge sharing within your organization. It's an essential aspect of using Yammer to its full potential.

Exercise

Exercise 1 – MCQ

Q 1. What is the primary purpose of Microsoft Yammer?
a. Video conferencing
b. social networking for organizations
c. Cloud storage and file sharing
d. Web-based email service

Q 2. How does Yammer enhance communication within organizations?
a. Through real-time document collaboration
b. By providing a platform for employees to connect and share updates
c. By offering video streaming services
d. Through advanced search capabilities

Exercise 2 – True/ False

Q 1. Microsoft Yammer is primarily focused on facilitating social networking and communication within organizations.

Q 2. Microsoft Yammer is primarily focused on facilitating social networking and communication within organizations.

Exercise 3 – Fill in the blanks

Q 1. Microsoft Yammer is a platform for ____________ communication and collaboration within organizations.

Q 2. Yammer provides a space for employees to post updates, ask questions, and engage in ____________ discussions.

Exercise 4 – Match case

1. Social Networking
2. Yammer Integration
3. Group Discussions
4. Cloud Storage

(A) Real-time document collaboration
(B) Facilitating communication within organizations
(C) Integration with Microsoft Office
(D) Sharing and updating posts

Exercise 5 – One word answer

Q 1. What type of discussions and updates are commonly found on Microsoft Yammer?

Q 2. What is one of the key benefits of using Yammer within organizations?

Exercise 6 – Small answer

Q 1. Explain how Microsoft Yammer enhances communication within organizations.

Q 2. How does Yammer's integration with Microsoft Office enhance productivity for users?

Exercise 7 – Long answer

Q 1. How does Microsoft Yammer promote internal communication and collaboration within organizations, and what are some of the key features that contribute to its effectiveness in fostering a sense of community among employees?

Q 2. How does Microsoft Yammer address data privacy and security concerns, ensuring that sensitive information shared within the platform is protected, and what measures are in place to guarantee compliance with data protection regulations?

Answers

Exercise 1 – MCQ

Ans: 1 b, 2 b

Exercise 2 – True/ False

Ans: 1 True, 2 False

Exercise 3 – Fill in the blanks

Ans: 1 Social, 2 Match Case

Exercise 4 – Match case

Ans: 1 B, 2 C, 3 D, 4 A

Exercise 5 – One word answer

Ans: 1 Group, 2 Communication

Chapter 12 - **Microsoft OneDrive**

Microsoft OneDrive is a versatile and powerful cloud-based file storage and synchronization service offered by Microsoft. It is designed to help individuals and organizations securely store, access, and share files and data from various devices with an internet connection. OneDrive is part of the Microsoft 365 suite of productivity tools, making it a seamless and integrated solution for users seeking a reliable way to manage and collaborate on their files.

Key features and characteristics of Microsoft OneDrive include:

Cloud-Based Storage: OneDrive provides users with the ability to store files, documents, photos, and other data in the cloud. This means that your files are stored on remote servers, ensuring accessibility from virtually anywhere with an internet connection.

Cross-Platform Compatibility: OneDrive is accessible across a wide range of platforms and devices, including Windows and Mac computers, iOS and Android smartphones and tablets, and via web browsers. This versatility ensures that users can access their files no matter what device they are using.

File Synchronization: OneDrive includes a synchronization feature that automatically keeps your files and folders up to date across all your connected devices. Changes made on one device are seamlessly mirrored on others.

Collaboration Tools: With OneDrive, you can easily share files and collaborate in real-time with colleagues or external partners. The service integrates with Microsoft 365 applications like Word, Excel, and PowerPoint, enabling collaborative editing and commenting.

Version History: OneDrive keeps a version history of your files, allowing you to recover previous versions or track changes over time. This is particularly valuable when working on collaborative projects.

Data Security: Microsoft places a strong emphasis on data security and compliance. OneDrive offers robust encryption, data loss prevention, and two-factor authentication to safeguard your files and ensure privacy and regulatory compliance.

Benefits of Using OneDrive

Utilizing Microsoft OneDrive brings a multitude of benefits to both individual users and organizations. Some of the primary advantages include:

Convenience and Accessibility: OneDrive provides the convenience of accessing your files from any device with internet access. This flexibility allows users to work on documents, view photos, or share files whether they are in the office, at home, or on the go.

Efficient Collaboration: OneDrive's integration with Microsoft 365 applications streamlines collaborative work. Users can co-author documents, leave comments, and work together on projects in real-time.

File Backup and Recovery: OneDrive offers automatic file backup and version history. This ensures that files are backed up and can be restored in case of accidental deletions or data loss.

Security and Compliance: Microsoft takes data security seriously, offering robust security features and compliance certifications. This makes OneDrive a trustworthy option for storing sensitive and regulated data.

Cost-Effective Storage: For Microsoft 365 subscribers, OneDrive offers ample cloud storage space, reducing the need for physical storage hardware and lowering storage costs.

Seamless Integration: OneDrive integrates seamlessly with Microsoft 365 applications like Word, Excel, PowerPoint, and Outlook. This integration enhances productivity and simplifies file management.

Personal and Professional Use: OneDrive caters to both personal and professional use cases. Individuals can use it to back up personal files, while businesses can take advantage of its collaboration features for team projects.

In summary, Microsoft OneDrive is a versatile cloud storage and collaboration solution that enhances productivity, accessibility, and security for users and organizations. Its integration with other Microsoft tools makes it a powerful choice for those looking to manage and collaborate on their files effectively.

12.1 Getting Started with OneDrive

Once you've downloaded OneDrive to your PC, you will see a cloud icon in the bottom right-hand corner of the status bar.

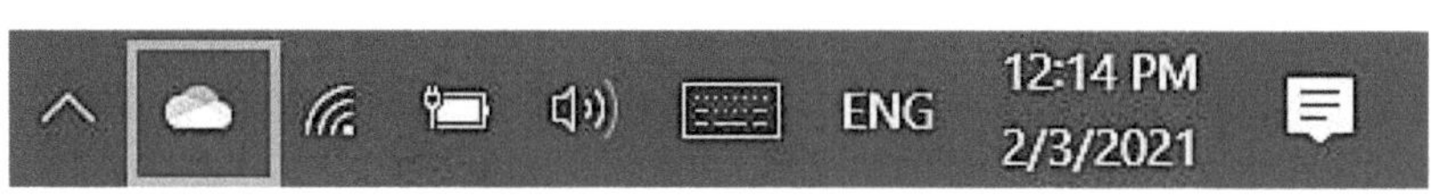

Click on the cloud icon.
The pop-up window will show you the files that have recently been synched.

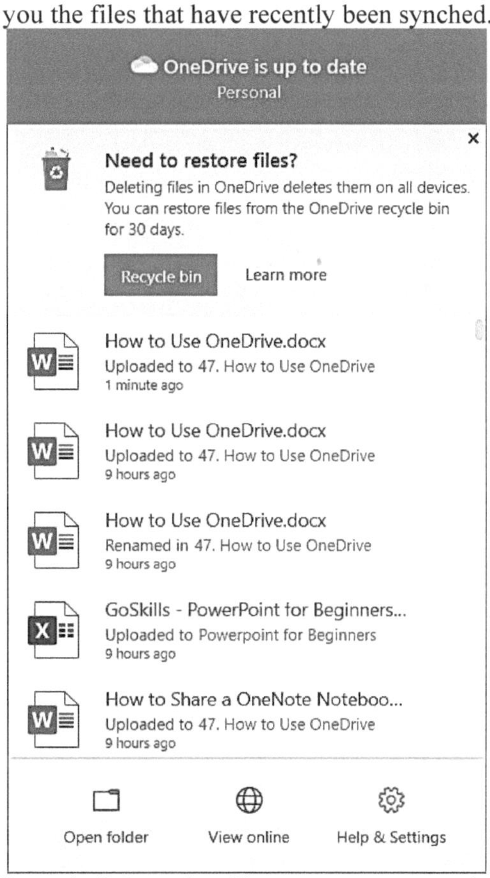

Hover over any file in the list and click on the ellipses to see more options.
From here, you can open the file, share the file with others, view the file online and see the version history. At the bottom, there are three actions: Open folder, View online, and Help and Settings.

Click Open folder
This will open File Explorer where you can see OneDrive and the folders and files in the cloud. This will look like regular files and folders on your PC with one small difference—the addition of a status column next to each file and folder.
The status column tells you the status of the file or folder.
A green circle with a tick: the file is synced and up to date on your PC and in the cloud.
Cloud icon: the file is only in the cloud. You can still open files only stored in the cloud through File Explorer. Just double-click to download.
Sync icon: the file is currently synching to the cloud.
Person icon: a person icon indicates the file has been shared.

Right-click on any file to see the contextual menu.
This menu contains many options. Essentially, things you can do with this file.
Let's explore some of the most important.

Navigating the OneDrive Interface

Once you've set up your OneDrive account and installed the app (if desired), it's important to familiarize yourself with the OneDrive interface. Here are some key elements:

Files and Folders: The primary interface of OneDrive displays your files and folders. You can organize them much like you would on your local device.

Navigation Bar: Use the navigation bar on the left to access various sections, including Files, Photos, Recent, Shared, and more.

Search: The search bar allows you to quickly find specific files or folders by searching for keywords or file names.

File Actions: You can select files to perform actions like deleting, moving, sharing, and downloading. These options are typically available in the top menu when you select one or more files.

Upload: Use the "Upload" button to add files or folders to your OneDrive storage from your local device.

Notifications: OneDrive may display notifications for file activity, sharing requests, or sync status.

Settings: Access your OneDrive settings by clicking on your profile picture or avatar. Here, you can manage account preferences, storage, and more.

12.2 Uploading and Managing Files

Uploading Files and Folders

Uploading files and folders to Microsoft OneDrive is a fundamental step in leveraging its cloud storage capabilities. Here's how you can easily upload your content:

Uploading Files:

Web Interface:

In your OneDrive interface on the web, click the "Upload" button.

Browse your computer to select the file you want to upload.

Click "Open" or "Upload" to add the file to your OneDrive.

Windows Explorer (PC) or Finder (Mac):

If you've installed the OneDrive app, you can simply drag and drop files from your local file system into the OneDrive folder on your device. This will automatically sync them to your cloud storage.

Mobile App (iOS/Android):

In the OneDrive app on your mobile device, tap the "+" or "Upload" button.

Select the file you want to upload from your device's storage.

Uploading Folders:

Web Interface:

On the web, click the "Upload" button and choose the option to upload a folder.

Select the folder from your computer to add it to your OneDrive.

Windows Explorer (PC) or Finder (Mac):

To upload a folder, simply drag and drop the entire folder into your OneDrive folder on your device.

Mobile App (iOS/Android):

In the OneDrive app, tap the "+" or "Upload" button.

Choose to upload a folder from your mobile device's storage.

Organizing Your OneDrive Files

Organizing your files in OneDrive helps you maintain a structured and efficient digital workspace. Here are some tips for effectively organizing your files:

Use Folders: Create folders to group related files. For instance, you can have separate folders for work documents, personal files, or specific projects.

Rename Files and Folders: Give your files and folders meaningful names to make them easy to identify. Avoid generic names like "Document1" or "Folder2."

Add Descriptions: You can add descriptions to your files and folders to provide context and information for yourself or collaborators.

Move and Rearrange: Use drag-and-drop functionality to move files and folders within your OneDrive, or within the OneDrive app on your device.

Star or Pin Important Files: Most OneDrive interfaces allow you to star or pin important files to keep them easily accessible.

Color Coding: Some versions of OneDrive let you color-code files or folders for quick visual identification.

Tags and Metadata: Use tags or metadata to categorize and classify your files.

File Versioning and Recovery

OneDrive offers robust file versioning and recovery features that are invaluable when working with documents and files. Here's how to manage file versions and recover files:

Version History: OneDrive automatically keeps a version history of your files. To access it, right-click on a file and choose "Version history." You can review previous versions and restore or download them.

Recover Deleted Items: If you accidentally delete a file, it's not lost forever. OneDrive retains deleted items in a "Recycle Bin" for a specified period (typically 30 days). You can restore files from the Recycle Bin or permanently delete them.

File Recovery: OneDrive provides a file recovery feature that allows you to recover files that have been deleted or become corrupted, even beyond the Recycle Bin period. This feature is particularly useful for restoring important files.

File Restore: This feature allows you to revert your entire OneDrive to a previous point in time, effectively rolling back changes if you encounter data loss or data corruption.

12.3 Sharing and Collaboration

Sharing Files and Folders

One of the key strengths of Microsoft OneDrive is its ability to facilitate easy sharing and collaboration on files and folders. Here's how to share files and folders with others:

Sharing Files:

Web Interface:

In your OneDrive interface on the web, select the file you want to share.

Click the "Share" button or right-click the file and choose "Share."

Enter the email addresses of the people you want to share the file with.

Set permissions (view only or edit) and optionally add a message.

Click "Send" to share the file.

Windows Explorer (PC) or Finder (Mac):

If you're using the OneDrive app, right-click the file you want to share.

Choose the "Share" option from the context menu.

Follow the on-screen prompts to share the file.

Mobile App (iOS/Android):

In the OneDrive app, select the file you want to share.

Tap the "Share" button and follow the prompts to share the file.

Sharing Folders:

Web Interface:

In OneDrive on the web, select the folder you want to share.

Click the "Share" button or right-click the folder and choose "Share."

Follow the same steps as for sharing files to invite collaborators and set permissions.

Windows Explorer (PC) or Finder (Mac):

To share a folder, right-click it and choose the "Share" option. Follow the on-screen prompts.

Mobile App (iOS/Android):

In the OneDrive app, select the folder you want to share.

Tap the "Share" button and follow the prompts to share the folder.

Collaborative Editing with Office Online

OneDrive seamlessly integrates with Microsoft Office Online, allowing you to collaborate in real time on documents, spreadsheets, and presentations. Here's how to start collaborative editing:

Web Interface:

Open a document in OneDrive using the web interface.

Click "Edit" or "Open in [Office App]" to launch the Office Online version (e.g., Word Online, Excel Online, PowerPoint Online).

Co-Authoring:

Multiple users can work on the same document simultaneously. Edits are instantly visible to all collaborators in real time.

Comment and Chat: Use the commenting and chat features to communicate with collaborators directly within the document.

Save Automatically: Changes are saved automatically as you work, ensuring that you and your collaborators always have the latest version of the document.

Real-time Co-Authoring

Real-time co-authoring in OneDrive allows multiple users to edit documents together at the same time. Here's how to make the most of this feature:

Web Interface:

Open a document in OneDrive on the web.

Click "Edit" to open the document in Office Online.

Collaborate in Real Time:

Collaborators can join the document in Office Online. Changes made by one user are immediately visible to others.

Track Changes: You can track changes and see who is currently editing the document by checking user icons or color-coded cursors.

Chat and Comment: Use the built-in chat and comment features to communicate and provide feedback while co-authoring.

Exercise

Exercise 1 – MCQ

Q 1. What is the primary purpose of Microsoft OneDrive?

a. Social Media Platform

b. Web Search Engine

c. Cloud Storage and File Sharing

d. Video Streaming Service

Q 2. What is the benefit of using OneDrive for document collaboration within Microsoft Office applications?

a. Real-time language translation

b. Screen sharing

c. Co-authoring and simultaneous editing

d. Video calling

Exercise 2 – True/ False

Q 1. True or False: OneDrive is a cloud storage service that allows users to store and access files from anywhere with an internet connection.

Q 2. True or False: OneDrive is a standalone application and is not integrated with other Microsoft products like Microsoft Office.

Exercise 3 – Fill in the blanks

Q 1. Microsoft OneDrive provides users with _______ storage space to store and manage their files and documents.

Q 2. OneDrive's integration with Microsoft Office enables real-time ___________ and collaboration on documents.

Exercise 4 – Match case

1. Cloud Storage
2. OneDrive Integration
3. Co-authoring
4. Web-Based Access

(A) Real-time document collaboration

(B) Storing and accessing files online

(C) Integration with Microsoft Office

(D) Accessing files from any device

Exercise 5 – One word answer

Q 1. What type of files and documents can you store in Microsoft OneDrive?

Q 2. What is the primary benefit of using OneDrive for document collaboration within Microsoft Office applications?

Exercise 6 – Small answer

Q 1. Explain how OneDrive's integration with Microsoft Office enhances document collaboration.

Q 2. How does OneDrive's web-based access feature make it convenient for users to access their files?

Exercise 7 – Long answer

Q 1. How does Microsoft OneDrive support the concept of remote work and enhance productivity for individuals and teams, especially in a world where flexibility and collaboration are increasingly important?

Q 2. How does OneDrive contribute to data backup and recovery, ensuring that critical files and documents are safeguarded from data loss and accidental deletions, and what strategies does it employ to maintain data integrity and availability for users?

Answers

Exercise 1 – MCQ

Ans: 1 c, 2 c

Exercise 2 – True/ False

Ans: 1 True, 2 False

Exercise 3 – Fill in the blanks

Ans: 1 Cloud, 2 Co-authoring

Exercise 4 – Match case

Ans: 1 B, 2 C, 3 A, 4 D

Exercise 5 – One word answer

Ans: 1 Files, 2 Collaboration

Chapter 13 - **Microsoft Skype**

Microsoft Skype, often simply referred to as Skype, is a powerful and popular communication platform that enables users to connect with others through voice and video calls, instant messaging, and collaborative features. Skype has become a staple in modern communication, bridging geographical gaps and allowing individuals and businesses to stay connected worldwide.

Key features of Microsoft Skype include:

Voice and Video Calls: Skype allows users to make voice and video calls over the internet, providing an excellent way to communicate in real time with friends, family, and colleagues, regardless of their location.

Instant Messaging: In addition to calls, Skype offers instant messaging capabilities. Users can send text messages, images, videos, and files to one another, making it a versatile communication tool.

Group Calls: Skype supports group voice and video calls, making it ideal for conferences, virtual meetings, and connecting with multiple people simultaneously.

Skype-to-Phone Calls: Skype allows users to call landlines and mobile phones from their computer or mobile device using Skype Credits or a subscription.

Screen Sharing: The screen sharing feature enables users to share their screen with others during a call, making it an invaluable tool for collaboration and technical support.

Skype for Business: Skype for Business is a business-oriented version of Skype that integrates with Microsoft 365 (formerly Office 365). It offers advanced features for professional communication and collaboration.

Benefits and Features

Microsoft Skype offers numerous benefits and features that make it an essential communication tool in today's digital age:

Global Connectivity: Skype transcends geographical boundaries, enabling individuals and businesses to connect with anyone worldwide, reducing the limitations of physical distance.

Cost-Effective: Skype offers a cost-effective way to make international and long-distance calls, especially with Skype-to-Phone calling options.

Real-Time Communication: Skype provides instant communication through voice and video calls, ensuring that messages and information are conveyed in real time.

Instant Messaging: The instant messaging feature allows users to exchange text messages, share files, images, and videos, making it versatile for both personal and professional use.

Collaboration: Skype's features, including group calls, screen sharing, and Skype for Business, enhance collaboration and teamwork among users.

Accessibility: Skype is available on various platforms, including Windows, Mac, iOS, Android, and the web, ensuring accessibility from different devices.

Security and Privacy: Microsoft places a strong emphasis on security, encryption, and user privacy, making Skype a safe platform for communication.

13.1 Getting Started with Skype

Setting Up Your Skype Account

Setting up your Skype account is a straightforward process that allows you to begin using this powerful communication platform. Follow these steps to get started:

Visit the Skype Website:

Open your web browser and go to the official Skype website at www.skype.com.

Click "Sign In":

In the upper-right corner of the Skype website, you will see a "Sign In" button. Click on it.

Create an Account:

If you don't have a Skype account, click on "Create one!" to start the account creation process.

Fill in Your Details:

You will be asked to provide your phone number or email address, your first and last name, and a password. Follow the on-screen instructions to fill in these details.

Verify Your Identity:

Skype may ask you to verify your identity by entering a code sent to your email or phone number.

Choose a Profile Picture:

After verification, you can add a profile picture to personalize your Skype account.

Start Using Skype:

Once your account is set up, you can start using Skype to make calls, send messages, and more.

Downloading and Installing Skype

Step 1: Visit the official website of Skype using any web browser like Google Chrome, Microsoft Edge, etc.

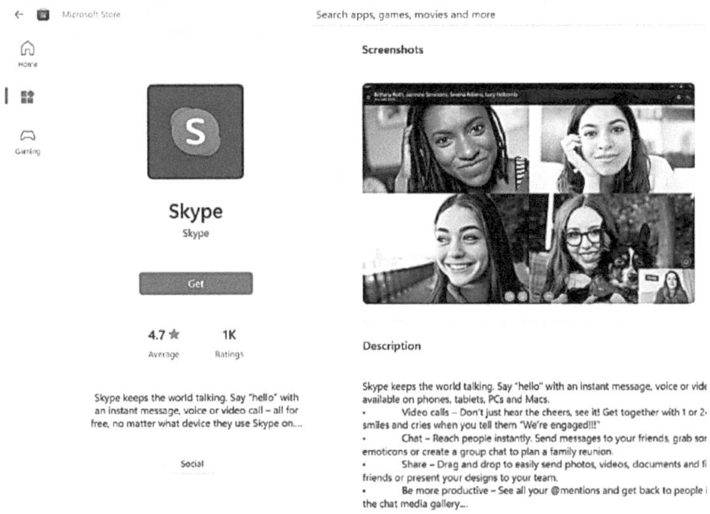

Step 2: Press the **"INSTALL"** button on the website to start the download of the Skype Application.

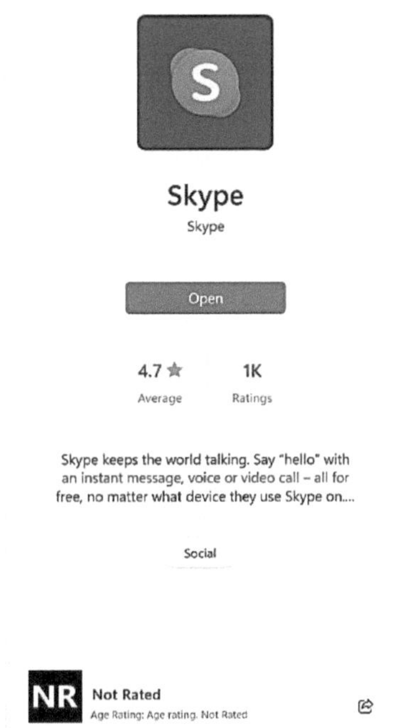

e

Step 3: It will then automatically re-direct you to the Windows Store App by Microsoft for the Windows device and the download will start in the background.

Step 4: After the download gets finished, the Skype app will get installed within 2-3 minutes and then show up on the all-programs list of the Start menu.

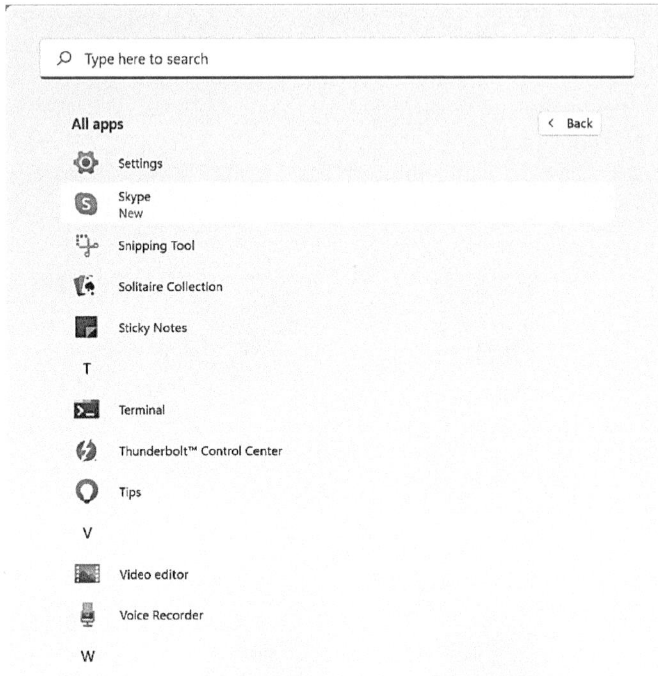

Step 5: Click on the Skype app to open it.

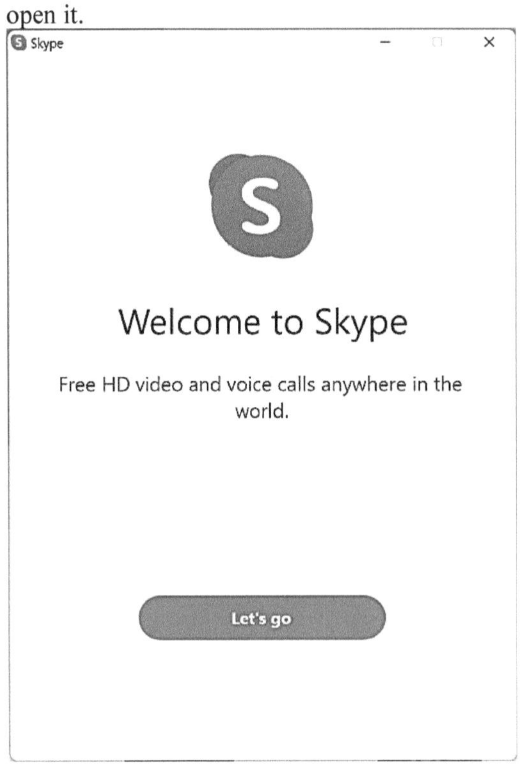

Step 6: After the Skype app opens up, it will show you a login button on the home page, where you have to use your login credentials (username and password) to login into your Microsoft account. If you don't have an existing account, then you have to create a new account.

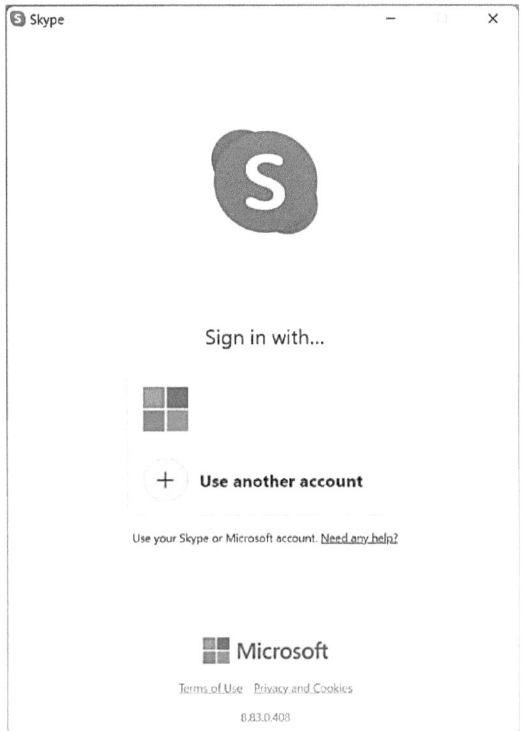

Step 7: Now, the Skype application will ask you to test the audio and video of your device through which your device is getting connected. It tests whether your microphone and camera are working properly or not.

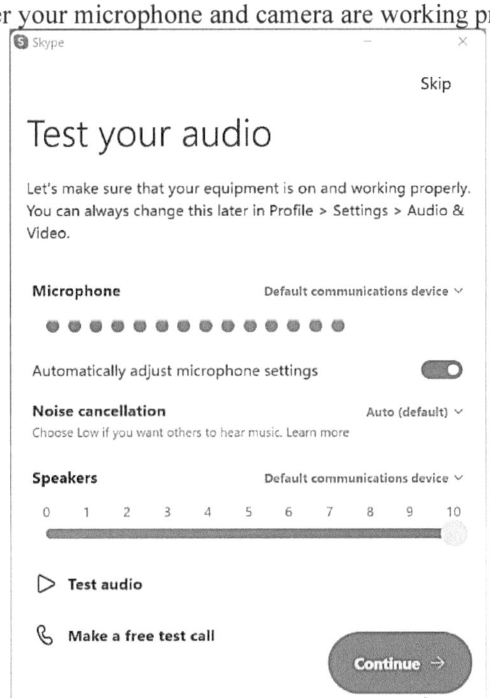

Step 8: Now, the home page of the Skype application looks like the following. To start a new Skype meeting click on the **Meet Now** button to start an instant meeting with other members.

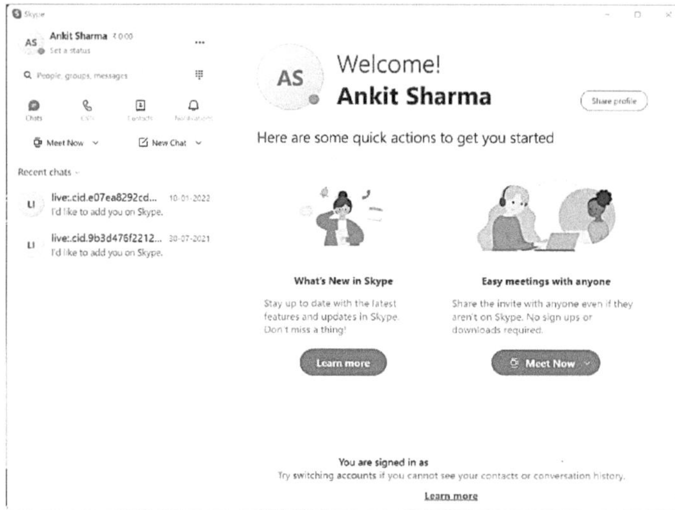

Navigating the Skype Interface

Once you've set up your Skype account and installed the app, it's essential to familiarize yourself with the Skype interface. Here are some key elements:

Contacts: In the "Contacts" section, you can find and add friends, family, or colleagues to your Skype contact list.

Chats: "Chats" display your chat history and allow you to send instant messages to your contacts.

Calls: In the "Calls" section, you can make voice and video calls, view your call history, and manage your call settings.

Meet Now: "Meet Now" lets you set up and join video meetings with just one click.

Notifications: Skype provides notifications for new messages, missed calls, and other activities.

Settings: Access your Skype settings by clicking on your profile picture or avatar. Here, you can manage your account preferences, privacy settings, and more.

Dial Pad: If you're using Skype for calling landlines or mobile phones, you'll find a dial pad for entering numbers.

13.2 Making and Receiving Calls

Making Voice and Video Calls

Skype provides a versatile platform for making voice and video calls, whether you're connecting with friends, family, or colleagues. Here's how to make voice and video calls using Skype:

Making Voice Calls:

Open Skype: Launch the Skype app on your computer or mobile device.

Sign In: Sign in to your Skype account if you're not already signed in.

Locate Your Contacts: Find the contact you want to call in your contact list. If they are not in your contacts, you can search for them using their Skype username, email address, or phone number.

Select the Contact: Click or tap on the contact's name to open a chat window.

Call Icon: In the chat window, click the phone icon to initiate a voice call.

Making Video Calls:

Open Skype: Launch the Skype app.

Sign In: Sign in to your Skype account.

Locate Your Contacts: Find the contact you want to video call.

Select the Contact: Click or tap on the contact's name to open a chat window.

Video Call Icon: In the chat window, click the video camera icon to initiate a video call.

Managing Contacts and Call History

Skype allows you to manage your contacts and access your call history easily. Here's how:

Managing Contacts:

Add Contacts:

Click "Contacts" in the Skype interface.

Select "Add Contact" and enter the Skype username, email address, or phone number of the person you want to add.

View Contacts:

Your contact list displays all your saved contacts. Click on a contact to initiate calls or send messages.

Organize Contacts:

You can create groups or categories for your contacts to keep them organized.

Call History:

View Call History:

Click on "Calls" in the Skype interface to access your call history. This shows a list of your recent calls.

Details and Actions:

For each call in the history, you can click on it to view details, such as the date and duration of the call, and you can take actions like calling back or sending a message.

Clear Call History:

If you want to clear your call history, you can do so from the call history section.

Skype Calling Features

Skype offers various features that enhance your calling experience. Here are some of the features you can use:

Speaker and Microphone: Skype allows you to switch between different audio devices (e.g., speakers, headphones, microphones) in the settings.

Mute and Unmute: During calls, you can mute and unmute your microphone to control your audio input.

Video On and Off: You can enable or disable your video camera during video calls.

Screen Sharing: Skype offers screen sharing, allowing you to share your screen with others during a call.

Add Participants: In group calls, you can add more participants to the call.

Recording Calls: Skype allows you to record voice and video calls, which can be valuable for keeping records of important conversations.

Call Quality: Skype offers settings to adjust the call quality based on your internet connection.

Call Transfer: In some versions of Skype, you can transfer calls to other contacts or devices.

Call Forwarding: Skype provides call forwarding options for those moments when you can't answer calls.

13.3 Messaging and Chat

Sending Instant Messages

Skype offers a convenient instant messaging feature that allows you to send text messages, images, videos, and files to your contacts in real time. Here's how to send instant messages using Skype:

Open Skype: Launch the Skype app on your computer or mobile device.

Sign In: Sign in to your Skype account if you're not already signed in.

Select a Contact: Locate the contact you want to message in your contact list. If the contact is not in your list, you can search for them using their Skype username, email address, or phone number.

Start a Chat: Click or tap on the contact's name to open a chat window.

Type Your Message: In the chat window, type your message into the text field at the bottom of the screen.

Send the Message: Hit the "Send" button (usually a paper airplane icon) or press "Enter" on your keyboard to send the message.

Managing Conversations and Chats

Managing your conversations and chats in Skype helps you stay organized and easily retrieve messages. Here are some key actions:

View Chat History: Skype automatically stores your chat history. You can view your previous conversations by clicking on the contact's name in your contact list.

Search Messages: Use the search feature to find specific messages or conversations quickly. Simply enter a keyword or phrase in the search bar.

Delete Messages: If you want to remove a specific message, right-click on the message and select "Remove Message" or a similar option.

Mark as Unread: To remember to respond to a message later, mark it as unread. Right-click on the message and choose "Mark as Unread."

Hide Conversations: You can archive or hide conversations you no longer need to keep the chat list organized.

Group Chats and Conversations

Skype allows you to have group chats, which are excellent for communicating with multiple people simultaneously. Here's how to create and manage group chats:

Create a Group Chat:

Click or tap on the "New Chat" button or icon.

Select "New Group Chat" and add the participants you want to include in the group chat.

Give your group chat a name and set a group photo if desired.

Start sending messages to the group.

Adding Participants to a Group Chat:

In an existing group chat, you can add more participants by clicking or tapping on the group name or photo.

Select "Add participants" and choose the contacts you want to include.

Leaving a Group Chat:

If you wish to leave a group chat, select the group and click "Leave" or "End Chat" to remove yourself from the conversation.

Group Chat Settings:

You can manage group chat settings, such as notifications and participant permissions, by accessing the group chat's settings or information.

Exercise

Exercise 1 – MCQ

Q 1. What is Microsoft Skype primarily used for?
a. Video Game Development
b. Project Management
c. Video Conferencing and Instant Messaging
d. Music Production

Q 2. Which feature in Skype allows users to see and communicate with each other through live video and audio?
a. Skype Chat
b. Skype Translator
c. Skype Meeting
d. Skype Video Call

Exercise 2 – True/ False

Q 1. Skype offers real-time language translation for voice and video calls.

Q 2. Skype can only be used on computers and laptops, and it's not available on mobile devices.

Exercise 3 – Fill in the blanks

Q 1. Microsoft Skype allows users to send instant ____________ to their contacts.

Q 2. Skype for Business provides a platform for online ____________ and collaboration within organizations.

Exercise 4 – Match case

1. Skype Chat
2. Skype Translator
3. Skype Meeting
4. Skype Video Call

(A) Online meetings and collaboration
(B) Live video and audio communication
(C) Real-time language translation
(D) Text-based instant messaging

Exercise 5 – One word answer

Q 1. What is the primary purpose of Skype for Business within organizations?

Q 2. What feature in Skype allows users to exchange text-based messages in real-time?

Exercise 6 – Small answer

Q 1. Explain how Skype Translator enhances communication in video calls.

Q 2. How does Skype for Business support online meetings and collaboration within organizations?

Exercise 7 – Long answer

Q 1. Can you provide an in-depth overview of Microsoft Skype, its key features, and its impact on communication and collaboration in today's digital world?

Q 2. How does Microsoft Skype's security measures and data protection contribute to user privacy and confidentiality during voice and video calls, and what steps are taken to ensure secure communication on the platform?

Answers

Exercise 1 – MCQ

Ans: 1 c, 2 d

Exercise 2 – True/ False

Ans: 1 True, 2 False

Exercise 3 – Fill in the blanks

Ans: 1 Messages, 2 Meetings

Exercise 4 – Match case

Ans: 1 D, 2 C, 3 A, 4 B

Exercise 5 – One word answer

Ans: 1 Collaboration, 2 Chat

Chapter 14 - **Microsoft Bing**

Microsoft Bing, commonly known as Bing, is a web search engine developed by Microsoft. Bing's primary function is to provide users with a powerful and intuitive platform for searching the internet, accessing information, and discovering digital content. As a search engine, Bing is designed to help users find websites, images, videos, news articles, maps, and much more by analyzing search queries and providing relevant search results.

Key features of Bing include:

- **Web Search**: Bing offers a comprehensive web search feature, allowing users to enter search queries and receive search results that match their queries.
- **Multimedia Search**: Users can explore and discover images, videos, and music through Bing's multimedia search capabilities.
- **News Search**: Bing provides access to the latest news and articles on a wide range of topics, helping users stay informed.
- **Maps and Directions**: Bing Maps is a mapping service that offers geographical information, directions, and 3D views.
- **Translation**: Bing Translator allows for text and web page translation across various languages.
- **Weather Updates**: Bing provides current weather conditions and forecasts for locations around the world.
- **Business and Local Search**: Users can search for local businesses, read reviews, and get directions to physical locations.
- **Intelligent Features**: Bing incorporates intelligent features such as voice search, predictive typing, and personalized search recommendations.
- **Visual Search**: Bing Visual Search enables users to search for information using images or photos as queries.
- **Microsoft Rewards**: Bing is integrated with the Microsoft Rewards program, offering users the opportunity to earn points for using Bing search.
- **Privacy and Customization**: Bing provides privacy controls and the ability to customize search preferences to tailor the search experience.

Why Use Bing?

There are several reasons why users choose to use Bing as their preferred search engine:

- **Comprehensive Search**: Bing offers a comprehensive search experience, providing access to a wide range of digital content, from websites and images to videos and news.
- **Multimedia Features**: Users can explore multimedia content, including images, videos, and music, all from within the Bing search interface.
- **Mapping and Directions**: Bing Maps offers detailed mapping and navigation features, making it a handy tool for travelers and those in need of location-based information.
- **Language and Translation Support**: Bing Translator is a valuable tool for translating text and web pages across multiple languages.
- **Local Business Information**: Bing's local search features help users find nearby businesses and read reviews to make informed decisions.
- **Personalization and Rewards**: Bing offers personalized search recommendations and integrates with Microsoft Rewards, allowing users to earn rewards for their search activity.
- **Privacy Controls**: Bing provides users with privacy controls, allowing them to manage their search data and preferences.

14.1 Using Bing for Web Search

Bing offers a straightforward and user-friendly interface for conducting basic web searches. To perform a basic web search on Bing:

- **Open Your Web Browser**: Launch your preferred web browser and go to the Bing homepage (www.bing.com).
- **Enter Your Query**: In the search bar at the top of the page, type in your search query. This could be a question, a keyword, a phrase, or any topic you want to learn more about.
- **Hit Enter or Click Search**: Press "Enter" on your keyboard or click the "Search" button, often represented by a magnifying glass icon.

Review Search Results: Bing will provide a list of search results relevant to your query. These results typically include website links, brief descriptions, and other pertinent information.
Explore Search Results: Click on the search results to access websites or gather more information about your query. You can also use the "Images," "Videos," or "News" tabs to filter results based on media type.

Advanced Search Operators
Bing allows users to refine their search results and perform more precise searches using advanced search operators. These operators enable you to specify criteria for your search. Here are some common advanced search operators you can use with Bing:
"AND" Operator: To find results that include both of two terms, use "AND" (e.g., "cats AND dogs" returns results containing both "cats" and "dogs").
"OR" Operator: To find results that include either of two terms, use "OR" (e.g., "cats OR dogs" returns results containing "cats" or "dogs").
"NOT" Operator: To exclude specific terms from your search results, use "NOT" (e.g., "cats NOT dogs" excludes results containing "dogs").
Quotation Marks: To search for an exact phrase, enclose the phrase in quotation marks (e.g., "New York Times" will return results with the exact phrase "New York Times").
Site Operator: To search within a specific website or domain, use "site:" followed by the website address (e.g., "site: wikipedia.org space exploration" searches for "space exploration" on Wikipedia).
Filetype Operator: To find specific file types, use "filetype:" followed by the file extension (e.g., "filetyped climate change" searches for PDF documents about "climate change").
Related Operator: To find web pages related to a specific URL, use "related:" followed by the website address (e.g., "related:www.nasa.gov" shows websites related to NASA's official site).

Search Filters and Options
Bing provides various search filters and options to help you refine your search results:
Filters: After conducting a search, you can use filters on the left side of the search results page to narrow down results by date, type, source, and more.
Video and Image Search: Use the "Videos" and "Images" tabs to filter results specifically for video or image content.
News Search: Click on the "News" tab to access the latest news articles related to your search.
Search History: Bing offers a search history feature to help you revisit previous queries.
Safe Search: You can adjust Safe Search settings to filter out explicit content from search results.
Location-Based Search: Bing may provide location-based results for queries related to businesses, services, and local information.

14.2 Exploring Bing's Multimedia Search

Image Search
Bing's Image Search feature allows you to explore a vast collection of images on the internet. Whether you're looking for pictures, graphics, artwork, or photos, Bing makes it easy to find and discover visual content. Here's how to use Bing's Image Search:
Access Bing: Open your web browser and navigate to the Bing homepage (www.bing.com).
Image Search: Click on the "Images" tab at the top of the Bing homepage. This will take you to the image search interface.
Enter Your Query: In the search bar, type your image search query. You can use keywords, phrases, or questions related to the image you want to find.
Search: Hit "Enter" on your keyboard or click the search icon to initiate the image search.
Review Image Results: Bing will display a grid of image results relevant to your query. You can scroll through the images to explore them.
View Image Details: Click on an image to view it in a larger size and access additional information, such as image source and related images.
Filter Options: On the left side, you'll find filter options to refine your search by image type, size, color, and other criteria.

Image Download: You can download images by clicking on them and selecting the "Download" option, if available.

Video Search

Bing's Video Search feature allows you to find and watch videos from various sources across the web, making it a valuable tool for discovering video content. Here's how to use Bing's Video Search:

Go to Bing: Visit the Bing homepage (www.bing.com) in your web browser.

Video Search: Click on the "Videos" tab at the top of the Bing homepage to access the video search interface.

Enter Your Query: In the search bar, enter your video search query. You can use keywords, video titles, or topics you're interested in.

Initiate Search: Press "Enter" on your keyboard or click the search icon to begin the video search.

Video Results: Bing will present a list of video results related to your query. You can click on any video thumbnail to watch it.

Filter and Sort: Use the filter options on the left side to sort results by relevance, date, and duration. You can also filter by source.

Watch Videos: Click on a video result to watch it directly on Bing or access the source platform.

Video Preview: Hover your mouse over video thumbnails to see a brief preview before clicking.

Music Search

Bing's Music Search feature allows you to explore information about songs, artists, albums, and even listen to music samples. Here's how to use Bing's Music Search:

Open Bing: Visit the Bing homepage (www.bing.com) in your web browser.

Music Search: Click on the "Music" tab at the top of the Bing homepage to access the music search interface.

Enter Your Query: In the search bar, type the name of a song, artist, album, or music-related query.

Initiate Search: Hit "Enter" on your keyboard or click the search icon to perform the music search.

Music Results: Bing will provide information related to your music query, including artist details, album information, song lyrics, and more.

Sample Music: If available, you can listen to music samples directly on the search results page to get a preview of the song.

Learn More: Click on music-related results to access more details about artists, albums, and related music content.

14.3 Staying Informed with Bing News

News Search

Bing News Search is a powerful tool for staying informed about the latest news and events from around the world. Here's how to use Bing for News Search:

Access Bing News: Visit the Bing homepage (www.bing.com) in your web browser.

News Search: Click on the "News" tab at the top of the Bing homepage. This will take you to the news search interface.

Enter Your Query: In the search bar, type in your news search query. You can use keywords, phrases, or topics to find news articles on a particular subject.

Initiate Search: Hit "Enter" on your keyboard or click the search icon to begin the news search.

News Results: Bing will present a list of news articles related to your query. The results are usually sorted by relevance and date.

Explore Articles: Click on a news article to read it in detail. You can also use the "Images" and "Videos" tabs to view multimedia related to the news.

Sort and Filter: Use the filter options on the left side to sort results by date, source, and more. You can also filter by specific categories, such as technology, sports, or politics.

Share News: You can share interesting news articles on social media or via email by using the share options provided.

Customizing News Feeds

Bing allows users to customize their news feeds to receive news articles that match their interests. Here's how to customize your news feed on Bing:

Sign In: If you're not already signed in, sign in to your Microsoft account or create one if needed.

News Interests: Click on "News Interests" or "My Interests" to access the customization options.
Add Interests: You can add specific news interests, topics, or categories that you want to follow. These interests will help Bing personalize your news feed.
Remove Interests: If you want to remove or change interests, you can easily do so by editing your preferences.
Stay Updated: Your personalized news feed will provide a curated selection of news articles that match your interests.

Bing News Alerts

Bing News Alerts is a valuable feature for staying updated on specific news topics or keywords. Here's how to set up Bing News Alerts:

Sign In: Ensure you're signed in to your Microsoft account.
News Alerts: Click on "News Alerts" or a similar option in your news feed or settings.
Create an Alert: Set up a new news alert by entering keywords, topics, or phrases you want to monitor.
Customize Alerts: You can choose the frequency of alerts (e.g., daily or weekly) and the method of notification (email or web notifications).
Save the Alert: Confirm your alert settings and save it. You will receive news updates related to your chosen topics.

Exercise

Exercise 1 – MCQ

Q 1. What is the primary purpose of Microsoft Bing?
a. Social Media Platform
b. Web Search Engine
c. Video Streaming Service
d. Email Service

Q 2. Which types of media can you search for using Microsoft Bing's multimedia search features?
a. Text and Documents
b. Images, Videos, and Music
c. Social Media Posts
d. Software Applications

Exercise 2 – True/ False

Q 1. Microsoft Bing provides advanced search operators to help refine search queries.
Q 2. Bing News Alerts can be set up to provide email notifications about specific news topics.

Exercise 3 – Fill in the blanks

Q 1. Microsoft Bing allows users to perform _______ search by entering keywords, phrases, or questions.
Q 2. Bing's advanced search operators help users specify particular search criteria and refine search _______.

Exercise 4 – Match case

1 Bing News Alerts
2. Multimedia Search
3. Advanced Search Operators
4. Web Search Engine

(A) Enhances search accuracy
(B) Provides email notifications
(C) Searches for images, videos, and music
(D) Refines search queries

Exercise 5 – One word answer

Q 1. What type of content can you find using Microsoft Bing's "Image Search" feature?
Q 2. What is the primary purpose of Bing News Alerts?

Exercise 6 – Small answer

Q 1. Briefly explain the role of Bing's advanced search operators in enhancing search results.
Q 2. How does Microsoft Bing contribute to making multimedia content, such as videos and music, easily accessible to users?

Exercise 7 – Long answer

Q 1. Can you provide an in-depth overview of Microsoft Bing, its features, and its significance in the world of online search and information retrieval?

Q 2.

Answers

Exercise 1 – MCQ

Ans: 1 b, 2 b

Exercise 2 – True/ False

Ans: 1 True, 2 True

Exercise 3 – Fill in the blanks

Ans: 1 Web, 2 Result

Exercise 4 – Match case

Ans: 1 B, 2 C, 3 D, 4 A

Exercise 5 – One word answer

Ans: 1 Images, 2 Notifications

Chapter 15 - **Microsoft Project**

Microsoft Project, often referred to as MS Project, is a comprehensive project management software developed by Microsoft. It is designed to assist project managers and teams in planning, executing, and controlling projects effectively. Microsoft Project is widely used in various industries and sectors, including construction, information technology, manufacturing, and more, to streamline project management processes.

Key features of Microsoft Project include:

- **Project Planning**: Users can create detailed project plans, including defining project goals, tasks, milestones, and timelines.
- **Resource Management**: Microsoft Project enables the allocation of resources, such as personnel, equipment, and materials, to tasks and projects.
- **Task Scheduling**: Users can set task dependencies and constraints to create realistic project schedules.
- **Gantt Charts**: Gantt charts help visualize project timelines, task relationships, and critical paths.
- **Tracking and Reporting**: Microsoft Project allows for real-time tracking of project progress and generates various reports for analysis and decision-making.
- **Integration**: It integrates with other Microsoft Office tools, such as Excel, Outlook, and SharePoint, for enhanced collaboration and data sharing.

Why Use Microsoft Project?

There are several compelling reasons to use Microsoft Project for project management:

- **Comprehensive Project Planning**: Microsoft Project offers a wide range of tools for detailed project planning, making it easier to define goals, tasks, and timelines.
- **Resource Management**: It allows for efficient allocation of resources, which is crucial for managing workload and ensuring that projects are adequately staffed.
- **Effective Task Scheduling**: The software helps in setting task dependencies, which ensures that tasks are completed in the right sequence.
- **Visibility and Control**: Microsoft Project provides a visual representation of project timelines and task relationships through Gantt charts, offering better control and monitoring.
- **Collaboration**: The integration with Microsoft Office 365 and SharePoint makes it easy for teams to collaborate and share project data.
- **Reporting and Analysis**: The software generates various reports and provides data for in-depth analysis, facilitating informed decision-making.
- **Historical Data**: Microsoft Project keeps a historical record of project data, which can be valuable for future projects and benchmarking.
- **Scalability**: It can be used for both small and large projects, making it a versatile tool for organizations of all sizes.

15.1 Getting Started with Microsoft Project

Step 1: Sign in to download Project

Go to www.office.com and if you're not already signed in, select **Sign in**.

Sign in with the account you associated with this version of Project. This account can be a Microsoft account (used with non-subscription versions), or work or school account (used with subscription versions).

Step 2: Install Project

Depending on your browser, select **Run** (in Edge or Internet Explorer), **Setup** (in Chrome), or **Save File** (in Firefox).

If you see the User Account Control prompt that says, **Do you want to allow this app to make changes to your device?** select **Yes**.

The install begins.

Your install is finished when you see the phrase, **"You're all set! Project is installed now"** and an animation plays to show you where to find the Project app on your computer.

Follow the instructions in the window to find Project, for example depending on your version of Windows, select **Start** and then scroll to find Project from your list of apps.

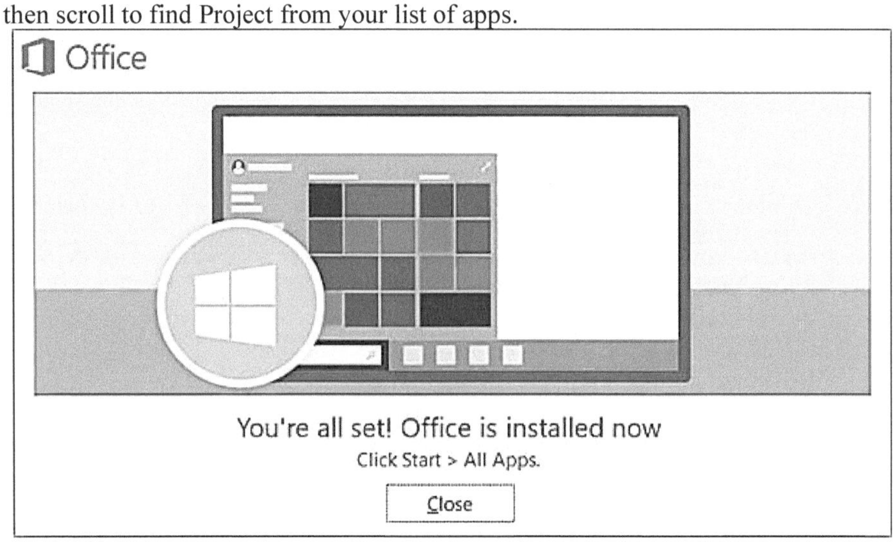

15.2 Project Planning and Setup

Before you dive into creating a project plan in Microsoft Project, it's essential to clearly define your project's goals and objectives. This initial step sets the direction for your project and helps ensure that everyone involved is on the same page. Here's how to define project goals and objectives:

Clarify the Purpose: Begin by understanding the purpose and scope of your project. What are you trying to achieve? Why is the project necessary?

Identify Stakeholders: Determine who the project stakeholders are. These are individuals or groups with an interest in the project's success, including sponsors, team members, and end-users.

SMART Objectives: Set SMART (Specific, Measurable, Achievable, Relevant, Time-bound) objectives. These objectives should be clear, quantifiable, attainable, relevant to the project, and have a defined timeline for completion.

Project Scope: Clearly define the project's scope by listing what is included and what is not included. This prevents scope creep and ensures focus.

Key Deliverables: Identify the key deliverables that must be produced during the project. These are tangible outcomes that help achieve project objectives.

Success Criteria: Establish the criteria that will be used to measure the success of the project. How will you know if the project has achieved its goals and objectives?

Document Goals and Objectives: Document the project goals and objectives in a project charter or a similar document that can be easily referenced throughout the project.

Creating a Project Timeline

Creating a project timeline in Microsoft Project is a critical step in project planning. It provides a visual representation of the project's schedule and helps with task sequencing and resource allocation. Here's how to create a project timeline:

Task Identification: List all the tasks that need to be completed to achieve the project objectives. Be as specific as possible.

Task Dependencies: Identify dependencies between tasks. Determine which tasks are dependent on others and establish their relationships (e.g., finish-to-start, start-to-start).

Estimating Durations: Estimate the duration of each task. How long will it take to complete each task, and what is the unit of measurement (hours, days, weeks)?

Resource Allocation: Assign resources (people, equipment, materials) to tasks. Make sure each task has the necessary resources for execution.

Gantt Chart: Use Microsoft Project's Gantt chart feature to create a visual representation of your project timeline. This chart displays tasks along a timeline, with dependencies and durations clearly indicated.

Critical Path: Identify the critical path in your project, which is the sequence of tasks that, if delayed, will delay the project's completion date.

Adjustments: As you build the project timeline, you may need to make adjustments to account for resource constraints, unexpected delays, or changes in project scope.

Setting Up Project Tasks and Milestones

In Microsoft Project, tasks are the building blocks of your project plan. Setting up tasks and milestones is crucial for a detailed project plan. Here's how to set up project tasks and milestones:

Task Names: Give each task a descriptive name that reflects the work involved. Task names should be clear and easily understandable.

Task Durations: Define the estimated duration for each task. This can be in hours, days, weeks, or other time units.

Task Dependencies: Establish relationships between tasks. Specify which tasks must be completed before others can start.

Task Assignments: Assign team members or resources to each task. This helps in workload distribution and resource management.

Milestones: Identify project milestones, which are significant points in the project's timeline. Milestones mark the completion of major phases or key achievements.

Task Descriptions: Provide task descriptions that outline the work to be done and any specific requirements.

Task Constraints: Set any constraints on tasks, such as deadlines, dependencies, or resource constraints.

Task Prioritization: Prioritize tasks to ensure that critical tasks are completed on time, especially if resources are limited.

Task Status: Track the status of tasks, indicating whether they are in progress, completed, or delayed.

Exercise

Exercise 1 – MCQ

Q 1. What is Microsoft Project primarily used for?

a. Graphic Design
b. Project Management
c. Video Editing
d. Web Development

Q 2. Which view in Microsoft Project provides a visual representation of a project's timeline and tasks?

a. Task Sheet
b. Gantt Chart
c. Resource Sheet
d. Network Diagram

Exercise 2 – True/ False

Q 1. Microsoft Project allows you to assign resources to tasks and track their progress.

Q 2. The critical path in a project is a sequence of tasks that can be delayed without affecting the project's completion date.

Exercise 3 – Fill in the blanks

Q 1. you can set task ____________ to define the sequence in which tasks should be completed.
Q 2. A project ____________ represents a significant achievement or point in a project's timeline.

Exercise 4 – Match case

1. Gantt Chart
2. Critical Path
3. Resource Allocation
4. Task Dependencies

(A) Assigning resources to tasks
(B) Visual representation of project timeline
(C) Sequence of tasks with no float
(D) Determining task order

Exercise 5 – One word answer

Q 1. What is the term for a major achievement or event in a project?
Q 2. What view in Microsoft Project provides a tabular layout of project tasks and their details?

Exercise 6 – Small answer

Q 1. Briefly explain the concept of a critical path in project management.
Q 2. How does Microsoft Project help with resource allocation?

Exercise 7 – Long answer

Q 1. Can you explain the process of setting up a project timeline in Microsoft Project, including the key steps and considerations?
Q 2. How does Microsoft Project enhance project collaboration and communication within a team?

Answers

Exercise 1 – MCQ

Ans: 1 b, 2 b

Exercise 2 – True/ False

Ans: 1 True, 2 False

Exercise 3 – Fill in the blanks

Ans: 1 Dependencies, 2 Milestone

Exercise 4 – Match case

Ans: 1B, 2 C, 3 A, 4cc D

Exercise 5 – One word answer

Ans: 1 Milestone, 2 Task Sheet

Chapter 16 - **Microsoft Publisher**

Microsoft Publisher is a versatile desktop publishing software application developed by Microsoft. It is designed to help users create a wide range of publications, from simple flyers and brochures to more complex documents like newsletters, business cards, posters, and even web publications. Publisher is an essential tool for individuals, businesses, and organizations looking to design and produce high-quality materials for both print and digital distribution.

Microsoft Publisher is a user-friendly desktop publishing program that provides a host of tools and features to create professional-looking documents. It stands out as an excellent choice for those who may not have extensive graphic design experience but still want to produce visually appealing and well-structured publications.

Key Features and Benefits

Microsoft Publisher offers several key features and benefits:

Templates: Publisher includes a wide range of customizable templates for various types of publications. These templates provide a solid starting point for creating documents and can be tailored to suit your specific needs.

Ease of Use: Publisher is known for its user-friendly interface, making it accessible for individuals with varying levels of design expertise. The drag-and-drop functionality, intuitive menus, and familiar Microsoft Office ribbon make it easy to get started.

Text and Typography Tools: The application offers powerful text and typography tools, allowing users to format and style text, adjust fonts, and create visually appealing content.

Graphics and Images: Publisher provides the ability to insert and manipulate images and graphics. Users can crop, resize, apply effects, and even draw shapes directly within the application.

Integration: It seamlessly integrates with other Microsoft Office applications, such as Word and Excel, simplifying the import and export of content.

Digital and Print Publishing: Publisher is suitable for both digital and print publications, making it versatile for a range of projects.

Customization: Users have control over layout, color schemes, and design elements, enabling them to create publications that align with their branding and messaging.

Professional Output: Publisher produces professional-looking documents that are suitable for business, marketing, and personal use.

Web Publications: Publisher allows for the creation of web publications, which can be published online for wider accessibility.

Compatibility: Publications created in Publisher can be saved in various file formats, including PDF, to ensure compatibility with different devices and platforms.

16.1 Getting Started with Microsoft Publisher

Getting started with Microsoft Publisher is a straightforward process that involves installation, familiarizing yourself with the interface, and creating or opening publications. In this section, we'll guide you through these initial steps to help you kick-start your journey with Publisher.

Installing Microsoft Publisher

Before you can start using Microsoft Publisher, you'll need to install the software on your computer. Here's how to do it:

For Windows Users: Microsoft Publisher is part of the Microsoft Office suite. If you have a Microsoft 365 subscription or a standalone version of Office, Publisher should already be included. If not, you can purchase and install it from the Microsoft Office website or through authorized retailers.

For Mac Users: As of my last knowledge update in September 2021, Publisher is not available for Mac. However, you can use alternative desktop publishing software that is compatible with Mac, or run Publisher on a Windows environment using virtualization software or Boot Camp.

Navigating the Publisher Interface

Once Publisher is installed, you'll need to familiarize yourself with the interface. The Publisher interface is user-friendly and shares common elements with other Microsoft Office applications. Here's an overview of the key components:

Ribbon: The ribbon is located at the top of the window and contains tabs with various commands and tools for creating and formatting your publication.

Quick Access Toolbar: This customizable toolbar allows you to access frequently used commands and functions.
Page Navigation: You can move between pages and access different parts of your publication using the page navigation tools located at the bottom of the screen.
Work Area: The central work area is where you create and edit your publication. It may include placeholders for text and images, depending on the template you're using.
Tools and Panels: Additional tools and panels, such as the Drawing Tools, Text Box Tools, and Graphics Manager, can be accessed through the ribbon to assist in design and layout tasks.

Creating a New Publication

Publisher is a desktop publishing application that helps you create visually rich, professional-looking publications.

With Publisher on your PC, you can:

Lay out content for a print or online publication in a variety of pre-designed templates.

Create simple items like greeting cards and labels.

Create complex projects like yearbooks, catalogs, and professional email newsletters.

Create with a template

Open Publisher.

If you're already in Publisher, select **File** > **New**.

Select or search for a template:

Select a **FEATURED** template.

Select **BUILT-IN** and select a template.

Search for a template using:

Search for online templates, or

One of the **Suggested searches**, or

View more templates online

Select **Create**.

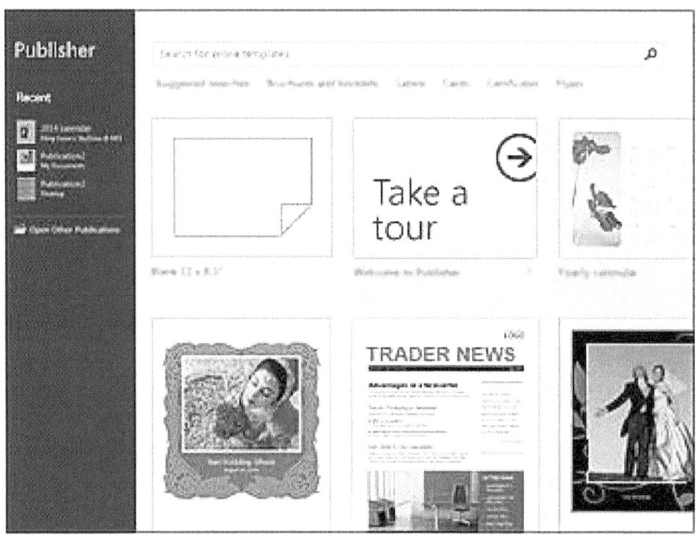

Add a text box

Select **Home** > **Draw Text Box**.

Drag the cross-shaped cursor to draw a box where you want to add text.

Type the text in the text box.

If the text doesn't fit in the text box, make the text box bigger, or link it to another text box.

Insert a picture
You can insert a picture from your computer, or insert an online picture from OneDrive or the web.
Select **Insert** > **Pictures** or
Insert > **Online Pictures**.

Find the picture you want and select it.
Select **Insert**.

Opening and Saving Publications
To open an existing publication or save your current work, use the following steps:

Opening a Publication:

Click the "File" tab.
Select "Open" to browse and locate the publication file you want to open.
Click "Open" to load the selected publication.

Saving a Publication:

Click the "File" tab.
Select "Save" or "Save As" to save your publication. "Save" updates the current file, while "Save As" allows you to specify a file name and location for a new copy of the publication.

16.2 Working with Text in Publisher

Microsoft Publisher, working with text is a fundamental aspect of creating publications. Whether you're designing brochures, flyers, or newsletters, text plays a crucial role in conveying your message effectively. This section covers various aspects of working with text, from adding and formatting text to using text styles and ensuring the correctness of your content.

Adding and Formatting Text

Adding Text:

Click on the text tool in the ribbon to select it.
Click on the location where you want to add text in your publication.
Start typing your text.

Formatting Text:

Highlight the text you want to format.
Use the formatting options in the ribbon to change font styles, sizes, colors, and alignment.
Adjust spacing and indentation to control text layout.
Apply effects such as bold, italics, underline, and more.

Text Boxes and Frames
Text boxes and frames are essential for controlling the placement and flow of text in your publication.
Creating Text Boxes:
Click the "Draw Text Box" tool in the ribbon.
Click and drag to create a text box.
Type or paste text into the text box.
Formatting Text Boxes:
Adjust the size and shape of text boxes.
Control text flow by linking text boxes.
Set text box borders and fills to enhance the design.
Using Text Styles
Text styles help maintain consistency and streamline text formatting across your publication.
Creating and Applying Text Styles:
Select a text element with the desired formatting.
In the ribbon, go to the "Format Text" tab.
Click "Create New Style."
Name the style and specify formatting options.
Click "OK" to create the style.
Apply the style to other text elements as needed.
Modifying Text Styles:
Update existing text styles to maintain a consistent look throughout your publication.
Spell Check and Proofreading
Ensuring the correctness of your text is crucial in professional publications. Microsoft Publisher provides tools for spell checking and proofreading.
Spell Check:
Click the "Review" tab in the ribbon.
Click "Spelling" to start the spell check.
Review and correct spelling and grammar errors as they are detected.
Proofreading:
Carefully proofread your content for errors in grammar, punctuation, and clarity.
Consider having others review your publication for a fresh perspective.

Exercise

Exercise 1 – MCQ
Q 1. Which type of documents can you create using Microsoft Publisher?
a. Spreadsheets
b. Presentations
c. Desktop publications
d. Databases
Q 2. What does a text box in Microsoft Publisher allow you to do?
a. Play videos
b. Insert images
c. Add and format text
d. Create shapes

Exercise 2 – True/ False
Q1. Microsoft Publisher is designed solely for creating spreadsheets.
Q2. Text boxes in Publisher are used for inserting images only.

Exercise 3 – Fill in the blanks
Q1. Microsoft Publisher is used for creating various types of __________ publications.
Q2. You can format text in Publisher by adjusting font styles, sizes, colors, and __________.

Exercise 4 – Match case
1. Text Box
2. Quick Access Toolbar
3. Spell Check
4. Graphics Manager

(A) A tool for spell checking and proofreading
(B) Allows you to create and format text
(C) A feature for inserting and manipulating images
(D) A customizable toolbar for frequently used commands

Exercise 5 – One word answer

Q1. What type of documents can you create using Microsoft Publisher?
Q2. What do you use to format text in Publisher?

Exercise 6 – Small answer

Q 1. Explain the purpose of a text box in Microsoft Publisher.
Q 2. How can you customize the Quick Access Toolbar in Publisher?

Exercise 7 – Long answer

Q 1. Imagine you're tasked with creating a professional brochure for a new product launch using Microsoft Publisher. Describe the step-by-step process you would follow, from choosing a template to finalizing the design. Include details about template selection, text and image placement, formatting, and any advanced features you might use to enhance the brochure's visual appeal and effectiveness.
Q 2. In a business context, elaborate on the significance of maintaining brand consistency and identity in publications created with Microsoft Publisher. How can the use of text styles and color schemes contribute to brand consistency? Provide specific examples and explain how Publisher's features enable businesses to adhere to their branding guidelines when creating marketing materials, such as flyers and brochures.

Answers

Exercise 1 – MCQ

Ans: 1 c,2 c

Exercise 2 – True/ False

Ans: 1 False, 2 False

Exercise 3 – Fill in the blanks

Ans: 1 desktop, 2 alignment

Exercise 4 – Match case

Ans: 1 B, 2 D, 3 A, 4 C

Exercise 5 – One word answer

Ans: 1 Publications, 2 Ribbon

Chapter 17 - **Microsoft ToDo**

Microsoft To Do is a simple and intelligent to-do list that helps you manage all your tasks in one place. You can work through your tasks for the day in My Day and create any number of additional lists to organize your work, groceries, travel, shopping, movies to watch - you get the idea!

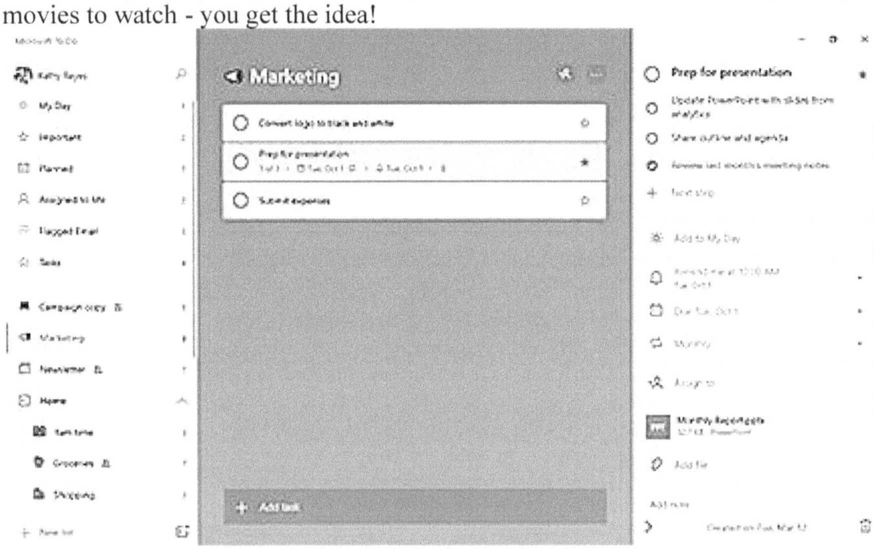

In each list you can add as many tasks as you like. Keep everything on track by setting due dates and reminders for each task and starring your most important tasks. Use steps to break down your larger tasks in to more manageable pieces and notes to record extra details. Since all of your tasks are stored on Exchange Online servers, they'll also appear automatically in Outlook tasks.

17.1 Project Planning

Define Project Goals
In this step, you will outline the primary objectives and expected outcomes of your project. Clearly defining your project goals is essential for providing direction and focus to your team.

Create Project Timeline
Creating a project timeline involves establishing a schedule that outlines the tasks, milestones, and deadlines for your project. It helps ensure that your project stays on track and is completed within the allocated time frame.

Allocate Resources
Allocating resources involves identifying and securing the necessary human and material resources required for the project. This includes determining who will work on the project and ensuring that they have the tools and support needed to complete their tasks effectively.

17.2 Gather Data

Gather Data
In the "Gather Data" phase, the focus is on collecting relevant information and data related to your project. This can involve conducting surveys, interviews, experiments, or acquiring existing data sources to support your research goals.

Analyze Findings
After data collection, the next step is to analyze the collected data and findings. This involves processing and interpreting the data to derive meaningful insights, patterns, and conclusions that will inform the project.

Literature Review
The "Literature Review" sub-section involves examining existing academic or industry literature and studies related to your project. It helps you understand what has already been documented on the topic and how your

project fits into the broader context. This process can provide valuable insights and inform your research direction.

17.3 Conceptual Design

Conceptual Design

In the "Conceptual Design" phase, you create a high-level, abstract representation of your project or product. This includes outlining the core concepts, features, and the overall architecture. It serves as the foundation for detailed design and development.

Prototyping

The "Prototyping" phase involves creating a working model or prototype of your project. This allows you to test and evaluate the concept in a tangible form, gather feedback, and make necessary adjustments before moving forward with the final product development.

Final Product Development

In the "Final Product Development" stage, you take the insights gained from the conceptual design and prototyping phases to build the actual product. This includes coding, manufacturing, and quality assurance, with the goal of delivering the end product as per the project's specifications and requirements.

Exercise

Exercise 1 – MCQ

Q 1. Which platform is Microsoft To Do available on?
a) Windows only
b) Windows and macOS
c) Windows, macOS, iOS, and Android
d) iOS only

Q 2. Which Microsoft service is closely integrated with Microsoft To Do for syncing tasks and lists across devices?
a) Microsoft Teams
b) Outlook
c) OneDrive
d) Microsoft Word

Exercise 2 – True/ False

Q 1. Microsoft To Do allows you to create multiple lists to organize your tasks.
Q 2. Microsoft To Do allows you to add sub-tasks within a task.

Exercise 3 – Fill in the blanks

Q 1. you can set ________ and due dates for your tasks to prioritize them.
Q 2. Microsoft To Do supports the creation of task ________ for more detailed information and checklists.

Exercise 4 – Match case

1. Reminders
2. My Day
3. Lists

A. Helps you focus on tasks you want to accomplish today.
B. Allows you to categorize and organize your tasks.
C. Enables you to set notifications for important tasks.

Exercise 5 – One word answer

Q 1. What is the primary purpose of Microsoft To Do?
Q 2. What is the feature called in Microsoft To Do that allows you to group related tasks together?

Exercise 6 – Small answer

Q 1. How can you share a task list with a colleague in Microsoft To Do?
Q 2. How can you mark a task as completed in Microsoft To Do?

Exercise 7 – Long answer

Q 1. Explain the process of creating a recurring task in Microsoft To Do.

Q 2.Describe the process of creating a reminder for a task in Microsoft To Do and how reminders can be customized.

Answers

Exercise 1 – MCQ

Ans: 1 c, 2 b

Exercise 2 – True/ False

Ans: 1 True, 2 True

Exercise 3 – Fill in the blanks

Ans: 1 due date, 2 notes

Exercise 4 – Match case

Ans: 1 C ,2 A, 3 B

Exercise 5 – One word answer

Ans: 1 Task Management, 2 lists

Chapter 18 - **Microsoft Power Platform**

Microsoft Power Platform is a suite of business application tools that empowers organizations to analyze data, automate processes, build custom applications, and create virtual agents. It provides a low-code, no-code environment for users to create solutions that address various business needs without extensive coding or development skills. The Power Platform consists of four key components:

Key Components of the Power Platform

Power Apps: Power Apps enables users to create custom business applications. It offers two primary types of apps: Canvas Apps, where you design the user interface, and Model-Driven Apps, which provide data-driven interfaces with a pre-built structure.

Power Automate: Formerly known as Microsoft Flow, Power Automate is an automation tool that allows users to create workflows and automate business processes. It can connect to a wide range of applications and services, triggering actions and responses based on predefined conditions.

Power BI: Power BI is a powerful business intelligence tool for data analysis and visualization. Users can connect to various data sources, transform data, create reports, and build interactive dashboards to gain insights and make informed decisions.

Power Virtual Agents: Power Virtual Agents lets you create chatbots or virtual agents to interact with users and provide automated responses. These chatbots can be integrated into websites, apps, and other services to improve customer service and engagement.

Benefits of Using Power Platform

Rapid Application Development: Power Platform allows organizations to develop custom solutions quickly, reducing the time and cost traditionally associated with application development. Non-technical users can participate in the development process, making it accessible to a broader audience.

Integration: It offers seamless integration with a wide range of Microsoft and third-party applications, allowing data to flow smoothly across systems. This integration streamlines business processes and enhances productivity.

Data-Driven Insights: Power BI, one of the Power Platform components, provides powerful data analytics and visualization capabilities, helping organizations gain valuable insights from their data to support informed decision-making.

Automation: Power Automate simplifies and automates routine tasks and workflows, reducing the need for manual processes and human intervention. This can lead to increased efficiency and reduced errors.

Low-Code/No-Code: Power Platform is designed for users with varying levels of technical expertise. Non-developers can create sophisticated solutions with minimal or no coding, while developers can extend and customize applications with code when necessary.

Scalability: Power Platform can scale to meet the needs of small businesses to large enterprises. Organizations can start with simple apps and expand to more complex solutions as their requirements grow.

Security and Compliance: The platform offers robust security and compliance features, ensuring that data and applications are protected and meet regulatory requirements.

18.1 Power Apps

1. **Creating and Customizing Apps**

Introduction to Power Apps: Power Apps is a low-code/no-code development platform that allows users to create custom applications without extensive coding. It's a part of the Microsoft Power Platform.

Creating a New App: Users can start by creating a new app from scratch or by using predefined templates to kickstart the development process.

Designing App Screens: Power Apps enable users to design the user interface by adding screens, navigation menus, and other elements.

Customizing the User Interface: You can customize the appearance of your app by changing colors, fonts, and layouts to align with your organization's branding.

Adding Controls and Elements: Power Apps offers various controls and elements like buttons, text input, galleries, and forms, which can be added to screens to create interactive apps.

Formulas and Expressions: Formulas and expressions are used to define the behavior and logic of your app. They are essential for implementing data validation, calculations, and conditional actions.

2. **Connecting to Data Sources**

   Data Sources in Power Apps: Power Apps can connect to a wide range of data sources, including Microsoft's Common Data Service (CDS), SharePoint, SQL Server, and other external sources.

   Connecting to Common Data Service (CDS): CDS is a centralized data storage service that is tightly integrated with Power Apps and can be used for building data models and entities.

   External Data Sources: You can connect Power Apps to external data sources using connectors, which facilitate data retrieval and updates from systems like databases, cloud services, and web APIs.

   Creating Data Tables and Entities: Power Apps allow you to create data tables and entities to organize and structure data for use within your apps.

   Data Integration and Transformation: Data integration involves pulling data from different sources and transforming it to meet the specific requirements of your app.

3. **Building Canvas Apps**

   Introduction to Canvas Apps: Canvas apps provide the flexibility to create highly customized apps with a drag-and-drop interface. You design the app screen by screen.

   Building Screens and Navigation: You can create multiple screens in your canvas app and define navigation between them.

   Working with Forms and Controls: Use forms and controls to collect and display data, and customize the user interface.

   Collecting and Patching Data: Power Apps provides functions like Collect and Patch to add, modify, or delete data in data sources.

   User Authentication and Security: You can implement user authentication and set access controls to ensure data security.

   Custom App Logic with Formulas: Formulas are used to define custom logic, validation rules, and business processes within your canvas app.

4. **Model-Driven Apps**

   Introduction to Model-Driven Apps: Model-driven apps are driven by data models, which define the structure and behavior of the app. These apps are more structured and are often used for business applications.

   Data Models and Entity Relationships: You create data models in the Power Platform and define entity relationships to manage complex data structures.

   Building App Components: Model-driven apps are built by assembling pre-defined components, like views, forms, charts, and dashboards.

   Configuring Views and Forms: You can configure views and forms to control how data is displayed and edited.

   Business Process Flows: Model-driven apps support business process flows for guiding users through complex processes.

   Role-Based Security: Role-based security allows you to control who can access what data and features within the app.

5. **Power Apps Components**

   Reusable Components: Power Apps components are reusable elements that can be used across multiple apps to maintain consistency in the user interface and functionality.

   Custom Controls and Components: You can create custom controls and components to address specific requirements that aren't met by built-in elements.

   Component Libraries: Component libraries help organize and manage your custom components.

   Building and Sharing Components: Custom components can be built and shared within your organization, making them accessible to others.

   Enhancing App Efficiency: Components improve app efficiency and maintainability by reducing redundancy and promoting reusability.

6. **App Deployment and Sharing**

   App Deployment Options: Apps can be deployed to various platforms, including web, mobile devices, and app stores (like Microsoft AppSource).

   Sharing Apps with Users: You can share apps with specific users or groups, controlling their access and permissions.

Publishing Apps to App Stores: If you wish to distribute your app more widely, you can publish it to app stores for broader access.

App Version Control: Version control allows you to manage app versions, ensuring that users always have access to the latest updates.

App Lifecycle Management: Effective app lifecycle management includes design, development, testing, deployment, and maintenance phases.

7. Integration with Power Automate

Automating Workflows with Power Automate: Power Automate is used to automate business processes and workflows. It can be integrated with Power Apps to trigger actions based on specific events.

Triggers and Actions: Triggers initiate a workflow, and actions are the steps that are performed in response to a trigger.

Building Flows for Power Apps: You can create flows in Power Automate that respond to actions in your Power Apps, creating seamless end-to-end processes.

Connecting Apps and Flow: The integration between Power Apps and Power Automate ensures that your apps can interact with various external systems and services.

Streamlining Business Processes: Automation and integration streamline business processes, reducing manual effort and increasing efficiency.

8. AI Builder in Power Apps

Introduction to AI Builder: AI Builder is a feature within Power Apps that allows you to add artificial intelligence capabilities to your apps.

Using AI Models in Apps: You can utilize pre-built AI models for tasks like object detection and form processing to enhance your applications.

Object Detection and Form Processing: AI Builder can automatically identify and extract data from images and forms.

Predictive Models: Predictive models can help you make data-driven predictions and decisions within your apps.

Custom AI Models: You can also create and train custom AI models to address specific business needs.

Improving User Experience with AI: The integration of AI enhances user experience by providing smart, automated features within your apps.

18.2 Power Automate

Power Automate is a cloud-based automation tool by Microsoft that allows you to create workflows to automate and streamline business processes and tasks.

Low-Code Automation: Power Automate provides a low-code/no-code environment, making it accessible to users with varying technical expertise.

`1. Creating Flows

Flow Creation: Users can create flows using a visual designer, where they define a series of actions and conditions to automate a process.

Flow Components: Flows consist of triggers, actions, and logical expressions to determine the flow's behavior.

2. Flow Types: Automated, Instant, Scheduled

Automated Flows: These flows are initiated automatically based on specific events or triggers, such as when a new email arrives or when a file is added to a folder.

Instant Flows: Instant flows allow users to manually trigger a flow when needed. They are often used for ad-hoc tasks.

Scheduled Flows: Scheduled flows are triggered at predefined intervals or times, automating tasks that need to occur regularly, like daily reports.

3. Triggers and Actions

Triggers: Triggers are the events that initiate a flow. They can be external events (e.g., email received) or internal events (e.g., a button click in Power Apps).

Actions: Actions are the steps or tasks that the flow performs in response to a trigger. They can include creating tasks, sending emails, updating databases, and more.

4. **Approvals and Notifications**

   Approvals: Power Automate enables the creation of approval flows where requests are sent to designated approvers for review and response.

   Notifications: Flows can send notifications, such as emails or mobile notifications, to keep users informed about specific events or actions.

5. **Flow Templates**

   Flow Templates: Power Automate provides a library of pre-built flow templates to help users get started quickly. These templates cover common use cases and can be customized to fit specific needs.

6. **Integration with Power Apps**

   Integration with Power Apps: Power Automate seamlessly integrates with Power Apps, allowing you to trigger flows from Power Apps and automate data processes within your applications.

   Enhanced Functionality: This integration enhances the functionality of Power Apps by enabling automated actions and processes.

7. **Flow Management and Monitoring**

   Flow Management: Users can manage and maintain their flows, including version control, updating, and troubleshooting.

   Flow Monitoring: Power Automate provides monitoring and reporting capabilities to track the performance of flows, identify issues, and view historical data.

18.3 Power BI

1. **Getting Started with Power BI**

   Introduction to Power BI: Power BI is a business intelligence tool by Microsoft that allows users to visualize and share data insights. It's available as a desktop application, a web service, and a mobile app.

   Power BI Components: Understanding the key components of Power BI, including Power BI Desktop, Power Query, Power View, and Power BI Service (cloud-based).

2. **Data Modeling and Transformation**

   Data Modeling: Creating data models in Power BI involves defining relationships between tables, managing hierarchies, and ensuring data accuracy.

   Data Transformation: Power BI provides Power Query, a powerful tool for data transformation, cleaning, and shaping. It allows you to load data from various sources and apply transformations.

3. **Creating Visualizations**

   Data Visualization Basics: Understanding the principles of effective data visualization, including choosing the right chart types and design best practices.

   Creating Visualizations: Using Power BI's drag-and-drop interface to create various visualizations, such as bar charts, line charts, pie charts, maps, and more.

   Interactive Visuals: Making visuals interactive with slicers, filters, and drill-through options.

4. **Building Reports and Dashboards**

   Reports vs. Dashboards: Distinguishing between reports and dashboards. Reports are detailed collections of visuals, while dashboards provide an overview with key visuals.

   Building Reports: Assembling visuals and designing layouts within Power BI reports.

   Building Dashboards: Creating dashboards by pinning visuals from multiple reports to provide a consolidated view of data.

5. **Power Query and DAX**

   Power Query: Exploring the Power Query Editor to transform and shape data from different sources before loading it into Power BI. Topics include data cleaning, merging, and appending data tables.

   DAX (Data Analysis Expressions): Understanding DAX formulas to create calculated columns, measures, and calculated tables. DAX is used for complex data calculations and aggregations within Power BI.

6. **Power BI Service**

    Power BI Service: An overview of the Power BI cloud service, which allows you to publish, share, and collaborate on reports and dashboards.

    Publishing Reports: Uploading Power BI reports to the Power BI Service for online sharing.

    Data Refresh: Managing data refresh schedules in the Power BI Service to keep reports up to date.

    Sharing and Collaboration: Collaborating with others by sharing reports and dashboards and setting up access permissions.

7. **Sharing and Collaboration**

    Sharing Reports: Understanding how to share Power BI reports with colleagues, including options for sharing links, embedding reports, and sharing via email.

    Collaborative Features: Exploring collaborative features like commenting, annotations, and discussions on report pages to facilitate team collaboration.

8. **Power BI Embedded**

    Power BI Embedded: Power BI Embedded allows developers to integrate Power BI reports and dashboards into custom applications and websites.

    Embedding Reports: How to embed Power BI reports into web applications using Power BI Embedded.

    Security and Licensing: Managing security, authentication, and licensing for embedded Power BI content.

    Customization: Customizing the appearance and behavior of embedded reports to fit the application's look and feel.

Exercise

Exercise 1 – MCQ

Q 1. Which components make up the Microsoft Power Platform?
A) Power Apps, Power Automate, SharePoint
B) Word, Excel, PowerPoint
C) Power Rangers, Spider-Man, Batman
D) None of the above

Q 2. What is the primary purpose of Power Automate within the Power Platform?
A) Creating custom applications
B) Automating business processes
C) Visualizing data insights
D) Sending emails

Exercise 2 – True/ False

Q 1. True or False: Power BI is used for data visualization and reporting.
Q 2. True or False: Power Platform consists of only two components, Power Apps and Power Automate.

Exercise 3 – Fill in the blanks

Q 1. Power Query is used for __________ and shaping data before loading it into Power BI.
Q 2. Power Platform can be integrated with Microsoft 365 applications like __________ for enhanced functionality.

Exercise 4 – Match case

1) Power Apps
2) Power Automate
3) Power BI

A) Data visualization
B) Low-code app development
C) Workflow automation

Exercise 5 – One word answer

Q 1. What is the name of the low-code, no-code development platform within the Microsoft Power Platform?
Q 2. What is the primary purpose of Power BI?

Exercise 6 – Small answer

Q 1. Provide one example of a data source that Power BI can connect to.

Q 2. How does Power Automate enhance workflow efficiency in organizations?

Exercise 7 – Long answer

Q 1. Explain the concept of data modeling in the context of Power BI and why it's important for creating effective data visualizations.

Q 2. Describe the key differences between Power Apps and Power Automate and give an example of how they can be used together in a business scenario.

Answers

Exercise 1 – MCQ

Ans: 1 A, 2 B

Exercise 2 – True/ False

Ans: 1 True, 2 False

Exercise 3 – Fill in the blanks

Ans: 1 transforming, 2 SharePoint

Exercise 4 – Match case

Ans: 1 B, 2 C, 3 A

Exercise 5 – One word answer

Ans: 1 Power Apps, 2 Visualization

Reference Video

MS Excel: https://youtu.be/E-9W-ak3GYM

MS Word: https://youtu.be/FchQby4CWgM

Microsoft Access: https://youtu.be/oilEviyIOpo

PowerPoint: https://youtu.be/4y6KnYYn32M